PRENTICE HA

Technology Applications

Online WorkText

Middle Grades

PEARSON

Prentice
Hall

Upper Saddle River, New Jersey
Needham, Massachusetts

ISBN 0-13-036332-4

1 2 3 4 5 6 7 8 9 10   07 06 05 04 03

(Acknowledgments continue on page 278, which constitutes an extension of this copyright page.)

Table of Contents

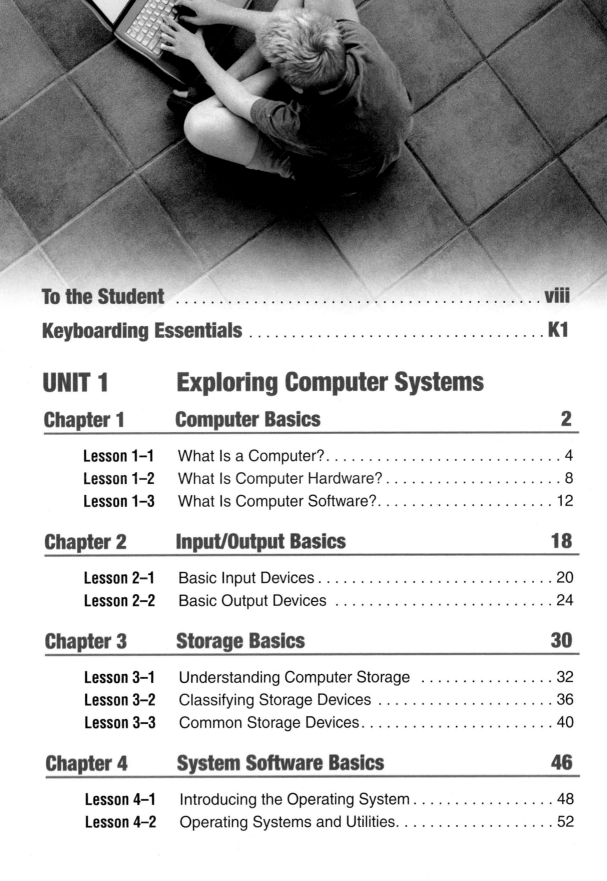

UNIT 2   Exploring Application Software

UNIT 5   Exploring Online Resources

UNIT 5   Exploring Online Resources

Computer Literacy Delivered Online, on CD-ROM, and in Print

Prentice Hall Technology Applications provides an exclusive flexible system for learning computer skills and applying them in all areas of your education.

Lighter BOOKBAG!

Available on CD-ROM!

Audio also available in Spanish

Interactive Tutorials

Multimedia exercises introduce you to technology concepts, including:

- **Computer Basics** Hardware, Software, Operating Systems & Utilities

- **Application Basics** Word Processing, Spreadsheets, Databases, Graphics & Multimedia

- **Exchanging Data** Telecommunications, Networks, E-mail, The Internet, Security & Ethics

Master Skills Anytime, Anywhere

All content in your WorkText can also be found online.

Practice and Application Activities

Reinforce computer skills through practice exercises in a variety of academic subjects, including:

- **Language Arts**
- **Social Studies**
- **Math**
- **Science**

Using Your WorkText

Chapter Overview

Each chapter begins with an introduction to concepts and a chapter outline.

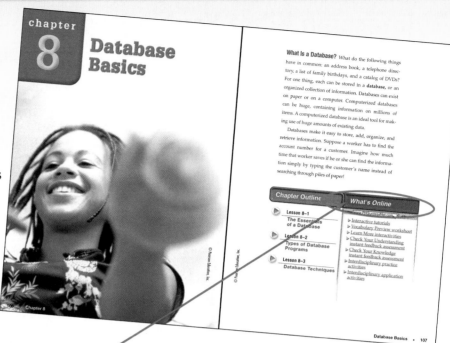

The Overview lists online activities and features from the *Prentice Hall iText*. All of the WorkText content is also available online!

Lesson Overview

Throughout each lesson you will find helpful tools that guide you through the learning process.

- **Objectives** Tasks you should be able to complete by the end of the lesson

- **As You Read** Ideas for how you can best organize information for maximum learning

- **Key Terms** Key words you should know after you complete the lesson

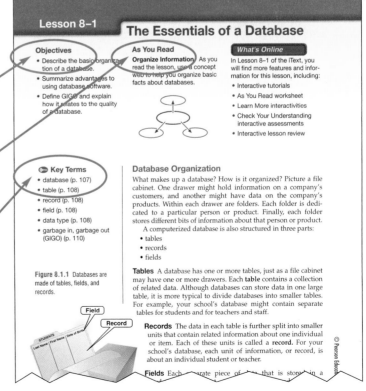

Reinforcing What You've Learned

At the End of Each Lesson

The Demonstrate Your Knowledge feature lets you show what you've learned through two types of exercises:

■ **Critical Thinking Questions** Open-ended questions providing in-depth skills challenge

■ **Activities** Hands-on exercises and creative projects to help you apply what you've learned

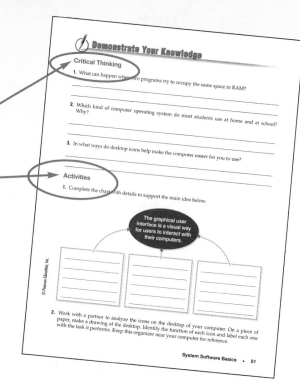

At the End of Each Chapter

■ **Use the Vocabulary** Matching exercises to check your understanding of key terms in the chapter

■ **Think Critically** Short-answer questions to demonstrate your understanding of concepts

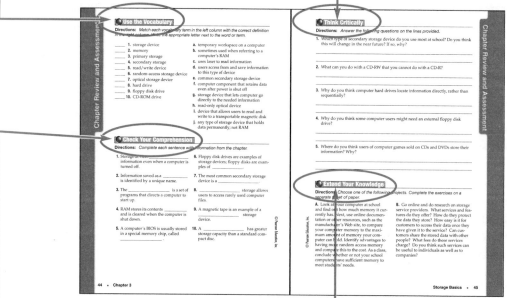

■ **Check Your Comprehension** Questions to self-check your reading comprehension

■ **Extend Your Knowledge** Projects incorporating all the skills you have learned in a fun and challenging activity

Keyboarding Essentials

Keying Correctly

FIGURE K-1
At the beginning of each class, adjust your workstation.

The human body is not designed for long sessions of repetitive movement. You might even know someone who has strained their hands and fingers by playing video games. Keyboarding can present similar dangers. When you key, you repeat many small movements with your hands and fingers. You might be keying for a long time. If you position yourself correctly, however, you can avoid strain and fatigue.

Even if you do not practice healthy keying techniques, you might not experience any problems while you are young and flexible. However, over the years, if you don't begin to key correctly, you will repeat thousands of stressful movements. You risk painful long-lasting injury that can reduce the quality of your life and your ability to work. It pays to develop healthy keying habits now.

ADJUSTING YOUR WORKSTATION

In a classroom you do not usually have much choice in the equipment you must use. However, flexible equipment and a little imagination can help you adjust your workstation.

Adjusting Your Keyboard and Mouse

You want your fingers to gently curve over the keys while your wrist is in a flat, neutral position.

- ◆ If wrist rests are available, place one in front of the keyboard as a guide. Never rest your arms, hands, or wrists while you are keying.

- ◆ Place your mouse or trackball at the same height as your keyboard, in easy reach of your preferred hand.

Adjusting the Slope of Your Keyboard

If your keyboard slants toward you, you need to adjust it so it is flat or slopes down away from you.

- ◆ Flatten the kickstand at the back of the keyboard.

- ◆ Alternatively, raise the front of the keyboard about ¾ inch by using door wedges, a wood strip, or a box.

TECHNIQUE TIP

Never rest your arms, hands, or wrists on anything while you are keying.

CORRECT KEYING POSTURE

After you have adjusted your workstation, you need to maintain the correct keying posture.

CHECKLIST

Keying Correctly

☑ Center your body on the J key, about a hand's length from the keyboard and directly in front of the monitor.

☑ Hold your head straight over your shoulders, without straining forward or backward.

☑ Position the monitor at eye level about arm's length away so you look down about 10 degrees.

☑ Elongate and relax your neck.

☑ Keep your shoulders down.

☑ Tilt your keyboard slightly down toward the monitor. This helps you keep your wrists neutral and your fingers relaxed and curled.

☑ Adjust your chair and keyboard so your elbows bend at right angles.

☑ Keep your arms close to your sides but free to move slightly.

☑ Keep your wrists relaxed and straight in a "neutral" position.

☑ Keep your back upright or tilted slightly forward from the hips. Keep the slight natural curve of your lower back. Use a cushion or adjust the chair to support your lower back.

☑ Keep your knees slightly lower than your hips.

☑ Adjust your chair so your feet are well supported. Use a footrest, if needed.

AVOIDING STRESS WHEN KEYING

There are two ways to avoid stress when keying. First, you need to maintain the correct keying posture as you key. Second, you need to take a short break every 20 to 30 minutes and perform stretching exercises designed to help you avoid strain, fatigue, and injury.

Maintaining a Correct Keying Position

It's easy to start keying by using the correct keying position. As we key, however, many of us lose our focus, and bad habits begin to creep in. It's important to check your keying position to make sure you are still keying correctly.

TABLE K-1: Maintaining a Correct Keying Position

Maintain a Correct Position		Avoid Stressful Positions	
	**FIGURE K-2** Maintain a correct upright posture.		**FIGURE K-3** Avoid slouching, extending your elbows, or bending your wrists.
	**FIGURE K-4** Maintain a neutral position with your hands.		**FIGURE K-5** Avoid twisting your hands inward or outward.
	**FIGURE K-6** Maintain a neutral wrist position with gently curled fingers.		**FIGURE K-7** Avoid bending your wrists or using an upward-sloping keyboard.

Stretching and Resting

When you key for a long time, your muscles stiffen. You become fatigued and risk injury. You build tension in many parts of your body, including your neck, arms, and wrists. To relieve the tension and reduce the threat of injury, you should stretch before you start keying. You should also take short breaks from keying every 20 to 30 minutes and stretch.

Stretch 1: Neck Stretch
Sitting tall, bring your chin toward your chest, stretching the back of your neck. Slowly repeat two times. See the following page.

FIGURE K-8

Stretch 2: Head Turn

Begin with your head in a neutral position. Look all the way to the right without moving your chest or upper back. Then look to the left. Slowly repeat two times.

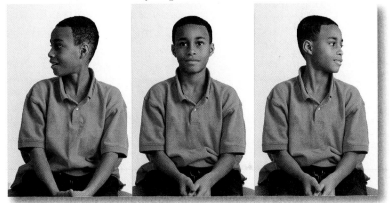

FIGURE K-9

Stretch 3: Head Tilt

Begin with your head in a neutral position. Bring your ear toward your shoulder without turning your head or lifting your shoulder. Hold for a count of five. Reverse directions.

FIGURE K-10

Stretch 4: Downward Wrist Stretch

With your left fingers pointing down and your palm in, place your right hand over your left knuckles. Extend your arms straight out. Gently press back with your right hand to a count of ten. Reverse hands. Repeat the stretches using a fist.

FIGURE K-11

Stretch 5: Upward Wrist Stretch

With your left fingers pointing up, place your right hand over your left palm. Extend your arms straight out. Gently press back with your right hand to a count of ten. Reverse hands. Repeat the stretches with fingers pointing down and the palm out.

FIGURE K-12

BENEFITS OF KEYING CORRECTLY

Training takes effort and time. If you already use a keyboard, you might have to re-teach your body to use correct techniques. You might ask yourself "Why make the effort? I'm already keying fast enough."

Just imagine you will probably be using a computer for the rest of your life. If you don't learn now, you will probably need to learn later. There's really no escaping it. Besides, if you learn to key correctly, you will:

- ✦ Increase your speed.
- ✦ Increase your efficiency, making fewer errors.
- ✦ Increase your effectiveness because you can see your work and screen while your hands are free to work.
- ✦ Stay healthy, avoid injury, and remain productive over your lifetime.

BREAKING BAD HABITS

Many of you might have been keying for years. However, without any formal training, you could easily have developed bad habits.

The best way to correct bad habits is to use natural breaks as checkpoints. For instance, look at your own habits at the end of each exercise, paragraph, or page you type. Consider your posture, sitting position, hand position, keying technique, and work habits.

To help you break your bad habits, here's a "Bad Habits Checklist." Check it when you start keying and when you take a break. If you know you have a particular bad habit, try to focus on the correction at the beginning of every keying session. Eventually the bad habit will be replaced by the good habit. It takes work, but it's worth it.

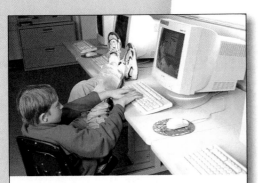

FIGURE K-13

Many of us have developed bad habits that we need to break.

TABLE K-2:   Bad Habits Checklist

Bad Habits	Correction
Slouching	Sit up straight with your feet flat and well supported.
Reaching too far for the keyboard or the mouse	Sit one hand's length from the keyboard. Keep elbows at right angles.
Leaning your hand on the keyboard or the wrist support	Hover your hands over the keyboard; curl your fingers slightly.
Bending your wrists forward, back, left, or right	Keep your forearms and wrists straight and in the neutral position.
Pounding the keys	Strike keys lightly.
Looking at the keyboard	Position the workstand close to the monitor at eye level. Keep your eyes on your work.
Raising your elbows	Keep your arms close to your body.
Raising your shoulders	Keep your shoulders relaxed, with your chest open and wide.
Keying with the wrong fingers	Practice with correct fingers until you establish the right habit. Your speed will then improve.

Learn the Home Keys

HOME KEYS

A	Use the **A** finger.
S	Use the **S** finger.
D	Use the **D** finger.
F	Use the **F** finger.
J	Use the **J** finger.
K	Use the **K** finger.
L	Use the **L** finger.
;	Use the **;** finger.

The semicolon (;) is typically used between two independent clauses in a sentence. In a sentence, key one space after a semicolon.

KEYBOARDING TIP

On **;** only the semicolon is colored. This is because the key is used for two different characters. In this lesson, you learn how to key the semicolon. In a later lesson you will learn how to key a colon.

LEARN AND PRACTICE

Begin keying by placing your fingers on the eight keys—called the *home keys*—**A S D F J K L** and semicolon **;** as shown below.

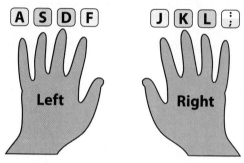

The index finger of your left hand should rest on **F**, your second and third fingers rest on **D** and **S**, and the little finger of your left hand rests on **A**. For your right hand, your index finger should rest on **J**, your second and third fingers rest on **K** and **L**, and your little finger rests on **;**.

From now on, the finger you use to press a key will be named for its home-key letter. For example, your left little finger is the **A** finger. Your right index finger is the **J** finger.

From the home keys, you can reach all the other keys on the keyboard. The keyboard diagram shows which home-key finger is used for each key. For example, you use the **D** finger to key all the keys in the band of green on the left. You use the **L** finger to key all the keys in the band of red on the right, and so on. When any finger is not actually pressing a key, you should keep it resting lightly on its home key.

The row of keys containing the home keys is called the *home row*. The row below the home row is the *first row*. The row above the home row is the *third row*.

NEW KEYS

Spacebar	Use the thumb of your writing hand.
Enter	Use the ⨆ finger.

Learn and Practice the Spacebar

Notice that on the keyboard diagram, the keys you have learned are darker and tinted with their background color. Now locate the Spacebar on the diagram. You use the Spacebar to insert spaces between letters and words. You press it by using the thumb of your writing hand (that is, the hand you use for writing). You do not use the thumb of your other hand.

Key the home-key letters, inserting a space after each letter by pressing the Spacebar quickly and lightly. (Drill lines are numbered. Do not key the green numbers.)

```
1  a s d f j k l ;
```

Learn and Practice Enter

You do not have to wait for a text line to be "full" before starting a new line. Pressing the Enter key starts a new line of text whenever you need one. You press Enter by using the ⨆ finger. Try to keep the J finger on its home key when you press Enter.

Now press Enter (↵) to start a new line.

Key each of the lines below twice. Press Enter (↵) after each line.

```
2  asdf jkl; asdf jkl; asdf jkl;↵
3  ;lkj fdsa ;lkj fdsa ;lkj fdsa↵
4  fd jk sa l; fds jkl dsa kl;↵
5  dfsa l;kj ddss kkll ffaa ;;jj fjdk ls;a↵
```

Learn and Practice Double-Space

You can add a blank line between lines of text by pressing Enter twice. This is how you *double-space* text. (Two consecutive Enters are sometimes referred to as a *double line-space*.)

Key a line of text, press Enter, and then key it again. After you key a line the second time, press Enter twice before keying a new line. Using this method, key each line twice, and double-space after each pair of lines.

```
6  adfs jlk; aj sk dl f; aaa jjj sd kl ldsk↵
7  fjjf dkkd slsl da l; ks fj ;f sss lll dl↵
8  kkd dlk ds ddd ;f ff ;; fdl; sl f; ds kl↵
9  a as dad sad fads lads lass falls flasks↵
```

TECHNIQUE TIP

Make sure your back is straight or tilted slightly forward from the hips.

TECHNIQUE TIP

Begin with your fingers curled and lightly touching the home keys.

LESSON 2

Review the Home Keys

REVIEW

The keyboard shows the keys you have learned so far. This lesson focuses on the keys highlighted in purple.

WARM UP

Key each line twice. Double-space after each pair of lines (remember, that means pressing Enter after you key the line the first time and pressing Enter twice after you key the line the second time).

```
1  asdf jkl; asdf jkl; asdf jk l; as df jkl↵
2  ;lkj fdsa ;lkj fdsa a;sl dkfj fdjk sa l;↵
3  fk dk sl a; fds jkl asd ;lkj k fd asf lj↵
4  sdl fdk kls ad; jfd salk klas dsf; flks;↵
```

PRACTICE

Key each line twice. Double-space after each pair of lines.

Left-Hand Focus
```
5  fdsa asdf ff dd ss aa fd sa ds af asf fd↵
6  asdf df df sd sd as as fa af das fad saa↵
7  fads df as dfaa ddfs fada dada fafa sasa↵
```

Right-Hand Focus
```
8  jkl; ;lkj jj kk ll ;; jk l; kl j; jk; jk↵
9  jkl; l; l; kl kl jk jk ;j j; ;lk ;lk kjj↵
10 jlkj l; jk jll lkjj kkjl klk jkkl; kllj;↵
```

Home Keys
```
11 asdf jkl; fjdk l;sa fjk jfd dkl kds; all↵
12 jk df dk jf sl a; fjd kds; akl kdsl dkll↵
13 adkl dajk kads lfds; ljds jfds lks; jdlk↵
14 as a dad; all lads; all fads; as a lass;↵
15 lads; dads; as sad; lass; as all; a fad;↵
```

TECHNIQUE TIP

Concentrate on pressing the correct keys. Read silently letter-by-letter as you key. In this Warm Up do not focus on your speed.

BREAKING BAD HABITS

Do not hammer your fingers on the keyboard. Strike keys with a light tap.

LESSON 3

Learn E and H

WARM UP

Key each line twice. Double-space after each pair of lines. Do not look at the keyboard when you are keying.

1 a dd aaa as asd sdf j jj jjj jk jkl jkl;↵
2 as ads ask; lass dada jask fads dads sad↵
3 lads dada daff; jajs ja salad dads; saks↵
4 jakk jall; jadd dajs ladd saddl aja had;↵

LEARN

Reach your **D** finger up and slightly left when you key **E**. Keep your **A** and **S** fingers anchored on their home keys. Reach your **J** finger directly left to key **H**. Keep the other right-hand fingers anchored on their home keys.

NEW KEYS

E Use the **D** finger.

H Use the **J** finger.

KEYBOARDING TIP

Press Enter at the end of every line unless you are told specifically to use word-wrap. From this point on, the Enter symbol (↵) is not shown.

PRACTICE

Key each line twice. Double-space after each pair of lines.

Practice e
5 d e d ddd eee de ede eed lee eel del eel
6 eee ddd lll eel led eee dell lee led lee
7 eee ddd elk elf sell eee ddd see lee fee

Practice h
8 j h jjj hhh jh hj jhj hjh jjj hhh jj hhh
9 aaa hhh ash sss ash hh ss aa has sa sash
10 ha had aha has heel she hee half hah has

Practice e and h
11 he he eh eh hhh eee she he eh she eh hee
12 hhh eee easel feed seed heed lead she he
13 jade desks head sake head lead seal jade
14 has heed; lad had; heel hale; seek sale;

Keyboarding Essentials • K11

LESSON 4 Learn R and I

Key each line twice. Double-space after each pair of lines. Concentrate on pressing the correct key each time.

1 ff fff ddd fd df jj jkj lkj fjk fdjk hhj
2 fed fej fek dek dell jade dale fake keel
3 lease lash lake ladle leak led leek feel
4 flea fled sea seal sell sleek shake heel

LEARN

NEW KEYS

R Use the F finger.

I Use the K finger.

Reach your F finger up and slightly left when you key R. Keep the other left-hand fingers anchored on their home keys. Reach your K finger up and slightly left to key I. Keep the other right-hand fingers anchored on their home keys.

TECHNIQUE TIP

Adjust your chair and keyboard so your elbows bend at right angles.

PRACTICE

Key each line twice. Double-space after each pair of lines.

Practice r
5 fff frf frf fff rfr rffr fff rrr fff rrr
6 ra are far raf dare reef fear free freed
7 red jar lard reel dark darker hares rare

Practice i
8 k kk iii kik kkk ikki iki kk ii kkk kiki
9 ii ll jj kij sill jik ilk fill dill kids
10 if is silk kid hid kill ilk kiss hi hide

Practice r and i
11 ri ire ride sir rife fire dire sire rise
12 if ride hire hare hers rides fries dries
13 lair fair hair raid rid dill drill frill
14 riff sheared shire sear fire liars fried

LESSON 5

Review E H R and I

REVIEW

The keyboard shows the keys you have learned so far. This lesson focuses on the keys highlighted in purple.

WARM UP

Key each line twice. Double-space after each pair of lines.

1 all ale ad else sled sell sale lass less
2 sheer shear share ail air rile lair fair
3 hash flea his head lead lease deals dash
4 here hares hire hair jars jeer rear dear

PRACTICE

Key each line twice. Double-space after each pair of lines.

Practice e and h
5 ddd dde ded dde eed ed deeds sea eel see
6 hhh hjh jhj jjj jjh hh ja had he has she
7 had shed he she jade lake head ease heed
8 deed heed seed heal seal fed easel lease

Practice r and i
9 rrr ffr frf rfr re are red her fair here
10 iii iki kik kki if ire dire kid lie like
11 rise iris frail rail err dear dire fires
12 sire fire liar lair rail hail jail riser

Practice e h r and i
13 heir hare hair heard hire here rare rear
14 lairs said share shire red her idea dare
15 jeers; sir fir hear; fare hare hair lair
16 sear shared; liars rails hired fired ire
17 hailed fresher fished rides herds shades

BREAKING BAD HABITS

Do not look at the keyboard. Keep your eyes on the screen or on your work.

NEW KEYS

T   Use the F finger.

O   Use the L finger.

BREAK ING

BAD HABITS

Do not rest your hands or arms on any support. Keep your hands over the keyboard as you key.

WARM UP

Key each line twice. Double-space after each pair of lines. Keep your fingers anchored on the home keys.

```
1  f ff fff fir fire fir fire fff ff fff ff
2  l ll lll lad lade lad lade lll ll lll ll
3  fall fell fill earl leaf field fife life
4  hall hall lire dire rare rash dash flash
```

LEARN

Reach your F finger up and right to key T. Keep your A, S, and D fingers anchored on their home keys. Reach your L finger up and slightly left to key O. Keep the other fingers of your right hand anchored on their home keys.

PRACTICE

Key each line twice. Double-space after each pair of lines.

Practice t
```
5  f ff ttt ftf tft fftt the that this tree
6  this tall tree; tear it; lift the tires;
7  at all; third three first; at tea three;
```

Practice o
```
8  o ll o oo lol olo old lot soak sold told
9  ode doe rot dot lot lost slot joke joker
10 oars are solid; oats look food; a lot of
```

Practice o and t
```
11 ff tt trt ll oo lo ol ooo of to too toto
12 foot fool tools loot took jots lots soot
13 hoot; odes to; store; lots of lost tools
14 hold those; if told; he dotes; too short
```

LESSON 7   Learn G and N

WARM UP

Key each line twice. Double-space after each pair of lines. Keep your wrists and fingers relaxed.

1 f ff fff fit file fail fir fr ftr ftt tf
2 j jj jjj jar jail has hill jhj jj hhj jj
3 feel foil life half heal this that those
4 joke hers rake fast haste hoist lash lid

NEW KEYS

G Use the F finger.

N Use the J finger.

LEARN

Reach your F finger directly right to key G. Keep the other fingers of your left hand anchored on their home keys. Reach your J finger down and left to key N. Keep the other fingers of your right hand anchored on their home keys.

TECHNIQUE TIP

When keying, hold your head straight, without tilting it forward or backward.

PRACTICE

Key each line twice. Double-space after each pair of lines.

Practice g

5 g gg ggg fgf fgtg tgf go gal got get lag
6 sag sage stag stage gas rag egg edge leg
7 dog ledge keg grog get tiger grade grail

Practice n

8 n nn nnn jnj jnhn hnjn no on in kin none
9 rind seen lane train lane lean nine lion
10 tan ten ton tin tones none nasal tinnier

Practice n and g

11 ff gg gg jj nn nn gn ng ing ing nag ring
12 nag anger gnarl range longer green grind
13 ring grand glean grin gone gentle ginger
14 tangle dangle strange slings and strings

LESSON 8

Learn Left Shift and Period

WARM UP

Key each line twice. Double-space after each pair of lines. Keep your fingers curved.

```
1  a aa aaa j jj jjj; a aa aaa j kk lll jkl
2  l ll lll lag lags land doll dill toil in
3  all lie like kite kin of ode or ore idea
4  lashes slides knell soil sails rill roil
```

LEARN

NEW KEYS

Shift Use the **A** finger.

Use Left Shift for right-hand capital letters (and for all other shifted right-hand characters).

> Use the **L** finger.
.

A period is used in abbreviations and to mark the end of a sentence. Typically, one space follows a period.

Reach your **A** finger down and left to press the Left Shift key. With Left Shift pressed, you can strike any right-hand key. Then release Left Shift. Reach your **L** finger down and slightly right to key **.** Keep your **J** finger on its home key.

PRACTICE

BREAK ING

BAD HABITS

Do not look at the keyboard. Keep your eyes on the screen or on your work.

Key each line twice. Double-space after each pair of lines.

Practice Left Shift
```
5   jJ Jj Jd kK Kk Kf lL Ll Ls JdJ fKKf sLLs
6   hH Hj Ha aHHa; Jill Hill Lee; Hall Iris;
7   Hi there Hello; Here he is; Leo the lion
```

Practice Period
```
8   a. l. s. k. d. j. f. e. r. t. i. o. n. a
9   adj. alt. art. e.g. gal. i.e. inf. sing.
10  in. ft. kil. gr. lit. orig. transl. del.
```

Practice Left Shift and Period
```
11  Kan. La. OH OK HI N.H. N.J. Jos. I. Kant
12  Long. Lat. N.H.L. Joe and Jed; King Lear
13  I see. I said. I sit. I sat. I do. I do.
14  Ode to Leo. Oh. His is. No. One. Listen.
```

Review Left Shift T O G N and Period

REVIEW

The keyboard shows the keys you have learned so far. This lesson focuses on the keys highlighted in purple.

WARM UP

Key each line twice. Double-space after each pair of lines. Concentrate on pressing the correct key each time.

1 t to to tot toe not note got gotten tote
2 jJ kK lL hH iI oO. Joke; Kids like Jake.
3 Joanne is terse. Nora nods. Kane is kin.
4 Kirk tends to the garden. Lana looks on.

TECHNIQUE TIP

Center your body on **J**, about a hand's length from the keyboard, directly in front of your monitor.

PRACTICE

Key each line once. Double-space after each group of lines.

Practice t and o

5 ttt ooo fff lll to too toot tot toe tote
6 to tone toner foot oat lot jot rote goat
7 toast knots trots lost stones toes ghost

Practice g and n

8 ggg nnn ggg nnn no go; gone; genes; sign
9 long longer longest longing song singing
10 no nod node; note done; gig agog; gotten

Practice Left Shift and Period

11 JKL; IO. KNOLL. Jr. Kg. Lg. Kg. Jds. Hd.
12 Kin are kind. Logan Hotel. Otis loiters.
13 L. L. H. H. K. K. J. J. I. I. I. Hi. No.

Practice t o g n Left Shift and Period

14 to go to. Nine tons. No one going. Ogden
15 green gnarl great gross gnats grain gilt
16 N.J.L. L.J.K. J.I.N.; Old Ohio. Old Hat.

LESSON 10 Learn C and U

WARM UP

Key each line twice. Double-space after each pair of lines. Strike the keys with a light tap.

```
1  d dd ddd sad sat dot dog done dotes adds
2  j jj jjj Jill Join hill her his hat hits
3  Lili held on. Jade is green. Jess holds.
4  does he dial one or three; drifted east;
```

NEW KEYS

C Use the D finger.

U Use the J finger.

LEARN

Reach down and slightly right with your D finger to key C. Keep the A and S fingers anchored on their home keys. Reach up and slightly left with your J finger to key U. Keep the K, L, and ; fingers anchored on their home keys.

TECHNIQUE TIP

Hold your head up and relax your neck.

PRACTICE

Key each line twice. Double-space after each pair of lines.

Practice c
```
5  d dd c cc dc dc dcd cad cat cater decade
6  lacks class clicks coins; Nick can cook.
7  lace cask flock shock Jack likes cheese.
```

Practice u
```
8  j jj u uu ju ju juj ujuj us use sue uses
9  due hue hurt huge urge; He is Uncle Kurt.
10 Used lutes and flutes; noun run nuts hut
```

Practice c and u
```
11 cur cue cut cud curt cute cuff cure curd
12 cull could cough couch accuse occur ouch
13 curls cushion curious cluck scour ruckus
14 such clubs culture course cruel function
```

LESSON 11

Learn W and Right Shift

WARM UP

Key each line twice. Double-space after each pair of lines. Keep your arms close to your sides but free to move.

```
1  s ss sss sash ski skits sour sell sister
2  so; does; sun; stars; sass; losses; dust
3  Hugh shares his fish. He leads us south.
4  sack; cast; usage; soccer; lesson; sense
```

LEARN

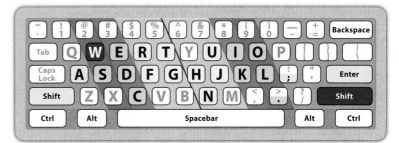

Reach up and slightly left with your **S** finger to key **W**. Keep your **F** and **D** fingers anchored on their home keys. Reach your **;** finger down and right to press the Right Shift key. (Keep your **J** and **K** fingers anchored on their home keys.) With Right Shift pressed, you can strike any left-hand key. Then release Right Shift.

PRACTICE

Key each line twice. Double-space after each pair of lines.

Practice w

```
5   s w ss ww sss ws sws wsw sss www sws wsw
6   saw awe dew draw jaw law wall well wills
7   sag wad owe we wan wall week wear wealth
```

Practice Right Shift

```
8   S; St; SA; W.A.G. F Fa Go Ta Da Ed We Fr
9   Fast Far Face Dad Dash Deal Sad Sash Add
10  AHA; Cold Drinks; Fine Sand; Grills Fish
```

Practice w and Right Shift

```
11  The Fresh Air Fund; The Far East; C.O.D.
12  WAAF Go slowly. Walt thinks; Tess walks;
13  Glow Aware Flaw Waist Rower Ewe Chew Few
14  Raw Flow Worn Waif Grown Stew Stow Worth
```

LESSON 12 Learn X and M

NEW KEYS

X Use the S finger.

M Use the J finger.

TECHNIQUE TIP

Keep your shoulders down.

WARM UP

Key each line twice. Double-space after each pair of lines. Keep your wrists relaxed.

1 s ss sss w ww www sw wsw sw saw sew swat
2 j jj u uu jiujitsu Julio jingle just jaw
3 Chris Wes Wendi sacks socks clock roasts
4 as is was SST Sid idle snack snake straw

LEARN

Reach down and slightly right with your S finger to key X. As you make the reach, keep your F finger anchored on its home key. Reach down and slightly right with your J finger to key M. Keep your K, L, and ; fingers anchored on their home keys.

PRACTICE

Key each line twice. Double-space after each pair of lines.

Practice x

5 s ss x xx sx xsx xs xss S X XSX six axis
6 ax axe axel ox oxen fox flex sax sox FAX
7 Rex hoax nix next index annex Saxons XXI

Practice m

8 j jj jm mj jmmj mmjm mm mmm JM MJ me mom
9 Milk makes more might. gamma mailman mum
10 mammoth makes mole mire magma Mark merge

Practice x and m

11 wax tax lax gum gem exam remix minx coax
12 mold mile mere more magic marred maximum
13 Tom Mix; Max; Mr. Maxwell; Ms. M. Maxine
14 maxim mixture axiom Manx matrix exclaims

LESSON 13

Review C U W X M and Right Shift

REVIEW

The keyboard shows the keys you have learned so far. This lesson focuses on the keys highlighted in purple.

WARM UP

Key each line twice. Double-space after each pair of lines.

1 Dd Ss Cc Jj Uu Ww Xx Mm cue cruel tuxedo
2 sugar smudge mail male malls urges under
3 Ursa Essex Tom mow met metric metal axle
4 Caitlin wash wish wells waxes masc. fem.

TECHNIQUE TIP

Key by using the correct reach; other fingers should remain in their home positions.

PRACTICE

Key each line twice. Double-space after each pair of lines.

Practice c and u

5 muck duck duct tuck luck lucid cull cuss
6 cute could crush crust touch truck scull
7 deuce stuck stack sticks success custard

Practice w and Right Shift

8 William Washi Wen Winslow Woodrow Wilson
9 Wolfgang Winona Wade Wheeler Wilma Wendi
10 Willow Wallace Wanda Ward Wes Walt Willa

Practice x and m

11 mix Mexican maximum maximal Maddox moxie
12 mixer Alex examined axmen taxman Maxwell
13 mass exits extremes exhumes sixth summer

Practice c u w Right Shift x and m

14 Cellist Cancels a Concert. Felix meowed.
15 Dexter Wexler Chuck chum chew chow exits
16 Sammie worries that few hear much music.

LESSON 14 Learn B and Y

WARM UP

Key each line twice. Double-space after each pair of lines. Do not look at the keyboard.

1 if elf fast fill fun effort effect faded
2 end hen den jail Julie hale hinge jogger
3 gas sash fish half fresh joshes freshman
4 Edward jest heft cleft gash grass jagged

NEW KEYS

B Use the F finger.

Y Use the J finger.

LEARN

Reach your F finger down and right to key B. Keep your A finger anchored on its home key. Reach your J finger up and left to key Y. Keep the other right-hand fingers anchored on their home keys.

BREAK ING

BAD HABITS

Do not reach far for the keyboard. Keep elbows at right angles but free to move slightly.

PRACTICE

Key each line twice. Double-space after each pair of lines.

Practice b

5 fff fbf bfb bbb fbf bbb fb bf baa be fib
6 bee bib bat bar rub dub cub club tub but
7 been bias bunt tuba stub beef bark about
8 cable rabbit cabbie ribbon rubber bubble

Practice y

9 jjj jyj yyj jjy jyj yyy jy yj yd jay hay
10 you yet yes say sty dry day aye fly away
11 joy jay jury ray rely yolk yen nosy body
12 Young York Yak yam yummy tiny teeny tidy

Practice b and y

13 Bryce buys a bulb to brighten the lobby.
14 Buddy the bulldog labors to bury a bone.
15 Brody yearns for a yacht; bye bye money.

LESSON 15 Learn V and P

WARM UP

Key each line twice. Double-space after each pair of lines. Key by using the correct reach.

```
1  ff gg bb fbf fans feels Biff baffles bye
2  j; Jill; lo; hi; his; hers; their; lake;
3  good friend; forge ahead; lost messages;
4  ironclad; tea for two; title match; I.D.
```

NEW KEYS

V Use the **F** finger.

P Use the **;** finger.

LEARN

Reach your **F** finger down and slightly right to key **V**. Keep your **A** and **S** fingers anchored on their home keys. Reach your **;** finger up and slightly left to key **P**. Keep the other right-hand fingers anchored on their home keys.

TECHNIQUE TIP

When using your **;** finger to reach for **P**, keep your right elbow close to your side.

PRACTICE

Key each line twice. Double-space after each pair of lines.

Practice v
```
5  fff fv fv vf fvv vfv vgf fvf fvv vet eve
6  vow van vat vex vote vast vase vest vary
7  ivy ever even envy eave avid alive above
```

Practice p
```
8  ;; ;p; pp; ;pp p; pp; ;p ppp pat pad ape
9  pep papa pass pond pane pick paste price
10 sap clap tape press supper paddle puddle
```

Practice v and p
```
11 pave peeve prove privy vamp VIP provider
12 vapors viper verve pivot private prevail
13 evil powers oval pools develop viewpoint
14 vampire approve overlap overpaid popover
```

LESSON 16 Learn Q and

WARM UP

Key each line twice. Double-space after each pair of lines. Strike each key with the correct finger.

1 as aim aide avid aster ashes adapt adept
2 key kid king kit kiss kiln milks kippers
3 okay lanes lake like lamb Luke live long
4 all alarm call rail raffle river Alabama

NEW KEYS

Q Use the **A** finger.

<, Use the **K** finger.

The comma is used to separate words and phrases for clearness.

LEARN

Reach your **A** finger up and slightly left to key **Q**. Keep your **D** and **F** fingers anchored on their home keys. Reach your **K** finger down and slightly right to key the comma **<,**. Keep your **L** and **;** fingers anchored to their home keys.

PRACTICE

Key each line twice. Double-space after each pair of lines.

Practice q

5 aa aq aqqa qqaa aqa qqa qa qua aqua quad
6 quit quay quite quick quill quilt quaint
7 equip equal squid squad quest quack Que.

Practice ,

8 k, kk, ki, jk, A, B, C, D, E, F, G, H, I
9 one, two, three, four; red, white, blue,
10 Joaquin owned a cat, a dog, and a mouse.

Practice q and ,

11 quiet, quota, quote, squat, squaw, squib
12 Raquel, quail, squirrel, sequel, conquer
13 equate, equator, Quincy, squares, squirt
14 Queen, quake, quasi, qualm, quirk, quash

BREAKING BAD HABITS

Do not bend your wrists forward, back, left, or right. Keep them relaxed and straight.

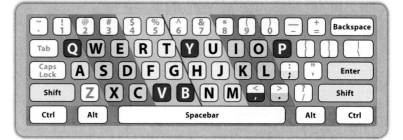

LESSON 17 Review B Y V P Q and <,

REVIEW

The keyboard shows the keys you have learned so far. This lesson focuses on the keys highlighted in purple.

WARM UP

Key each line twice. Double-space after each pair of lines.

1 fad frail Frank Alfred bug bud bush vast
2 hen Hanna vary very your young yell yelp
3 bevy; pamper; prove; pixie; posh; gladly
4 year, ache, acre, squish, piquant, quint

TECHNIQUE TIP

Make sure your back is straight or tilted slightly forward from the hips.

PRACTICE

Key each line twice. Double-space after each pair of lines.

Practice b and y
5 byte ruby abyss shabby tabby bygone days
6 bay birthday yellow belly bully boundary
7 gabby cubby abbey bubbly burly hobby buy

Practice v and p
8 vapor vapid pensive pave preview prevent
9 Vice President V.I.P. overpaid passivity
10 Pablo plays the vibraphone very happily.

Practice q and ,
11 Quite, squab, quickens, quibble, quantum
12 Queens, quits, toque, quarrels, quantity
13 Quinn squashed it quickly and then quit.

Practice b y v p q and ,
14 pay pry bypass bumpy pebbly pygmy opaque
15 brave, vinyl, brevity, behave very badly
16 Bowery Boys, Marquis, Beverly, Quasimodo

LESSON 18 Learn Z and ;

NEW KEYS

Z Use the **A** finger.

; Use Left Shift and the **;** finger.

The colon (:) is used in numerical expressions and to direct attention to information that follows (as in "For example:").

SPACING TIP

In a sentence, you use one space after a colon.

WARM UP

Key each line twice. Double-space after each pair of lines. Keep your wrists relaxed and straight.

1 debut past perk park chances dares tries
2 flurry hurry scurry enjoy delays happens
3 salve settles vessel vassal caste create
4 Frasier will pursue a career in finance.

LEARN

Reach your **A** finger down and slightly right when you key **Z**. Keep the left-hand fingers anchored on their home keys. Keying the colon is like keying a capital letter. Hold down the Left Shift key and strike **;**. Then release Left Shift.

PRACTICE

Key each line twice. Double-space after each pair of lines.

Practice z
5 a az aza zza zaz aqza za azq zza zap zoo
6 zoom zest zeal Zen zinc zone cozy zipper
7 Zuni fizz fuzz zigzag zebra zero pizzazz
8 zip quiz lazy mezzo muzzle zenith frozen

Practice :
9 ; ;: :: ;: :; ::: Sirs: Ext: As follows:
10 Memo To: From: Date: Subj: RE: CC: ATTN:
11 To Whom It May Concern: Dear Madam: Ref:

Practice z and :
12 Dear Elizabeth: To: Mrs. Dezanne Ziegler
13 Puzzle answer: ZIP Code: Zone: Size: NZ:
14 Zoe: Zora: Oz: Ziggy: Ezra: Zelda: Buzz:

LESSON 19 Learn

WARM UP

Key each line twice. Double-space after each pair of lines. Keep your eyes on the page and not on the keyboard.

```
1 fizz fuzz dizzy gaze buzzer prized gizmo
2 Abbot alley fast has lasts dash flag lab
3 play; pram; pads; my pals; swamps; pique
4 Name: Address: FAX: cars, planes, trains
```

NEW KEYS

 Use the finger.

The apostrophe (') has many purposes. Use it to form contractions (don't) and possessives (John's).

Use Left Shift and the finger.

Use quotation marks (" ") to enclose direct quotations, to emphasize words, and to display certain titles.

LEARN

Reach your finger right to key an apostrophe. Keep the **J**, **K**, and **L** fingers anchored on their home keys. To key a quotation mark, hold down Left Shift, reach your finger right, and strike.

PRACTICE

Key each line twice. Double-space after each pair of lines.

Practice '
```
5 ;' ;';' ';'; 's s' it's I'm isn't aren't
6 Jill's Dave's Omar's didn't don't aren't
7 isn't hadn't should've would've could've
```

Practice "
```
8 ;" ";"; "x" "y" "A" "B" "My Way" "Okay."
9 "Not me." "Maybe soon." "See you later."
10 "Just enough," she said. "Oh, we agree."
```

Practice ' and "
```
11 "It's Magic" "Let's Dance" "That's Life"
12 "Don't hang up." "I'll call." "I'm Sue."
13 "Malcolm's moved the boxes," Rubin said.
14 It's the book "Emma" for Mr. Hu's class.
15 "Lillie won't travel on New Year's Eve."
```

BAD HABITS

Do not hammer your fingers on the keyboard. Strike keys with a light tap.

LESSON 20

Learn — and ?/

Key each line twice. Double-space after each pair of lines. Hold your head straight, without leaning it forward or backward.

1 "Let's go pick apples," Sophie proposed.
2 Paul's parrot piped up, "I'm not Polly."
3 Shipped to: Paul Lopez; PS: Please RSVP.
4 Piper liked papaya; Piper's aunt didn't.

NEW KEYS

— Use the ; finger.

A hyphen (-) is used to divide words between lines. It is also used for compound words.

?/ Use the ; finger.

A diagonal (/), often called a forward slash, is used in abbreviations, in fractions, and to express alternatives or relationships.

LEARN

To key a hyphen, reach your ; finger up and slightly right and strike —. Keep the J finger anchored on its home key. To key a diagonal, reach your ; finger down and slightly right and strike ?/. Keep the other right-hand fingers anchored on their home keys.

PRACTICE

Key each line twice. Double-space after each pair of lines.

Practice -
5 ;p; ;p-p; ;-; ;-; -er one-on-one T-shirt
6 side-by-side, after-effects, part-timers
7 toll-free, good-humored, close-captioned

Practice /
8 ;/; ;//; ;//;/ a/b I/we he/she East/West
9 true/false, owner/manager, and/or, AM/FM
10 his/her, on/off, either/or, input/output

Practice - and /
11 best-case/worst-case, high-rise/low-rise
12 left-hand/right-hand, mid-week/mid-month
13 paper-thin/see-through, ice-cold/red-hot
14 tax-exempt/tax-sheltered one-way/two-way

SPACING TIP

In normal use, do not space before or after the diagonal.

LESSON 21

Review Z ; " — and ? /

REVIEW

The keyboard shows the keys you have learned so far. This lesson focuses on the keys highlighted in purple.

WARM UP

Key each line twice. Double-space after each pair of lines. Begin with your fingers curled and lightly touching the home keys.

1 brazen shilly-shally sizzle crazy quartz
2 Don's fez, Via: tilt-a-whirl willy-nilly
3 mightn't hadn't "Don't say such things."
4 http://www.si.edu "wall-to-wall" mi./hr.

PRACTICE

Key each line twice. Double-space after each pair of lines.

Practice z and :
5 Price per dozen: Prize: Size: Zookeeper:
6 Zone: Bronze medal: Tarzan: Waltz: Czar:

Practice ' and "
7 "Neither a borrower nor a lender be." S.
8 "Don't just say 'Don't' like that's it."

Practice - and /
9 street-smart/quick-witted/sharp-sighted;
10 He/she must give a blow-by-blow account.
11 She provides on-site support for E-mail.

Practice z : ' " - and /
12 "door-to-door" 'self-employed' in-house:
13 log-jam low-flying "Long-Range" two-term
14 Zig Lenz: Writer/Producer; life-or-death
15 A day of dappled sea-born clouds. -Joyce

SPACING TIPS

Remember: Do not key a space before or after a hyphen in a hyphenated word. Do not key a space before or after a diagonal.

LESSON 22

Learn Caps Lock and

NEW KEYS

Caps Lock   Use the **A** finger.

Use Caps Lock to key capital letters without pressing Right Shift or Left Shift.

?/   Use Left Shift and the **;** finger.

Use a question mark (?) at the end of a sentence that asks a question.

TECHNIQUE TIP

The Caps Lock key works only on letter keys. You still have to press Left Shift to key punctuation such as a question mark, a colon, or a quotation mark.

WARM UP

Key each line twice. Double-space after each pair of lines. Focus on your technique, not on speed.

1 AR append alternate Aswan Dallas daisies
2 Q.E.D. client-server peer-to-peer hi-res
3 Pass/Fail E/G/B/D/F play-by-play on-site
4 La Paz quizzical A-OK on-again/off-again

LEARN

Reach your **A** finger left to press **Caps Lock**. Keep all other fingers on their home keys. (Once you press **Caps Lock**, it stays on until you press it again.) The question mark is a shifted diagonal. Press Left Shift, reach your **;** finger down and slightly right, and strike **?/**.

PRACTICE

Key each line twice. Double-space after each pair of lines.

Practice Caps Lock

5 NBA, NFL, AND NCAA ANNOUNCE RULE CHANGES
6 ASPCA FINDS LOST DOG; ROVER RETURNS HOME
7 IMAGINE: MEN WALK ON MOON; READ ABOUT IT

Practice ?

8 ;/; ;?; :?? ?:? ?;? ?/?/? Who? How? Why?
9 Me? When? Soon? What day? Are you going?
10 Can you? Would you? Could you? Call me?

Practice Caps Lock and ?

11 VISITOR FROM SPACE? AN ECONOMIC SETBACK?
12 PRESIDENT'S TRIP ON HOLD? TWO TEE TIMES?
13 VIKINGS IN THE NEW WORLD? KENNEWICK MAN?
14 MASSIVE CALCULATION ERRORS TO BLAME? US?

LESSON 23 · Learn Tab

NEW KEYS

Tab Use the **A** finger.

Press Tab to align items into columns or to indent text for paragraphs. Tabs are automatically set every half-inch.

LEARN

Reach up and left with your **A** finger to key Tab. Keep the **F** finger on its home key. Keep your elbows close to your sides.

SPACING TIP

Do not key a space before or after pressing Tab.

PRACTICE

Key each line twice. Press Tab where you see an arrow. Double-space after each pair of lines.

Practice Letters and Tab

5 aba→ bcc→ cdd→ dee→ efe→ ghh→ hii→ ijj
6 jkk→ llm→ mnn→ opo→ qrr→ stt→ uvw→ xyz
7 DMA→ UPS→ CPU→ CRT→ LCD→ IRQ→ KBD→ I/O

Practice Short Words and Tab

8 all→ ad→ cat→ cot→ dot→ lot→ rot→ not
9 be→ bit→ bat→ do→ to→ tot→ in→ the
10 if→ so→ then→who→ call→to→ tell→me
11 TO→ BE→ OR→ NOT→ TO→ BE→ THAT→IS

Practice Indenting with Tab

Key the following text as a paragraph. Use word wrap. To indent the paragraph, press Tab where you see the arrow.

12 →   Qatar is an independent Arab state
13 in the Middle East, bordering the
14 Persian Gulf. It is a major exporter of
15 oil and natural gas.

LESSON 24 — Review Caps Lock and Tab

REVIEW

The keyboard shows the keys you have learned so far. This lesson focuses on the keys highlighted in purple.

WARM UP

Key each line twice. Double-space after each pair of lines.

1 A diller a dollar, a ten o'clock scholar
2 Everyone's seen a movie, no? We did not.
3 a/b/c/d/e/f/g/h/i/j/k/l/m/n/o/p/q/r/s/t/
4 Del thinks he's all that. Al thinks not.

PRACTICE

Key each line twice. Double-space after each pair of lines. Where you see an arrow, press Tab.

Practice Caps Lock

5 PHASE One; PHASE Two; PHASE Three; RESET
6 MONDAYS, WEDNESDAYS, and FRIDAYS AT NINE
7 Jamal: WISHING YOU A VERY HAPPY BIRTHDAY

Practice ?

8 Who said that? Why? Where is Paul going?
9 Well, which is it? What? You don't know?
10 How are you? Yes? No? Do you? Won't you?

Practice Tab

11 eucalyptus→hemlock→ sycamore→ larch
12 hickory→   dogwood→chestnut→ willow

Practice Caps Lock ? and Tab

13 TO:→ FR:→ RE:→ CC:→ FAX:→EXT:→FL:→ DEPT:
14 VOL→ HIGH→LOW→ DATE→OPEN→CHG→ YTD→ INT
15 ADRIANA, did ALEJANDRO call the station?
16 Narrator: WHO KNOWS WHICH WAY THEY FLED?

BREAK ING

BAD HABITS

Do not look at your hands when keying. Look at your monitor or your book.

Technology Applications

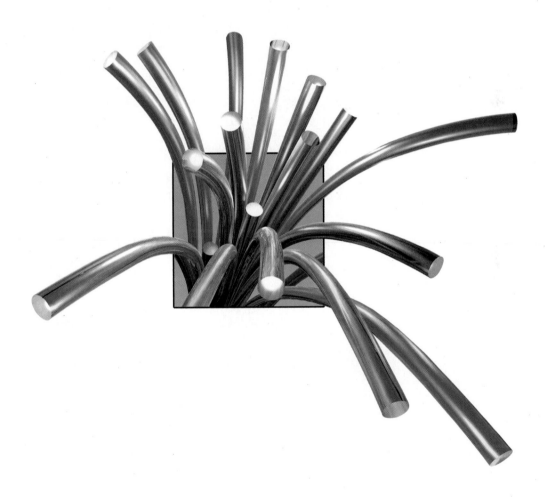

Computer Basics

© Pearson Education, Inc.

How Do Computers Work? The answer to this question can be very long and complicated, even though computers work in a fairly simple way. At its core, a computer contains a set of on/off switches; by turning these switches on and off very rapidly, the computer can represent information. Imagine a wall covered with a thousand light bulbs, each with its own on/off switch. By turning switches on and off in a certain way, you could use the lights to spell words or create pictures. Computers work in a similar way.

But a computer cannot use its switches without instructions. That's where software and you, the user, come into play. By giving the computer instructions and data to work with, you and your software programs tell it how to work its switches—turning them on and off millions of times each second.

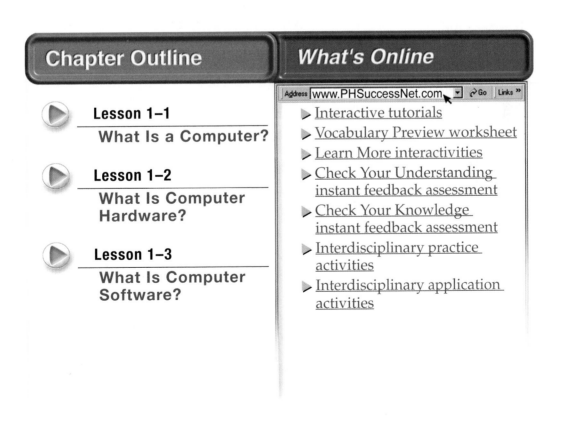

Chapter Outline

▶ **Lesson 1–1**
What Is a Computer?

▶ **Lesson 1–2**
What Is Computer Hardware?

▶ **Lesson 1–3**
What Is Computer Software?

What's Online

Address www.PHSuccessNet.com Go Links »

▶ Interactive tutorials
▶ Vocabulary Preview worksheet
▶ Learn More interactivities
▶ Check Your Understanding instant feedback assessment
▶ Check Your Knowledge instant feedback assessment
▶ Interdisciplinary practice activities
▶ Interdisciplinary application activities

What Is a Computer?

Objectives

- Describe the four operations of computers.
- Contrast analog and digital computers.
- Explain why data and instructions for computers are coded as 0s and 1s.
- Identify three benefits of computers.

As You Read

Sequence Information Use a sequence chart to help you organize the four operations of computers as you read the lesson.

What's Online

In Lesson 1–1 of the iText, you will find more features and information for this lesson, including:

- Interactive tutorials
- As You Read worksheet
- Learn More interactivities
- Check Your Understanding interactive assessments
- Interactive lesson review

🔑 Key Terms

- computer (p. 4)
- input (p. 4)
- bit (p. 4)
- byte (p. 4)
- processing (p. 5)
- output (p. 6)
- storage (p. 6)

Computer Basics

A **computer** is a machine that changes information from one form into another by performing four basic actions. Those actions are input, processing, output, and storage. Together, these actions make up the information processing cycle. By following a set of instructions, called a program, the computer turns raw data into organized information that people can use. There are two kinds of computers:

- Analog computers measure data on a scale with many values. Think of the scales on a mercury thermometer or on the gas gauge of a car.
- Digital computers work with data that has a fixed value. They use data in digital, or number, form. The computers that run programs for playing games or searching the Internet are digital computers.

Input

Input is the raw information, or data, that is entered into a computer. This data can be as simple as letters and numbers or as complex as color photographs, videos, or songs. You input data by using a device such as a keyboard or digital camera.

Bits of Data Data is entered into a computer in a coded language. The building blocks of that language are units called **bits.** *Bit* is short for *binary digit*. Each bit is a number, or a digit. A bit can have only two possible values—0 or 1.

Bits Into Bytes Every letter, number, or picture is entered into the computer as a combination of bits, or 0s and 1s. The bits are combined into groups of eight or more. Each group is called a **byte.** Each letter or number has a unique combination of bits.

© Pearson Education, Inc.

For instance, the letter *A* is coded as 01000001. The number *1* is 00110001.

Even images are formed by combinations of bytes. Those combinations tell the computer what colors to display and where to put them.

Processing

The second step of the information processing cycle is called **processing.** In this step, the computer does something to the data.

Coded Instructions   What the computer does depends on the instructions, or program, given to the computer. The instructions are also written in binary code, using combinations of 0s and 1s. They might tell the computer to add two numbers, or they might have the computer compare two numbers to see which is larger.

Speed of Processing   Computers can process data very rapidly, performing millions of operations every second. The ability to process data with lightning speed is another reason computers are so valuable.

Math You ordinarily count using the decimal, or base 10, system. That system has 10 values, 0 through 9. But you can express many numbers using those values. You simply add additional places—the 10s, the 100s, and so on. Each place is 10 times larger than the previous place. In a binary system, the quantity represented by each place is 2 times the previous quantity. In an 8-digit binary number, the places are the 1s, 2s, 4s, 8s, 16s, 32s, 64s, and 128s.

Figure 1.1.1 Each computer component plays a role in one of the system's four primary functions.

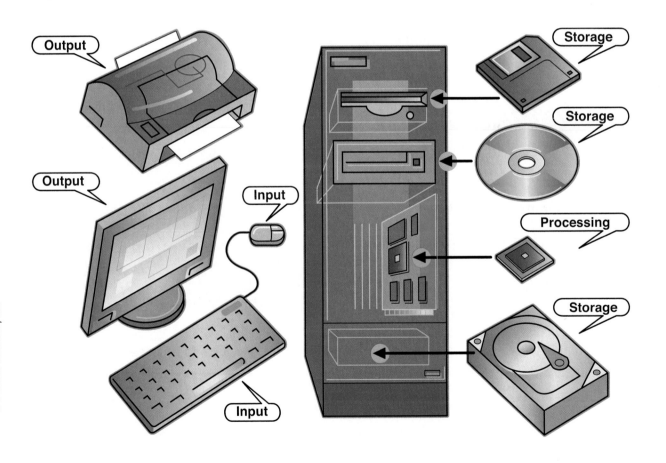

Technology @ School

In some schools, students' work is collected over the year in electronic portfolios. These portfolios reflect a range of the students' work on many projects during the school year. The computer's ability to store this information is perfect for portfolio work.

Think *About* It!

Think about how an electronic portfolio might be used. Circle each item that you think could be in an electronic portfolio.

➤ multimedia presentations
➤ maps
➤ paper-and-pencil homework
➤ poetry
➤ lab report

Output

The third step shows what happens after the computer processes the data. This is the **output** step. If the program tells the computer to add two numbers, the output stage displays the result. To create output, the computer takes the bytes and turns them back into a form you can understand, such as an image on the screen or a printed document.

Output can take many forms. A program might convert the 0s and 1s into a report. It might become an image you are drawing on the computer. If you are playing a game, the output might be a car zooming along a road and the sound of its engine. A computer provides output through a device such as a monitor, speaker, or printer.

Storage

The fourth operation is **storage,** in which the computer saves the information. Without storage, all the work you do on the computer would be lost. Computers have a temporary memory that is used during the processing stage. When the computer is turned off, however, any data in that temporary memory is lost.

By storing the data in a permanent form, you can access the information over and over. This is another great advantage of computers—what you do one day can be saved and reused on another day.

Real-World Tech

Robots at Work Some output is very unusual. Computer-controlled robots work in some auto factories. Their output is cars. The robots are perfect for the tasks that take place on an assembly line. These tasks are done over and over again without change. For instance, robots weld parts together and paint car bodies.

What is a disadvantage to workers of bringing in robots to do tasks such as factory work? What can businesses and workers do to make that less of a problem?

_____

_____

_____

Demonstrate Your Knowledge

Critical Thinking

1. What is the difference between analog and digital computers?

_____

_____

2. Why must all data in a digital computer be in the form of 0s and 1s?

_____

3. What are three benefits of computers?

_____

_____

Activities

1. Look at the graphic organizer below. Complete the spider map by identifying the four steps in information processing. Then write at least two facts about each step.

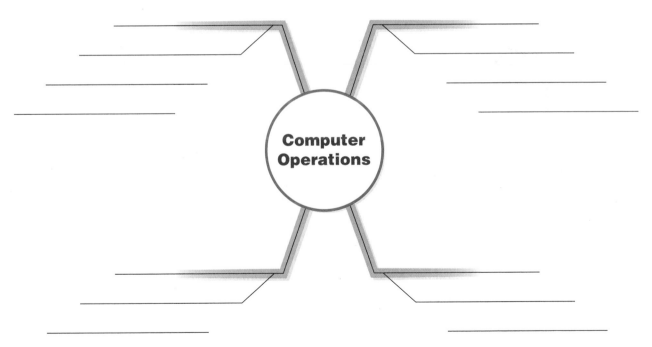

2. As you move through your home, school, and community for a day, keep a log of how computers are used. Each time you see a computer in use, identify how it is being used. Report your findings to the class. Then discuss the widespread role of computers in our society.

What Is Computer Hardware?

Objectives

- Summarize how a CPU and RAM work together.
- Contrast primary and secondary storage.
- Compare the features of three secondary storage devices.
- Identify three types of connectors and the peripherals that use each.

As You Read

Compare and Contrast Use a chart to help you compare and contrast computer hardware as you read.

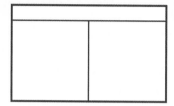

What's Online

In Lesson 1–2 of the iText, you will find more features and information for this lesson, including:

- Interactive tutorials
- As You Read worksheet
- Learn More interactivities
- Check Your Understanding interactive assessments
- Interactive lesson review

🔑 Key Terms

- hardware (p. 8)
- central processing unit (CPU) (p. 8)
- random access memory (RAM) (p. 8)
- peripheral (p. 10)

Figure 1.2.1 Intel's Pentium® 4 is one type of processor.

What Is Hardware?

When you think about a computer, you probably picture its **hardware,** the computer's physical parts. You use hardware devices such as a keyboard or mouse to input data. The processor is a hardware device that turns the raw data into usable information. Hardware devices such as a monitor or a disk drive show output and store data for later access.

Inside the Case

Much of a computer's hardware is found inside the computer case, hidden from view. Most of this hardware is used for processing and storing data.

Processing Devices Perhaps the most important piece of hardware in a computer is the **central processing unit,** or **CPU.** This is the device that processes data. The CPU is a small, thin piece of silicon attached to a circuit board. The CPU is covered with tiny electrical circuits. By moving data along these circuits in specific ways, the CPU can do arithmetic and compare data very quickly.

Primary Storage Some hardware used to store data is inside the computer case near the CPU. The computer uses **random access memory,** or **RAM,** to store data and instructions while the computer is working. In this way, the CPU can quickly find the data it works with. This type of storage is called primary storage. Data in RAM is lost when the computer is turned off.

Secondary Storage Devices Other pieces of storage hardware are secondary storage. The following devices let you store data permanently—even when the computer is turned off.

- Hard drives use a stack of disk platters to store large amounts of information permanently inside the computer.
- Floppy disk drives record data on removable floppy disks. The drives are mostly inside the computer's case. You can put a removable disk in the opening and save data onto that disk. If a computer has a floppy disk drive, you can copy data from a hard disk drive to a floppy disk or vice versa.
- CD-ROM drives or DVD-ROM drives are storage devices. Like floppy disk drives, these are mostly inside the computer case but have an access door in which either a CD or DVD is placed. The drive can read data recorded on the CD or DVD.

Secondary Storage Capacity Floppy disks store the least amount of data. They hold just under one and one half megabytes of data. A megabyte is just over a million bytes. Hard disk drives can hold more data. Many computers now have hard drives that can store several gigabytes. A gigabyte is just over a billion bytes.

A CD-ROM can hold several hundred megabytes. It can store entire encyclopedias, including pictures, maps, and sound. A DVD-ROM, which can hold several gigabytes of information, stores much more than a CD-ROM.

Career Corner

Service Technician Computer hardware sometimes fails. When that happens, people call service technicians. These people work for computer companies. They might work in the offices of the company that employs them, or they might travel to business sites to fix machines. Technicians need to know about software and hardware because problems are sometimes caused by a computer's programs and not by its equipment.

Figure 1.2.2 Today's computers have a great deal of storage capacity, with hard drives holding 20 gigabytes of data or more.

CD-ROM/DVD-ROM drive

Monitor

Speaker

The CPU and hard drive are inside this case.

Keyboard

Mouse

Peripherals

For most desktop systems, input devices, such as the keyboard and mouse, are separate from the case. So are output devices, such as monitors and printers. Hardware that is separate but can be connected to the case is called a **peripheral.**

Not all computers have all this equipment as peripherals. Apple's iMac® computers include the monitor as a physical part of the main system. Other computers may have built-in storage devices. Portable computers have the keyboard, a type of mouse, and a monitor all attached to the main unit.

Cables Peripherals need to be connected to the computer so that data can be moved back and forth. Each peripheral is linked to the computer by a cable with a plug. The plug joins the computer at a connector on the computer case.

Connectors There are several main types of connectors, or ports:

- Serial ports move data one bit at a time. For example, they connect computers to phone lines for Internet access.
- Parallel ports move data in groups. They are typically used to connect printers to computers.
- Multiple device ports, such as Small Computer Systems Interface (SCSI) and Universal Serial Bus (USB) ports, connect several peripherals to a computer at one time. They all move data faster than serial ports can.

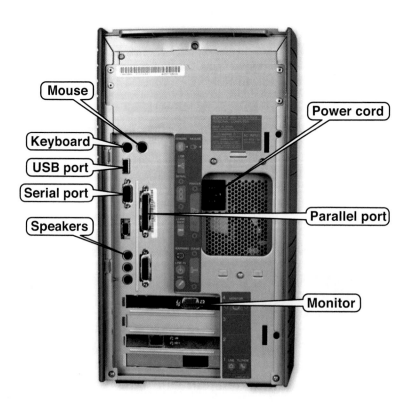

Figure 1.2.3 Personal computers have a variety of special ports, so you can connect many different devices to them.

© Pearson Education, Inc.

Demonstrate Your Knowledge

Critical Thinking

1. How does RAM work with the CPU?

_____

_____

2. How do floppy disks, hard drives, CDs, and DVDs compare in storage capacity?

_____

_____

3. What are three different connectors between peripherals and the main unit, and which peripherals connect to each of them?

_____

_____

Activities

1. Look at the Venn diagram below. Write details about primary storage in the left circle. Write details about secondary storage in the right circle. Include common details in the area where the circles overlap.

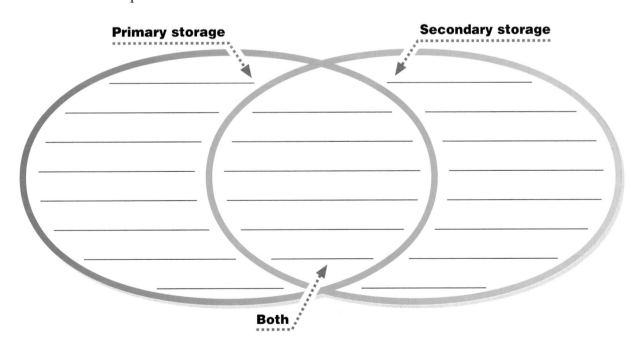

2. Look at your computer. Make a chart and, in the first column, list all the peripherals attached to it. Categorize them as input or output devices.

What Is Computer Software?

Objectives

- Describe what an operating system does.
- Summarize why compatibility is an issue for computer users.
- Explain what utility software does.
- Identify four types of application software and ways to obtain them.

As You Read

Classify Information Use a concept web to help you classify different types of computer software as you read.

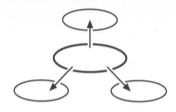

Key Terms

- software (p. 12)
- system software (p. 12)
- application software (p. 13)
- operating system (OS) (p. 13)
- compatibility (p. 13)
- utility software (p. 14)

What Is Software?

Hardware includes all the physical pieces that make up a computer. Hardware is useless without software, however. **Software** includes all of the programs that tell a computer what to do and how to do it. Think of a computer as a sports team. Hardware is the players, and software is the coach. No matter how talented the players are, the team will only perform properly if the coach gives it the right instructions.

Types of Software

Software is divided into two main types: system software and application software. **System software** includes programs that

Figure 1.3.1 The Macintosh® operating system is an example of system software.

help the computer work properly. You are probably more familiar with **application software,** which are programs designed to help you do tasks such as writing a paper or making a graph. This type of software also includes programs that allow you to use the computer to listen to music or play games.

System Software

There are two types of system software: operating systems and system utilities. Both help computers run smoothly.

Operating Systems The **operating system (OS)** lets the hardware devices communicate with one another and keeps them running efficiently. It also supports the hardware when applications programs are running. The two most widely used operating systems are the Macintosh® OS and Microsoft® Windows®.

Compatibility Operating systems are designed for particular processors. The Macintosh® OS runs on computers with Motorola® processors. Windows® runs on computers with processors made by Intel® or which are made to work like Intel® chips.

For some years, the systems did not have **compatibility.** That is, programs written for one OS did not run on the other. In addition, each OS formats files in its own way, which prevented sharing files between the two systems. Now, Macintosh® computers can run many Windows® programs. To some extent, each system can read files created on the other system.

Technology @ Home

A backup program copies data that is stored on a computer's hard drive. If anything happens to the hard drive, the data on the backup CDs or disks will not be lost. Backups can be used for data files, program files, or both.

Think *About* **It!**
Before backing up your hard drive, think about the value of each file saved on it. Next to each item below, sequence the importance of each file using a scale of 1 (lowest) to 5 (highest).

- a program for which you have a CD
- a report that you spent four hours on
- a file not used for a year
- family photos
- stored files of a game

Spotlight on...

BILL GATES

66 *Bill Gates has the obsessive drive of a [computer] hacker working on a tough technical dilemma, yet [he also] has an uncanny grasp of the marketplace, as well as a firm conviction of what the future will be like and what he should do about it.* 99

Steven Levy,
Writer

Bill Gates has a simple idea about the future of computing. "The goal," he says, "is information at your fingertips." It will not surprise anyone if Gates and his company, Microsoft®, play a major role in making that goal become a reality. Gates started writing software in high school. He and a childhood friend, Paul Allen, wrote a programming language to run on a machine called the Altair, the first personal computer. Allen and Gates then formed Microsoft®, which is now one of the leading software companies in the world.

A software program's version is usually indicated by a number, such as "Version 4" or "Version 8.5." Software is upgraded to remove programming errors and to add new features. Some revisions are major, and the version number jumps from, for example, 9.0 to 10. Minor fixes typically change the number after the decimal point, such as 10 to 10.2.

Think *About* It!

Below, circle the item if you think it would be worthwhile for you to buy the new version of the program.

▷ a program you use all the time that is moving from 4.3 to 5.0

▷ a program you rarely use that is moving from 2.2 to 2.3

▷ a program you often use that is moving from 5.1 to 5.2

▷ a program you often use that is moving from 1.0 to 3.0

System Utilities Programs that help the computer work properly are called **utility software.** They usually do maintenance and repair jobs that the operating system cannot do itself. Some utility programs repair damaged data files or save files in certain ways so they take up less space. Others translate files created in one OS so they can be read and worked on in another.

Application Software

There are many different applications. They can be grouped into four main categories:

- Productivity software helps people be more productive at work. People use these programs to write reports, prepare financial plans, and organize data.
- Graphics software makes it possible to draw, paint, and touch up photos.
- Communication software allows computers to connect to the Internet and to send e-mail.
- Home, education, and entertainment software helps people manage their money or figure their taxes. Other products can be used to learn new skills or simply to have some fun.

Custom Software There are two ways to obtain application software. Some organizations need software programs to do very specific jobs. They hire people to write custom software designed to do those jobs. Because these programs are custom written, they are usually quite expensive.

Off-the-Shelf Software Most people use software to do standard jobs. They might want to write letters or keep track of their CD collection. They can choose from many ready-made programs to handle these common tasks. These are called "off-the-shelf" programs because stores and companies that sell software from the Internet stock them. Because software publishers can sell many copies of this software, it costs much less to develop than custom software costs.

Figure 1.3.2 You can buy off-the-shelf software in many places, from computer stores to department stores.

© Pearson Education, Inc.

Demonstrate Your Knowledge

Critical Thinking

1. What two tasks do operating systems carry out?

_____

_____

2. Which two issues created compatibility problems between Mac OS® and Windows® machines?

_____

_____

3. What are two examples of utility programs?

_____

_____

Activities

1. Complete the graphic organizer below by writing two of the four types of application software in each box. In the spaces below the type of software, write a task that can be done using that type.

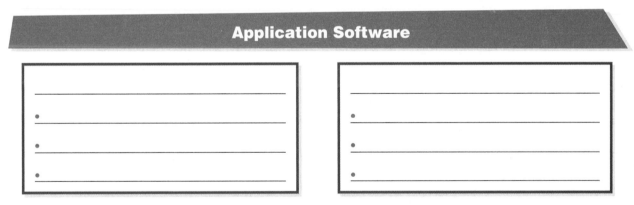

2. Interview three people who own computers. Ask them how they obtained their application software. Find out how satisfied they are with that method of acquiring the software. Report your findings to the class. Discuss the advantages and disadvantages of each method.

Use the Vocabulary

Directions: *Match each vocabulary term in the left column with the correct definition in the right column. Write the appropriate letter next to the word or term.*

_____ **1.** input

_____ **2.** bit

_____ **3.** byte

_____ **4.** output

_____ **5.** hardware

_____ **6.** central processing unit

_____ **7.** random access memory

_____ **8.** peripheral

_____ **9.** software

_____ **10.** utility software

a. program that tells the computer what to do

b. group of 8 bits

c. area where data and instructions are stored while the computer is working

d. physical parts of a computer

e. raw data entered into a computer

f. program that does maintenance or repair tasks

g. part of a computer that processes data

h. basic unit of data a digital computer can understand

i. hardware separate but connected to the computer

j. the results of the computer's processing

Check Your Comprehension

Directions: *Complete each sentence with information from the chapter.*

1. A _____ is a machine that changes information from one form into another.

2. _____ is a basic operation of computers.

3. Data and instructions in computers are coded with a _____ because computers only understand two values.

4. The CPU uses _____ to hold data it is working on.

5. Data in RAM is _____ when the computer is turned off.

6. A _____ is an example of a connector that works with only one kind of peripheral.

7. SCSI and USB connectors connect _____ peripherals at the same time.

8. Programs and files created on either Macintosh or Windows operating systems _____ files differently.

9. _____ software is used to connect to the Internet and send e-mail.

10. Off-the-shelf software is _____ expensive than custom software because publishers sell more units.

Think Critically

Directions: *Answer the following questions on the lines provided.*

1. How do analog and digital computers differ?

_____

_____

2. Which benefit of computers—the ability to use any kind of data, the ability to work rapidly, or the ability to access stored data again and again—do you think is the most important? Why?

_____

_____

3. What are the differences between primary and secondary storage?

_____

_____

4. Why might the operating system be called a computer's most important software?

_____

_____

5. What type of application software do you use most? Explain.

_____

_____

_____

Extend Your Knowledge

Directions: *Choose one of the following projects. Complete the exercises on a separate sheet of paper.*

A. Look at a computer. Create a five-column chart. In the first column, list all the hardware that you can identify. In the remaining columns, state whether each item is used for inputting, processing, outputting, or storage. Examine how the different pieces are connected to the computer. What other hardware do you think the computer has that you cannot see? What kinds of hardware were usually peripherals? Which were usually in the computer's case? What exceptions did you identify? Share your findings with the class.

B. Interview both a young person and an adult who use computers regularly, either at work, at school, or at home. Ask them what tasks they do with the computer that they used to do without it. Have them compare how much easier or faster it is to do those tasks now. Ask them what tasks they do on the computer that they could never have done without it. Finally, ask them what impact they think computers have had on society. Summarize your findings to report on how computer technology has changed people's lives.

Input/Output Basics

Input and Output If you think of the computer as a person, its brain would be the central processing unit, or CPU. Like a brain, a CPU receives and organizes data from many different sources into useful information.

Also, like a person, a computer needs more than just a brain to work properly. It needs a way to receive the unorganized data and to show the results of its processing of the data. The brain receives data through the senses: sight, hearing, smell, taste, and touch. It shows the results of its processing of the data through speech, movement, and writing. The CPU receives its data from input devices such as the keyboard and mouse. It shows the results of its processing through output devices such as a monitor, printer, or speakers.

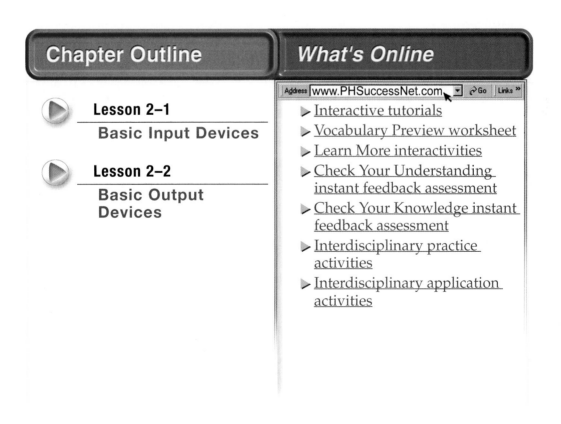

Chapter Outline

▶ **Lesson 2–1**
Basic Input Devices

▶ **Lesson 2–2**
Basic Output Devices

What's Online

Address www.PHSuccessNet.com ▾ ⬀ Go   Links »

▷ Interactive tutorials
▷ Vocabulary Preview worksheet
▷ Learn More interactivities
▷ Check Your Understanding instant feedback assessment
▷ Check Your Knowledge instant feedback assessment
▷ Interdisciplinary practice activities
▷ Interdisciplinary application activities

Basic Input Devices

Objectives

- Distinguish among four types of input.
- Compare and contrast basic input devices.
- Discuss the health risks of using some input devices.

As You Read

Organize Information Use a concept web to help you organize information about basic input devices as you read.

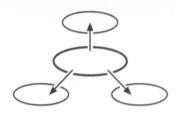

🔑 Key Terms

- command (p. 20)
- pointer (p. 21)
- speech recognition (p. 22)
- digital camera (p. 22)
- scanner (p. 22)
- repetitive strain injury (RSI) (p. 22)

What Is Input?

Input is any kind of information, or instructions, that is entered into a computer's memory. There are four basic types of input: data, software instructions, user commands, and responses.

Data Words, numbers, images, and sounds that you enter into a computer are data. This is the raw material that a computer processes.

Software Instructions To perform any job, a computer must follow instructions from a software program. Software typically is installed from a CD onto the hard drive. Launching a program moves it into the computer's RAM. That makes the program available to the CPU—and to you.

User Commands A **command** is an instruction that tells a software program what action to perform. For example, to open a program, save your work, or close a program, you must issue a command to the computer.

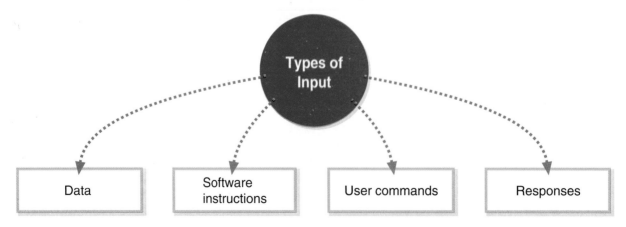

Responses Sometimes a program asks you to enter information or make a choice so that it can carry out a command or process data. For example, if you try to close a program without saving your work, the program will ask if you wish to save it. Before you can continue, you must input a response.

What Is an Input Device?

An input device is any hardware used to input data.

Keyboard The most common input device is the keyboard, which is used to input text, symbols, and numbers. The keyboard can also be used to enter commands and move the cursor around the screen.

Pointing Devices A pointing device is used to move the insertion point and issue commands. A mouse is a common pointing device. Moving the mouse over a surface moves a **pointer** on the screen. Clicking a mouse button inputs commands or changes the position of the insertion point in a document. Small computers, such as notebooks, often use a touchpad, or trackpad, as the pointing device. It is built into the computer. Moving your finger on the touchpad moves the pointer.

Technology @ Work

Some people have disabilities that prevent them from working a mouse with their fingertips. Two companies make joysticks that can be controlled by mouth. Moving the stick up and down or from side to side moves the cursor on the screen.

Think *About* It!
Circle each mouse action that you think needs to be considered in an adaptive input device for people with physical disabilities.

➤ select text
➤ scroll through a document
➤ create art in a drawing program
➤ click the mouse button to select a menu option
➤ cut text

Spotlight on...

DOUG ENGLEBART

66 *We were looking for the best—the most efficient—device. We . . . said 'let's test them,' and determine the answer once-and-for-all. . . . It quickly became clear that the mouse outperformed all the [other devices].*99

Doug Englebart

In the 1960s, Doug Englebart created the mouse—a device that could be used to move a cursor around a computer screen.

The first mouse was a crude wooden box with two round discs on the bottom and a button on the top. The long cord that connected it to a computer looked like a tail.

A visionary, Englebart also thought computers could be used as writing machines, or word processors.

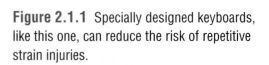
You might think that repetitive strain injury only affects adults who work all day at a computer. Researchers are trying to find out if children can also be affected by repeated use of the keyboard and mouse. They have learned that children run some risk of injury.

One thing that can reduce this risk is to have the keyboard and mouse positioned lower than the computer. Many students, though, prefer to have these devices on top of a table. They want to be able to see the keys as they type!

Joystick The joystick is a lever that can be moved in all directions to move objects on the screen. The programs that use the joystick the most are computer games or those that simulate flying a plane. Joysticks typically have buttons that are used to input commands.

Microphone To input sounds, you can use a microphone. A computer must also have a sound card to record and play back sounds. **Speech recognition** software lets you use a microphone to input by speaking aloud. Software programs change your words into data, commands, or responses. This software helps people who may have difficulty typing.

Digital Cameras and Scanners You can input images by using digital cameras or scanners. A **digital camera** takes and stores photos in a digital form that the computer can work with. Some store photos on a removable disk that you can put into a piece of hardware similar to a disk drive. You can either input the photos right away or save them to a disk and input them later. Many cameras connect to the computer by a cable or a wireless link to input pictures.

Scanners are devices that let you copy printed images into a computer. The scanner changes the printed image into a digital form.

Modem A modem allows one computer to input data into another computer. Computers must be connected by cables or phone lines. Many people use modems to connect their computers to the Internet.

Health Risks of Some Input Devices

When you use a keyboard or mouse a lot, you make the same hand movements over and over again. This can cause damage to nerves in the hand. The problem is called **repetitive strain injury,** or **RSI.** New keyboards have been designed to reduce RSI. Some people who suffer from this problem use a mouse controlled by foot pedals or some other kind of pointing device.

Figure 2.1.1 Specially designed keyboards, like this one, can reduce the risk of repetitive strain injuries.

Demonstrate Your Knowledge

Critical Thinking

1. What kind of input instructs a computer to take an action, such as copy a file or print a report?

_____

_____

2. How are a mouse and a joystick alike? Different?

_____

_____

3. How do some input devices cause or contribute to health risks?

_____

_____

Activities

1. Complete the graphic organizer below by listing the uses of each input device.

Input Device	Uses
Keyboard	
Mouse, Touchpad	
Joystick	
Microphone	
Digital camera	
Scanner	
Modem	

2. Open a draw program and create a simple illustration. Save the drawing by using the mouse to move among the program's menus and by using the keyboard to type in a file name. Close the file. Then, use the File menu to open the drawing again. Change the drawing and save it again. Make a list of the input devices that you used in this activity.

Basic Output Devices

Objectives

- Distinguish among the four types of output.
- Compare and contrast basic output devices.
- Explain how visual display systems work.
- Summarize printing technology.

As You Read

Outline Information Use an outline format to help you organize information about output as you read.

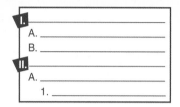

What's Online

In Lesson 2–2 of the iText, you will find more features and information for this lesson, including:

- Interactive tutorials
- As You Read worksheet
- Learn More interactivities
- Check Your Understanding interactive assessments
- Interactive lesson review

🔑 Key Terms

- output device (p. 25)
- cathode ray tube (CRT) (p. 25)
- liquid crystal display (LCD) (p. 26)
- impact printer (p. 26)
- nonimpact printer (p. 26)

What Is Output?

After a computer has processed data, it provides the results in the form of output. There are four types of output: text, graphics, video, and audio.

Text Characters such as letters, symbols, and numbers are called text. To be considered text, the characters must be organized in a coherent way. For example, random letters on a page are not considered text, but paragraphs in a book report are text.

Graphics Drawings, photographs, and other visual images are called graphics.

Video Moving images are known as video. Images captured by a digital video camera, and which can be played on a computer, are one example of video. The use of animation is another example.

Audio Sound output is called audio. This includes music or speech that the computer plays through its speakers or headphones.

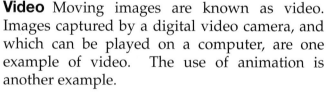

Figure 2.2.1 This is a CRT monitor—an output device for displaying text and graphics.

What Is an Output Device?

An **output device** is any piece of hardware that displays or plays back the result of computer processing in one of the four forms of output. For example, monitors and printers create a visual record of the processing completed by the computer.

Monitors

The computer displays information on a monitor, a hardware device that receives and shows images on a screen. The images the monitor displays change as the computer processes data.

CRTs The most common type of monitor is the **cathode ray tube,** or **CRT.** In a CRT, the monitor receives electrical signals from the computer. The signals cause "guns" in the CRT to shoot a stream of electrons at the back of the screen. The electrons strike materials called phosphors, which begin to glow. The glowing phosphors appear as points of light on the screen.

A monochrome monitor has only one gun and can produce images in only one color. A color monitor has three electron guns. Each one shoots a beam of a different color: red, blue, or green. The color that appears on the screen depends on the relative strength of the beams hitting the phosphor. A CRT mixes the strength of the beams to produce different colors on the screen.

Technology @ School

Some schools have a special kind of monitor that is an educational tool. The SMART Board™ allows teachers and students to project text and images onto a special monitor mounted on the wall. Not only is the image visible to all students, but it can also be manipulated and changed, making learning more interactive.

Think *About* **It!**
Think about ways the SMART Board can be used at school. Underline ONLY the examples below for which you think the SMART Board would be useful.

➤ solve math problems
➤ play music
➤ edit text
➤ display reports
➤ meet in groups

Real-World Tech

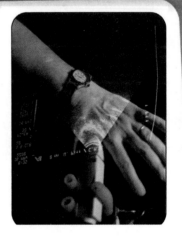

Sonic Flashlight Researcher George Stetten developed an ultrasound scanner, called a sonic flashlight, to help doctors treat their patients. Stetten's device uses sound waves to create three-dimensional (3-D) images of a part of the body. Stetten's portable device displays the 3-D image on a thin mirror. It gives doctors the ability to provide an on-the-spot, accurate diagnosis.

How do you think computers can be used to help address health-care issues?

_____

_____

_____

Test Engineer Before equipment is manufactured and sold, it needs to be designed. New models, called prototypes, have to be tested.

The work of test engineers is to make sure that the equipment works the way it is supposed to. If it does not, the test engineer has to explain to the design team what went wrong.

Figure 2.2.2 A dot matrix printer (on the left) is an impact printer. A photo printer (on the right) is a nonimpact printer.

LCDs CRTs are heavy and take up a lot of space. As a result, they cannot be used with portable computers like notebooks. Portable computers, therefore, use a **liquid crystal display,** or **LCD.** In an LCD, two transparent surfaces are placed on either side of a layer of cells containing tiny crystals. Electrical signals sent to the crystals cause them to form images on the surface.

LCDs use less power than CRTs. While they cost more than CRTs, they are becoming more common on desktop computers.

Printers

A printer makes a paper copy of the display shown on a monitor. There are two basic types of printers: impact printers and nonimpact printers.

Impact Printers An **impact printer** receives signals from the computer that cause hammers or pins to press a ribbon covered in ink. The ribbon then strikes a sheet of paper. Impact printers are usually inexpensive, but they can be noisy. Also, the quality of the image they produce is poor compared to that of nonimpact printers. Dot matrix printers are one kind of impact printer. They are widely used by businesses to provide multiple copies of printed multipart forms and labels.

Nonimpact Printers Most of the computer users today use **nonimpact printers,** such as inkjet and laser printers, to produce paper copies. Inkjet printers make images by spraying a fine stream of ink onto the paper. Laser printers do not use ink. Instead they use a powder called toner. Heat fuses the toner to the paper, creating an image.

Demonstrate Your Knowledge

Critical Thinking

1. Give an example of each of the four types of output.

_____

_____

2. Why do you think monitors are among the most common output devices?

_____

_____

3. How do CRTs compare to LCDs?

_____

_____

Activities

1. Complete the chart below to compare and contrast the two main types of printers.

Impact Printers	Nonimpact Printers
• _____	• _____
• _____	• _____
• _____	• _____

2. Interview a computer user about the printers he or she uses. Ask the person to identify the type of printer, what capabilities it has, how fast it prints, how frequently it is necessary to replace ink cartridges or toner, and other questions about operating the device. Finally, ask the person to evaluate the printer: How easy is it to use? How good a job does it do? Compare your findings with those of your classmates. Is there general agreement about the different types of printers?

Use the Vocabulary

Directions: *Match each vocabulary term in the left column with the correct definition in the right column. Write the appropriate letter next to the word or term.*

_____ **1.** command
_____ **2.** pointer
_____ **3.** speech recognition
_____ **4.** digital camera
_____ **5.** scanner
_____ **6.** repetitive strain injury
_____ **7.** cathode ray tube
_____ **8.** liquid crystal display
_____ **9.** impact printer
_____ **10.** nonimpact printer

a. produces images by sending electrical signals to crystals

b. software that turns spoken words into input

c. device with hammers or pins that strike a ribbon to leave ink on paper

d. lets you input printed images into a computer

e. produces images by making phosphors glow

f. follows a mouse's movements

g. device such as an inkjet or laser printer

h. takes photographs that a computer can read

i. condition caused by making the same movements again and again

j. instruction to a software program to take an action

Check Your Comprehension

Directions: *Circle the correct choice for each of the following.*

1. Which type of input provides answers to questions issued by programs?
   a. commands
   b. data
   c. responses
   d. software

2. Which device can be used to connect a computer to the Internet?
   a. keyboard
   b. modem
   c. pointing device
   d. scanner

3. Which of the following devices can be designed to reduce the problem of RSIs?
   a. scanner
   b. digital camera
   c. monitor
   d. keyboard

4. What do output devices provide?
   a. data to be processed
   b. software code
   c. text and images only
   d. results of processing

5. How many colors can a monochrome monitor display?
   a. one
   b. two
   c. three
   d. four

6. What kind of output device would NOT be used to output images?
   a. CRT
   b. LCD
   c. printer
   d. speaker

Think Critically

Directions: *Answer the following questions on the lines provided.*

1. Why are microphones or digital cameras unlikely to cause the damage that is found in repetitive strain injury?

_____

_____

2. Are you likely to use a joystick to complete schoolwork? Why or why not?

_____

_____

3. Why is speech recognition software useful for people who have difficulty typing?

_____

_____

4. How is video similar to ordinary graphics? How is it different?

_____

_____

5. Why are workers likely to prefer inkjet or laser printers to impact printers?

_____

_____

Extend Your Knowledge

Directions: *Choose one of the following projects. Complete the exercises on a separate sheet of paper.*

A. Open a word-processing program. Go back to the beginning of Lesson 2–1 of this component. Use the keyboard to input the paragraph that starts with the sub-heading "Keyboard." Input the paragraph a total of five times. Each time you do so, time yourself. Print the five paragraphs. Compare the five times. Determine whether you were able to type faster and more accurately with practice.

B. Open a word-processing program. Find a file that you created and saved previously. Open the file. Use both the keyboard and the mouse to move around in the document and to print it. Write a paragraph explaining which device you thought was easier to work with and why.

Storage
Basics

Why Do Computers Store Data? Computer storage is like the backpack you bring to school. Both store things until you are ready to use them. Your backpack stores books and school supplies; most computers store software and data.

Computer storage devices can store information for long periods of time. This lets you create a file today, save it, and then use it again in the future. In this chapter, you will learn why storage is necessary and how information is stored. You will also examine some of the storage devices you are likely to find on today's computers.

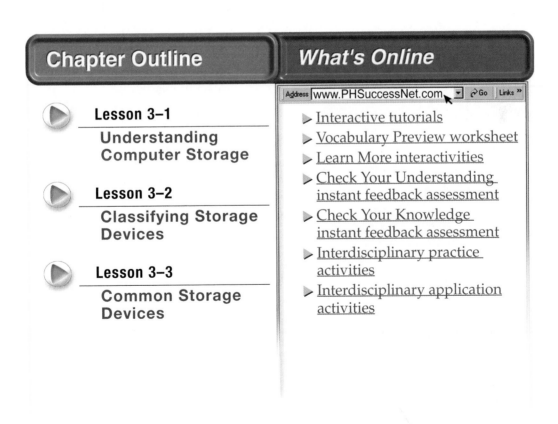

Chapter Outline

▶ **Lesson 3–1**
   Understanding Computer Storage

▶ **Lesson 3–2**
   Classifying Storage Devices

▶ **Lesson 3–3**
   Common Storage Devices

What's Online

Address www.PHSuccessNet.com ▼ | ⌀Go | Links »

▶ Interactive tutorials
▶ Vocabulary Preview worksheet
▶ Learn More interactivities
▶ Check Your Understanding instant feedback assessment
▶ Check Your Knowledge instant feedback assessment
▶ Interdisciplinary practice activities
▶ Interdisciplinary application activities

Understanding Computer Storage

Objectives

- Explain the need for storage devices for computers.
- Distinguish between memory and storage.
- Distinguish between storage devices and media.

As You Read

Organize Information Use an outline to help you organize information about computer storage and storage devices as you read.

```
I.  _____
    A. _____
    B. _____
II. _____
    A. _____
        1. _____
```

Key Terms

- storage device (p. 32)
- file (p. 32)
- Basic Input/Output System (BIOS) (p. 33)
- memory (p. 33)

Computer Storage Devices

Where do you store the books, pencils, and notebooks that you need for school? Many students keep them in a backpack. When class is about to begin, they pull out the items they need. When class is finished, they put the items back into their backpacks.

This is similar to the way **storage devices** work. They are the computer's hardware components that retain data even after the power is turned off. Suppose you turned off your computer without saving your work to a storage device. All your work would be lost. Without storage devices, you would have to re-create all of your work every time you wanted to use it.

Why not keep all of a computer's software and data available at all times? Because no one needs to use every program or file every time they work on the computer. For example, you might be doing word processing today, but creating a computer drawing tomorrow. There is no need to have both programs open at the same time if you are not using both of them.

Files A computer stores data and program instructions in files. A **file** is a collection of related information or program code, which has been given a unique name.

Figure 3.1.1 Like a backpack, a computer's storage devices hold things until you need them.

© Pearson Education, Inc.

The type of file people most often use is called a document. A document can be any kind of data file that a user can create, save, and edit. For example, you can use a word-processing program to create a letter, which is one type of document. A digital photo is another type of file.

System Startup Computer storage devices are a key part of a computer's startup process. Without a storage device to hold startup information permanently, a computer would not know what to do when you turned it on.

When you start a computer, it looks for information that tells it what to do. The **Basic Input/Output System,** or **BIOS,** is a set of programs that tells the computer equipment how to start up. When a computer is built, the BIOS is set up with this basic information. Usually, the BIOS instructs the computer to look for the operating system. The operating system contains all the commands required to run the computer. It provides the tools you need to operate the system and enables programs to run on the computer.

Memory and Storage

When people talk about computer **memory,** they usually mean a set of chips that acts as a temporary workspace in the computer. This memory, called random access memory, or RAM, stores data and program instructions while they are needed by the CPU.

RAM and ROM are different in two important ways, as the following chart shows. First, ROM stores its contents permanently, even when the computer is turned off. RAM, on the other hand, only stores its contents temporarily; if the computer loses power, RAM's contents are lost.

Second, because ROM stores instructions that are needed only by the computer, you seldom need to think about ROM or the information it holds. But RAM holds data and programs while they are being used. As you use the computer, you constantly work with the contents of RAM.

Connections

Science The study of memory does not only apply to computer science. Some psychologists have noted similarities in the ways human and computer memories function.

Some research supports an input-output model of human memory. They see memory as a storage device that is limited in capacity. According to this theory, how much a person can learn (input) may be limited by how much he or she forgets (output).

ROM and RAM

	Storage	Holds
ROM	Permanent	Startup instructions and configuration information for the computer
RAM	Temporary	Program instructions and data that are being used by the CPU

Figure 3.1.2 Nearly all PCs use the three storage devices and media shown here.

Storage Versus Memory New computer users sometimes get confused about temporary memory (RAM) and permanent storage (disks and disk drives). They will say "memory" when they actually mean to say "storage." To avoid this problem, remember two key differences between storage and memory:

- The two work differently. Remember that RAM uses chips to temporarily store information. These chips depend on a constant supply of power to keep their contents; when the power is lost, the chips lose their contents. Storage uses different methods to store data permanently, so it isn't lost when the power is turned off.
- A PC has more storage capacity than memory. Even though some PCs can hold as much as 1GB of RAM, their hard drives will be many times larger.

Storage Media and Storage Devices

Storage has two components: storage media and storage devices.

Storage Media In terms of storage, a medium is an object that physically holds data or program instructions. Floppy disks, magnetic tapes, and compact discs are examples of storage media. (The word *media* is the plural of *medium*.)

Storage Devices A storage device is a piece of hardware that holds the storage medium, sends data to the medium, and retrieves data from the medium. Floppy disk drives, hard drives, CD-ROM and DVD-ROM drives, and tape drives are all examples of storage devices.

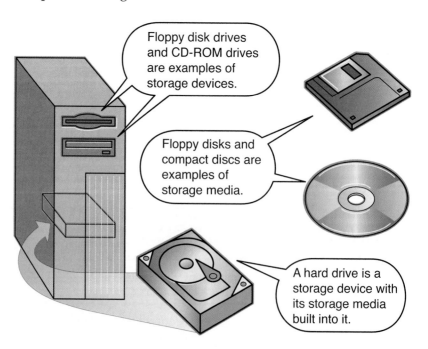

© Pearson Education, Inc.

Demonstrate Your Knowledge

Critical Thinking

1. What is the purpose of storage devices in a computer?

_____

_____

2. What is the role of RAM in a computer?

_____

_____

3. What is the difference between storage devices and storage media?

_____

_____

Activities

1. Complete the following chart to list the similarities and differences between RAM and ROM.

RAM and ROM	
Similarities	**Differences**
_____	_____
_____	_____
_____	_____
_____	_____
_____	_____
_____	_____
_____	_____

2. With a partner, conduct research to learn about trends in computer storage devices. Make a class list of students' findings. Then, discuss why new storage devices are in development.

Classifying Storage Devices

Objectives

- Explain how computer storage devices are classified.
- Compare and contrast primary, secondary, and archival storage devices.
- Describe the categories of storage devices.

As You Read

Classify Information Use a spider map to help you classify storage devices as you read.

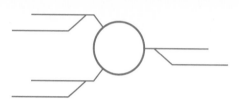

What's Online

In Lesson 3–2 of the iText, you will find more features and information for this lesson, including:

- Interactive tutorials
- As You Read worksheet
- Learn More interactivities
- Check Your Understanding interactive assessments
- Interactive lesson review

Key Terms

- primary storage (p. 36)
- secondary storage (p. 36)
- archival storage (p. 36)
- read-only device (p. 37)
- read/write device (p. 37)
- sequential storage device (p. 38)
- random access storage device (p. 38)
- optical storage device (p. 38)

Figure 3.2.1 Compact discs and digital video discs are popular storage media.

Hierarchy of Storage Devices

Computer storage devices are sometimes classified in a hierarchical structure—that is, primary or secondary.

Primary Storage Devices The term **primary storage** is sometimes used to describe the main memory, or RAM, in a computer. This is because when the CPU needs data or instructions, it looks in memory before looking anywhere else.

Most knowledgeable computer users, however, avoid using the term *storage* when talking about RAM. This is because RAM works very differently from storage devices such as disks or tapes. RAM also loses any data it contains when the computer is turned off, while disks and tapes can hold data permanently.

Secondary Storage Devices The term **secondary storage** is sometimes used to describe devices that can store data permanently, such as a hard drive, floppy disk, compact disc, or tape. This is because the computer will look for data on one of these devices if the data is not in RAM.

Many kinds of secondary storage devices can hold much more data than a computer's RAM can. (Floppy disks are the main exception to this.) For example, while most of today's PCs have a few hundred megabytes of RAM, they have hard drives that can store several gigabytes of data.

Because they can store data permanently (or until you erase it), secondary storage devices are sometimes called **archival storage** devices. This refers to the fact that you can store data on a disk or tape and then put it away for a long time, only using it again when you need it.

© Pearson Education, Inc.

Categories of Storage Devices

Storage devices (but not RAM) are divided into three categories. Each category has two options based on the device.

Read-Only Versus Read/Write   A **read-only device** can only read data from the storage medium. You cannot change the data on the medium or save new data onto it. A CD-ROM drive is an example of a read-only device, because it does not have the capability to write data onto a disc.

The media used with read-only devices come with data already saved on them. Music CDs or software programs on CDs are CD-Rs. Your CD-ROM drive will be able to play the music or read the program instructions from the disc, but you can't change the disc's contents. Standard DVD players are another example of a read-only device.

A **read/write device** not only can read data from the storage medium, but can write data onto the medium, as well. These devices let you read data from a disk or tape, make changes to the data, and save new data onto the medium. Hard drives, floppy disk drives, tape drives, CD-Rewritable drives (CD–RW), and DVD-RAM drives are commonly used examples of read/write devices.

You probably use a variety of storage devices in your home. Some of these may be computerized, while others are not.

Think *About* **It!**
Some of these devices are based on read-only technology, while others are based on read/write technology. Underline each storage device in the list that is based on read-only technology.

➤ answering-machine
➤ CD-ROM
➤ CD burner
➤ DVD-ROM

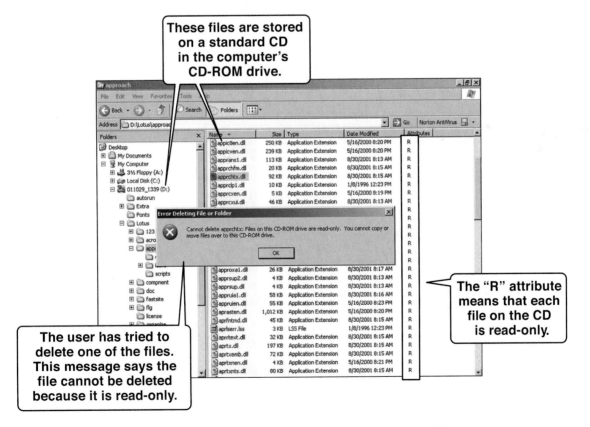

Figure 3.2.2 If you try to delete a file from a read-only storage device, you will see an error message.

© Pearson Education, Inc.

Technology @ School

Schools often use both magnetic and optical storage devices. These can be used to show films, broadcast famous speeches, and provide research for a school paper.

Think *About* It!

Below, circle the devices that use magnetically sensitive materials. Underline the devices that use optical storage.

- laserdiscs
- videotapes
- cassette tapes
- compact discs
- floppy disks

Sequential Versus Random Access When equipped with a tape drive, a computer can store data on a long piece of tape, similar to a cassette tape. A tape drive is an example of a **sequential storage device,** which requires the computer to scan from the beginning of the medium to the end until it finds the data it needs. This type of storage is cheaper but slower than other types of storage. Today's computer tapes can store 200 GB or more of data. But it can take several minutes to locate a piece of data on a high-capacity tape.

A **random access storage device** lets a computer go directly to the needed information. The device does not have to search the entire medium to find data. For this reason, random access storage devices are much faster, and more expensive, than sequential devices. A hard drive is an example of a random access storage device.

Magnetic Versus Optical Storage Magnetic storage devices are specially treated disks or tapes that record information using magnetically sensitive materials. These devices use electricity to shift magnetic particles so they form a pattern. That way, the computer can read and store the information. Common magnetic storage devices include hard drives, floppy disk drives, and tape drives.

Other storage devices use laser beams to read information that has been stored on the reflective surface of a disc. These are called **optical storage devices.** Popular types of optical storage devices for computers include CD-ROM and DVD-ROM drives.

Spotlight on...

HIGH-CAPACITY PORTABLE STORAGE

Devices such as Apple's iPod and Creative Labs' NOMAD MuVo function as both MP3 players (meaning they can play audio files saved in the popular MP3 format) and as high-capacity, transportable storage devices.

By plugging them into a computer, you can use these tiny storage devices to download files or transfer information from one computer to another. They can store, at minimum, 5GB of data. (That's at least 1,000 songs!) Yet, they are only about the size of a deck of cards and weigh about six ounces.

Demonstrate Your Knowledge

Critical Thinking

1. Suppose you back up your work for this class on a floppy disk. What type of storage device are you using?

_____

_____

2. On what kind of storage device—read-only or read/write—do you think a manufacturer of computer games supplies its products? Why?

_____

_____

3. Why can a random access storage device access information faster than a sequential storage device?

_____

_____

Activities

1. Complete the chart below to summarize details that you have learned about computer storage devices.

Storage Device	Read-Only vs. Read/Write	Sequential vs. Random	Magnetic vs. Optical
Hard drive			
Floppy disk drive			
Tape drive			
CD-ROM			
CD-RW			

2. Many PCs include CD-RW drives so users can record data onto CD-Rs and CD-RWs. Research the differences between CD-Rs and CD-RWs and the advantages and disadvantages of each.

Common Storage Devices

Objectives

- Differentiate between internal and external storage devices.
- List commonly used magnetic storage devices.
- Summarize optical storage options.

As You Read

Classify Information Use a T-chart to help you classify information about magnetic and optical storage devices as you read.

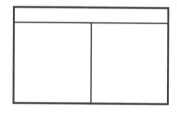

What's Online

In Lesson 3–3 of the iText, you will find more features and information for this lesson, including:

- Interactive tutorials
- As You Read worksheet
- Learn More interactivities
- Check Your Understanding interactive assessments
- Interactive lesson review

🔑 Key Terms

- hard drive (p. 40)
- floppy disk drive (p. 40)
- CD-ROM drive (p. 41)

Figure 3.3.1 If you removed your PC's internal hard drive, it would look something like this.

Internal and External Storage Devices

Storage devices can be installed in your computer or connected to it. A storage device installed inside your computer is called an internal storage device. One that is positioned outside your computer is referred to as an external storage device. External hard drives are becoming more popular, as they provide an easy way to add more storage capacity to a PC.

Common Magnetic Storage Devices

The most common magnetic storage device installed in computers is a **hard drive.** You cannot see the hard drive because it is installed inside your computer. Often, a small flashing light on the front of a computer shows when the hard drive is in use. External hard drives are becoming more popular, as they provide an easy way to add more storage capacity to a PC.

Floppy Disk Drives A **floppy disk drive** is a storage device with a slot that accepts floppy disks. These are often internal storage devices, but they may also be external. In either case, the device can read and write data on a floppy disk, or diskette, which uses magnetics to store information. Because the amount of information floppy disks can hold is very limited in terms of today's needs, some computers no longer have built-in floppy disk drives.

Zip and Jaz Drives Other forms of magnetic storage devices include Apple's iPod, a portable storage/playback device, and Zip and Jaz drives. These drives are similar to floppy disk drives; however, they are slightly larger in size and use a special disk or cartridge to store much more information—often 100 times more!

Magnetic Storage Devices

Device	Capacity
Hard drive	10 GB – 200 GB
Floppy disk	1.44 MB
iPod	5 GB – 20 GB
Jaz drive	2 GB
Zip drive	100 MB – 750 MB

Magneto-Optical (MO) Drives One type of drive combines both magnetic and optical drive technologies. A magneto-optical drive uses a removable disk that is inserted via a slot in the front of the drive. These drives can be internal or external. Their disks can store several gigabytes of information.

Online Storage You also can store information on a remote computer—one that is not your own. Usually, these computers are located on the Internet. To use online storage, you must contact a storage service provider, or SSP. This is usually done using the Internet but can also be done over the telephone or in person. The SSP sets up a contract with the user to clarify who has access and the amount and kind of information to be stored. Many businesses use online storage as a way to keep backup copies of their important data and to archive data they no longer need.

Common Optical Storage Devices

Optical storage devices let you store a lot of information and transport it easily. The most common optical storage device is known as a **CD-ROM drive.** These drives are read-only drives. You can access data from them but cannot use them to write data onto a CD.

A button on the front of the drive opens a tray on which you insert a CD. You push the button to close the tray, so you can use the disc's contents. Laserdisc drives, still used in some settings, operate in much the same way. The tray must be opened and the disc inserted before a laser can read the microscopic patterns of data encoded on the surface of the disc.

Career Corner

© Pearson Education, Inc.

CD Capacity A standard compact disc can hold 650 MB of data, or 74 minutes of audio. A newer type of compact disc can store 700 MB, or 80 minutes of audio. It also can be easily moved from one computer to the next.

Standard CD-ROM drives are read-only devices, but newer types of compact disc drives can write data as well as read it. One such device is the CD-Recordable (CD-R) drive, which can read standard CDs and write data onto special CD-R discs. You can write data onto a CD-R disc only once, however; once data is on the disc, it cannot be deleted or changed. Depending on the drive and recording software you use, you may be able to write data onto different parts of a CD-R disc at different times.

A CD-Rewritable (CD-RW) drive can write data onto special CD-RW discs. These discs allow you to change, overwrite, and erase data, in much the same way that you can use a floppy disk. CD-RW discs, however, don't work in all compact disc drives and can't be used for audio.

Digital Video Discs When you have very large storage requirements, consider the digital video disc, or DVD. One DVD can hold up to three times the information as a standard compact disc. Like compact discs, the letters following the initials *DVD* will let you know whether the disc is read-only or whether you can add information to it. With DVD-CD-RW and DVD-RAM, you can read and write to the discs. With DVD-ROM, you can only read information from the discs.

Figure 3.3.2 CDs and DVDs are popular components in both computers and home entertainment centers.

© Pearson Education, Inc.

Demonstrate Your Knowledge

Critical Thinking

1. What do you think is one advantage and one disadvantage to internal storage devices?

_____

_____

2. Why do you think CD-ROM drives are standard equipment on most computers sold today?

_____

_____

3. If you wanted to make a backup copy of all the files on your hard drive and store them in a different building, what storage device would best meet your needs? Why?

_____

_____

Activities

1. Complete the concept web below with three statements about ways optical storage devices read and write information.

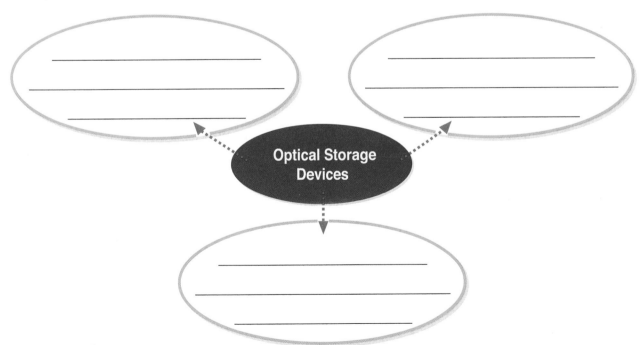

2. Most laserdiscs are found primarily in schools. Ask your teacher or school librarian to teach you how to access, operate, and manipulate information from this device and then let you use it. In writing, compare and contrast laserdiscs with compact discs.

Use the Vocabulary

Directions: *Match each vocabulary term in the left column with the correct definition in the right column. Write the appropriate letter next to the word or term.*

_____ **1.** storage device

_____ **2.** memory

_____ **3.** primary storage

_____ **4.** secondary storage

_____ **5.** read/write device

_____ **6.** random-access storage device

_____ **7.** optical storage device

_____ **8.** hard drive

_____ **9.** floppy disk drive

_____ **10.** CD-ROM drive

a. temporary workspace on a computer

b. sometimes used when referring to a computer's RAM

c. uses laser to read information

d. users access from and save information to this type of device

e. common secondary storage device

f. computer component that retains data even after power is shut off

g. storage device that lets computer go directly to the needed information

h. read-only optical device

i. device that allows users to read and write to a transportable magnetic disk

j. any type of storage device that holds data permanently; not RAM

Check Your Comprehension

Directions: *Complete each sentence with information from the chapter.*

1. Storage devices _____ information even when a computer is turned off.

2. Information saved as a _____ is identified by a unique name.

3. The _____ is a set of programs that directs a computer to start up.

4. RAM stores its contents _____ and is cleared when the computer is shut down.

5. A computer's BIOS is usually stored in a special memory chip, called _____ .

6. Floppy disk drives are examples of storage devices; floppy disks are examples of _____.

7. The most common secondary storage device is a _____.

8. _____ storage allows users to access rarely used computer files.

9. A magnetic tape is an example of a _____ storage device.

10. A _____ has greater storage capacity than a standard compact disc.

Think Critically

Directions: *Answer the following questions on the lines provided.*

1. Which type of secondary storage device do you use most at school? Do you think this will change in the near future? If so, why?

   _____

   _____

2. What can you do with a CD-RW that you cannot do with a CD-R?

   _____

   _____

3. Why do you think computer hard drives locate information directly, rather than sequentially?

   _____

   _____

4. Why do you think some computer users might need an external floppy disk drive?

   _____

   _____

5. Where do you think users of computer games sold on CDs and DVDs store their information? Why?

   _____

   _____

   _____

Extend Your Knowledge

Directions: *Choose one of the following projects. Complete the exercises on a separate sheet of paper.*

A. Look at your computer at school and find out how much memory it currently has. Next, use online documentation or other resources, such as the manufacturer's Web site, to compare your computer memory to the maximum amount of memory your computer can hold. Identify advantages to having more random access memory and compare this to the cost. As a class, conclude whether or not your school computers have sufficient memory to meet students' needs.

B. Go online and do research on storage service providers. What services and features do they offer? How do they protect the data they store? How easy is it for customers to access their data once they have given it to the service? Can customers share the stored data with other people? What fees do these services charge? Do you think such services can be useful to individuals as well as to companies?

chapter
4
System Software Basics

What Is An Operating System?

Have you ever wondered what happens when you turn on your computer? For many users, just seeing that the computer starts and that they can begin working is enough to meet their needs. But to become a more knowledgeable user, you should know how your computer works. One of the main behind-the-scenes contributors is the operating system.

The operating system is like the control center of your computer: it controls everything that happens with your computer. The operating system makes sure that files are stored properly on storage devices, software programs run properly, and instructions to peripherals are sent, among other jobs. Without an operating system, your computer would not be able to perform even basic tasks.

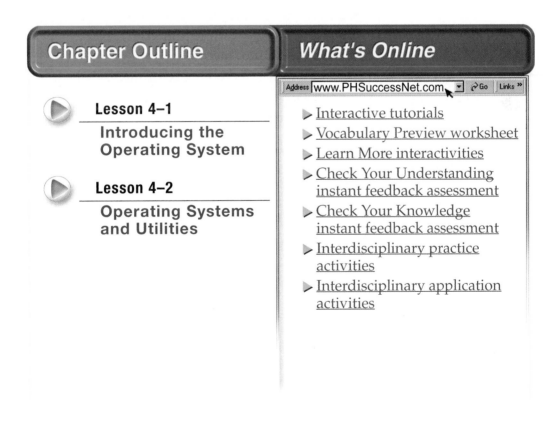

Chapter Outline

▶ **Lesson 4–1**
  Introducing the Operating System

▶ **Lesson 4–2**
  Operating Systems and Utilities

What's Online

Address www.PHSuccessNet.com ▾ ↻Go Links »

▶ Interactive tutorials
▶ Vocabulary Preview worksheet
▶ Learn More interactivities
▶ Check Your Understanding instant feedback assessment
▶ Check Your Knowledge instant feedback assessment
▶ Interdisciplinary practice activities
▶ Interdisciplinary application activities

Introducing the Operating System

Objectives

- Explain what an operating system is and what it does.
- Identify types of operating systems.
- Describe a graphical user interface.

As You Read

Organize Information Use a concept web to help you collect information about operating systems as you read.

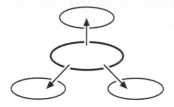

What's Online

In Lesson 4–1 of the iText, you will find more features and information for this lesson, including:

- Interactive tutorials
- As You Read worksheet
- Learn More interactivities
- Check Your Understanding interactive assessments
- Interactive lesson review

Key Terms

- interface (p. 48)
- crash (p. 48)
- graphical user interface (GUI) (p. 50)
- desktop (p. 50)
- icon (p. 50)

What Operating Systems Do

An operating system (OS) is a set of instructions designed to work with a specific type of computer, such as an IBM® PC or a Macintosh® computer. The OS controls all the computer's functions. It also provides an **interface,** the on-screen tools you use to interact with the computer and your programs. The operating system performs several tasks:

- manages the central processing unit (CPU) so that processing tasks are done properly
- manages computer memory
- manages files stored on the computer's disks
- manages input and output devices
- loads application programs into memory

Avoiding Conflicts In most computers, especially personal computers, the operating system is stored on the hard drive. Before you can use the computer, a portion of the operating sytem must be loaded into memory. This is true of all programs; they may permanently reside on a disk but must be copied into RAM before you can use them.

Some operating systems enable a computer to run more than one program at a time. To do this, the operating system has to assign each program some space in RAM, and then protect that space. Otherwise, conflicts can occur when two programs try to occupy the same space in RAM. When this happens, one or both of the programs may **crash,** or stop working, until the conflict is resolved.

Types of Operating Systems

All computers require an operating system. There are four kinds of operating systems.

Real-Time Systems Real-time operating systems are used to control large equipment, such as heavy machinery and scientific instruments, and to regulate factory operations. In order for these systems to run, they require very little user interaction.

Single-User/Single-Task Systems This kind of system lets one person do one task at a time. An example is the operating system that controls a handheld computer.

Single-User/Multitasking Systems A multitasking system allows the computer to perform several jobs, either one after the other or at the same time. For example, you could use your computer to write a letter as it downloads a page from the Internet and prints another letter. Most desktop and laptop computers today use this kind of system. Windows® and the Macintosh® OS are examples of this type of operating system.

Multi-User Systems These systems allow many individuals to use one large computer. The OS balances all the tasks that the various users ask the computer to do. UNIX is an example of this type of operating system.

Real-World Tech

An Operating System—in Your Dog? Robots are devices that can move and react to input from sight, hearing, touch, and balance. How are those "senses" and those reactions controlled? Through an operating system, of course! Robots are used to explore outer space and to do factory jobs. Now, however, they're also available as pets. Some robotic "dogs" can learn their own name and your name. They can show joy, anger, and surprise through lights, sounds, and gestures.

For what purposes do you think robots would be useful or fun? Write your ideas below.

_____

_____

_____

© Pearson Education, Inc.

The User Interface

The operating system's user interface lets you start programs, manage disks and files, and shut down the computer safely. To start the OS, you turn the computer on. During the startup procedure, the OS places part of itself into the computer's memory.

Desktop Nowadays, computer operating systems are based on visual displays. The **graphical user interface,** or **GUI** (GOO-ee), lets you use a mouse to interact with the workspace on the computer screen, called a **desktop.**

Icons On the screen, pictures called **icons** represent various resources on the computer. An icon might represent a program, a document, a hardware device, or a Web site. You click or double-click an icon to perform an action, such as starting a program or opening a file.

Options The operating system lets you change some features of the desktop, such as the look of the background or the placement of the icons. You can also change how other things work on your computer, such as keyboard functions and the speed at which the cursor blinks on the screen. The computer's manual or the Help feature allows you to explore these options.

Figure 4.1.1 Customizing the keyboard's operation in Microsoft® Windows® XP

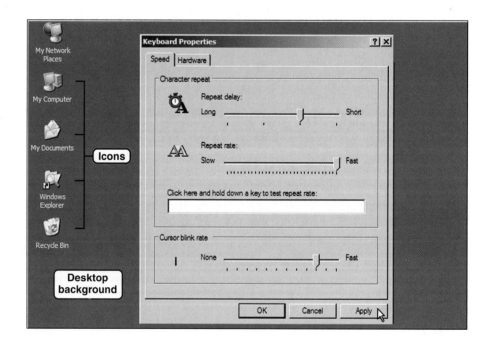

Demonstrate Your Knowledge

Critical Thinking

1. What can happen when two programs try to occupy the same space in RAM?

_____

_____

2. Which kind of computer operating system do most students use at home and at school? Why?

_____

_____

3. In what ways do desktop icons help make the computer easier for you to use?

_____

_____

Activities

1. Complete the chart with details to support the main idea below.

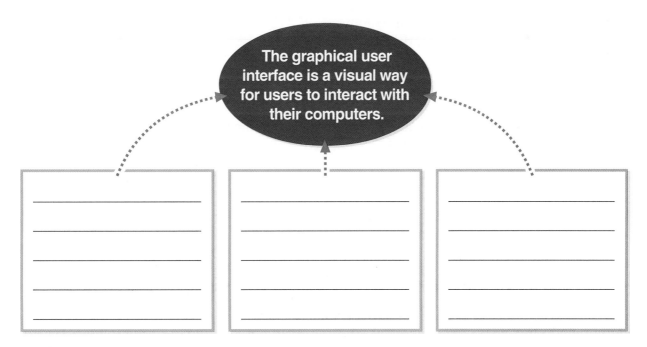

The graphical user interface is a visual way for users to interact with their computers.

2. Work with a partner to analyze the icons on the desktop of your computer. On a piece of paper, make a drawing of the desktop. Identify the function of each icon and label each one with the task it performs. Keep this organizer near your computer for reference.

Operating Systems and Utilities

Objectives

- Examine different operating systems.
- Discuss the function of the file manager in an operating system.
- Describe how system utilities help operating systems function.

As You Read

Outline Information Use an outline to help you note details about operating systems and system utilities as you read.

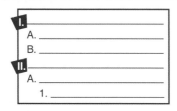

What's Online

In Lesson 4–2 of the iText, you will find more features and information for this lesson, including:

- Interactive tutorials
- As You Read worksheet
- Learn More interactivities
- Check Your Understanding interactive assessments
- Interactive lesson review

Key Terms

- driver utility (p. 54)
- Plug and Play (PnP) (p. 54)
- backup utility (p. 54)
- file compression utility (p. 54)

Popular Operating Systems

Three operating systems dominate the computer world—Microsoft® Windows®, the Macintosh® OS, and UNIX. The computer you use at school or at home probably has a version of Windows® or the Macintosh® OS installed. UNIX, and adaptations of it, is most often found running on large business or scientific networks.

Mac® OS In 1984, Apple® became the first computer maker to sell consumers a personal computer equipped with a graphical user interface (GUI). *Macintosh®* names both the computer and its operating system. Easy for beginners to use, some version of the Mac® OS runs all Macintosh® computers.

Microsoft® Windows® Although Microsoft® Windows® was not the first OS to have a GUI, the Windows® OS is currently the market leader, installed on more than 90 percent of personal computers.

UNIX and Linux UNIX was one of the first operating systems ever written. It was designed to work on powerful business and scientific computers. Later versions of UNIX have been developed to work on microcomputers, or personal computers.

One of these versions of UNIX, a system called Linux, has gained great attention in recent years. Linux works with an optional GUI and is very fast compared to other operating systems. Technically, Linux is free and can be downloaded from the Internet. But most users buy it with other features on a disc, and it is now challenging Apple® and Microsoft® for a share of the operating-system market.

System Utilities: File Management

Utility software is a collection of programs that help you maintain and repair your computer. Today, many types of utilities are built into the operating system. Probably the most important utilities are file managers, which let you work with data stored on your computer.

Organizing Files The operating system, programs, and data are all stored in files, each with a name. Files can be grouped together into folders. Folders can be divided into subfolders.

Using Files You can use an operating system's file manager to perform several tasks:
- create new folders or subfolders
- move or copy items between folders or to other disks
- delete files and folders
- launch applications

Finding Files You can use the file finder utility from your operating system to help you look for a file. This utility can search for a file by its name, type, date, or even by looking for specific data inside the file.

Technology @ Home

GUI designers choose icons that most people recognize.

Think *About* **It!**
Circle each item represented by an icon on a home computer.

➢ music files
➢ e-mail
➢ Internet browser
➢ printer
➢ text files
➢ antivirus software

Figure 4.2.1 Windows® Explorer® is one of two file management utilities built into Windows® XP.

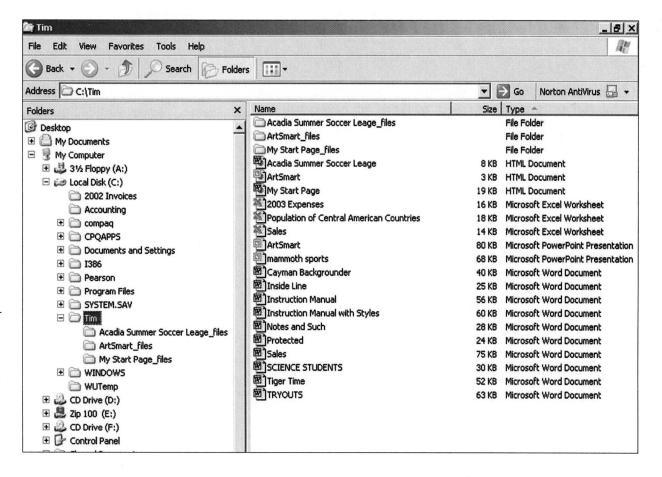

© Pearson Education, Inc.

Figure 4.2.2 Backing up data with Windows® XP Backup Utility Program

System Utilities: Other Jobs

Your operating system probably has utilities that can help with routine maintenance and other jobs.

Driver Utilities A **driver utility** contains data needed by programs to operate input and output devices such as a mouse and printer. Operating systems that have **Plug and Play (PnP)** capability can automatically detect new PnP-compatible devices. Otherwise, you will be prompted to insert the disk that came with the equipment to load the driver.

Program Utilities Before you can use a program, you must install it on your hard drive. In Windows®, you can use the Add/Remove Programs utility to ensure that your program installs properly. You can use the same utility to remove a program you no longer need.

Backup Utilities **Backup utility** programs automatically copy data from the computer's hard drive to a backup storage device, such as a floppy disk or a CD. Businesses and individuals routinely use backup utilities to ensure data is not lost if a computer or disk drive fails. You, too, should regularly back up your computer data.

File Compression Utilities **File compression utilities** are programs that reduce the size of files without harming the data. These programs make it easier to copy and send files.

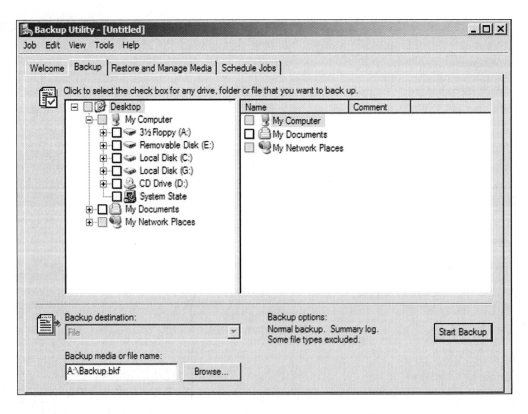

Demonstrate Your Knowledge

Critical Thinking

1. How are Microsoft® Windows® and Macintosh® operating systems alike? Different?

_____

_____

2. Why is it a good idea to organize files into folders and subfolders?

_____

_____

3. What options might you have for installing a new printer on your computer?

_____

_____

Activities

1. Complete the chart below to show the purpose of various system utilities.

Utility	Purpose
File managers	
Driver utilities	
Program utilities	
Backup utilities	
File compression utilities	

2. Create a simple word-processing document that includes your name and class schedule. Create a folder named with your initials. Create two subfolders, each named with your initials and a number (for example, dst1 and dst2). Save the word-processing document in one of the subfolders. Then, move it to the second subfolder. List the steps you took.

Use the Vocabulary

Directions: *Match each vocabulary term in the left column with the correct definition in the right column. Write the appropriate letter next to the word or term.*

_____ **1.** interface

_____ **2.** crash

_____ **3.** graphical user interface

_____ **4.** desktop

_____ **5.** icon

_____ **6.** driver utility

_____ **7.** Plug and Play

_____ **8.** backup utility

_____ **9.** file compression utility

a. area on a computer screen where you perform work

b. to stop working

c. program that controls input/output devices

d. picture that represents something on a computer

e. on-screen tools that let you use the computer

f. program that copies a file onto another medium

g. lets you use a mouse to work with the computer

h. capable of detecting compatible devices

i. reduces file size without harming data

Check Your Comprehension

Directions: *Circle the correct choice for each of the following.*

1. Which of the following is NOT usually handled by the operating system?
   a. managing programs
   b. dealing with input/output devices
   c. publishing Web pages
   d. interacting with the user

2. Which kind of computer operating system usually requires the least amount of user interaction?
   a. real-time systems
   b. single-user/single-task systems
   c. single-user/multitask systems
   d. multi-user systems

3. Which of the following is a key part of a graphical user interface?
   a. command words
   b. cursors
   c. memory
   d. icons

4. Which operating system is found most often on large business and scientific computers?
   a. Microsoft® Windows®
   b. Mac® OS
   c. UNIX
   d. Linux

5. Which of the following do operating systems, application programs, and user data have in common?
   a. They are all system utilities.
   b. They are all Windows®-based.
   c. They are all created by the user.
   d. They are all stored in files.

6. What kind of utility is used to reduce the size of a file?
   a. driver utility
   b. program utility
   c. backup utility
   d. file compression utility

⬤ Think Critically

Directions: *Answer the following questions on the lines provided.*

1. What kind of computer operating system do you think small, sophisticated devices such as PDAs use? Why?

_____

_____

2. What effect do you think the development of graphical user interfaces had on the number of people using computers? Why?

_____

_____

3. Which kind of utility program do you think is most important to your computer? Why?

_____

_____

4. What are two ways that you can launch an application program?

_____

_____

5. Why is it a good idea to back up your important files?

_____

_____

⬤ Extend Your Knowledge

Directions: *Choose one of the following projects. Complete the exercises on a separate sheet of paper.*

A. Go to Help in a Microsoft® Windows® operating system. Find out how it is organized, but make no changes to the system settings. Follow the same process on a Macintosh® computer. Which Help section was easier to use? Provide reasons for your preference. Discuss your conclusions as a class.

B. Find ads in computer magazines or on the Web that are sponsored by companies that sell backup and file compression utilities. Make a chart to summarize the features of three products in each category. Note which operating system each product works with and its price. Summarize your findings in a brief report.

chapter
5
Application Basics

What Is Application Software?

Application software is a type of program, such as word-processing or spreadsheet software, that directs a computer to perform one or more tasks. Think about all the things a computer can help you do. You can write letters and reports. You can look up information, record songs, play games, chat with friends, and more. Application software makes it possible for your PC to perform such tasks.

There are many different types of application software (sometimes called applications), each best suited for a certain purpose. Some programs perform specific jobs. Others do many different tasks. Once you become familiar with application software, you can make choices to help your computer work faster and more efficiently.

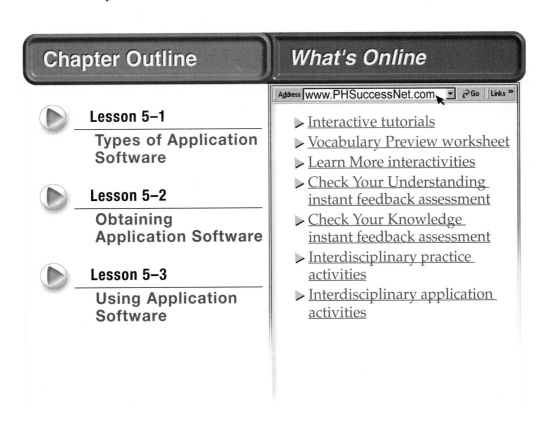

Chapter Outline

Lesson 5–1
Types of Application Software

Lesson 5–2
Obtaining Application Software

Lesson 5–3
Using Application Software

What's Online

Address www.PHSuccessNet.com   Go   Links »

- Interactive tutorials
- Vocabulary Preview worksheet
- Learn More interactivities
- Check Your Understanding instant feedback assessment
- Check Your Knowledge instant feedback assessment
- Interdisciplinary practice activities
- Interdisciplinary application activities

Lesson 5–1

Types of Application Software

Objectives

- Identify widely used types of application software.
- Compare and contrast three types of application software.
- Decide what kinds of applications will work best for you.

As You Read

Compare and Contrast Use a three-column chart to compare three different types of application software. Write each type as a column header and list the features below the header.

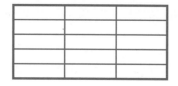

What's Online

In Lesson 5–1 of the iText, you will find more features and information for this lesson, including:

- Interactive tutorials
- As You Read worksheet
- Learn More interactivities
- Check Your Understanding interactive assessments
- Interactive lesson review

Key Terms

- application software (p. 59)
- personal information manager (PIM) program (p. 60)
- integrated software (p. 61)
- office suite (p. 62)

Why Use Application Software?

Application software performs a specific job or task. For example, some applications help astronomers research stars. Others help doctors care for their patients. It is important to choose applications that can do the jobs you want done. The most common types of application software include:

- word processors for writing letters and reports
- spreadsheets for working with numbers and doing math
- databases for storing and finding information
- presentation graphics for creating slide shows
- telecommunications for using the Internet and e-mail
- **personal information manager (PIM) programs** for storing phone numbers and addresses and creating schedules

Popular Stand-alone Programs

Application	Program
Database	Corel® Paradox, FileMaker® Pro, Lotus® Approach, Microsoft® Access
Graphics	Corel® Presentation, Lotus® Freelance Graphics, Microsoft® PowerPoint
Spreadsheet	Corel Quattro® Pro, Lotus® 1-2-3, Microsoft® Excel
Word Processor	Corel® WordPerfect, Lotus® WordPro, Microsoft® Word®

Types of Application Software

Application software falls into three basic categories: stand-alone programs, integrated software, and office suites. These forms differ in their features (the tasks they do) and in cost. Wise computer users choose the type of software that best fits their needs, their computers, and their pocketbooks.

Stand-alone Programs Software that specializes in one task is called a stand-alone program. Because each program—such as a word processor, database, or spreadsheet—is dedicated to just one application, stand-alone programs can have many useful and advanced features. However, stand-alone programs may cost more than other forms of application software.

Because they focus on one kind of job, stand-alone programs usually have many very specialized features. Word processors, for example, give users tools to print labels and envelopes.

Integrated Software Buying multiple stand-alone programs might require too much memory in your computer or may cost too much. You might want to do more with the software than a stand-alone program is capable of handling.

Integrated software programs combine the basic features of several applications into one package. They are not as powerful or as complete as their stand-alone counterparts, nor do they specialize in one application. However, integrated software usually is less costly and is fairly easy to use. These programs let you do basic work in several applications such as word processors, databases, spreadsheets, graphics, and more.

People use integrated software programs because the applications work in similar ways. That is, you often can use many of the same commands. You also can use data from one program in another. Popular integrated programs include Apple-Works® and Microsoft® Works.

Connections

The Arts Software applications can be created to help make life easier for many different types of people. A software application called Goodfeel® converts printed sheet music to Braille, allowing blind musicians greater access to music. Before this software was created, blind musicians often had to wait months for sheet music to be converted by hand.

Spotlight on...

ROBERT LISSNER

66 *Originally released in 1984 by Apple Computer, [AppleWorks] has gone on to become one of the best selling computer programs of all time, on any computer.* 99

Steven Weyhrich
Apple II History

Written between 1982 and 1984 by Rupert (Robert) Lissner, AppleWorks was one of the first and most successful integrated software packages of all time. Originally named "Apple Pie," AppleWorks® was marketed for the new Apple® computer. For the first time, a program successfully integrated word processing, database, and spreadsheet modules, and used similar commands in each. It also allowed users to share files among the modules. Today, several programs use *Works* as part of their name, a credit to Robert Lissner and his "piece of the pie."

© Pearson Education, Inc.

Applications Basics • **61**

Figure 5.1.1 Popular productivity suites include a word-processing program, a spreadsheet, an e-mail program, and other applications.

Office Suites What if you need to use the advanced features of several stand-alone programs? You might select an **office suite.** Although one suite may differ from another, in general office suites combine several programs such as word processing, spreadsheets, databases, and graphics. Like integrated software, the programs in office suites have a common look and feel. But office suites contain more than the basic software found in integrated programs. They contain the actual stand-alone programs with all their features.

Office suites generally cost more than integrated software, but usually they are cheaper than buying the stand-alone programs separately. Some popular office suites include:

- Microsoft® Office (with Word®, Excel®, PowerPoint®, Outlook®, and Access® in the Windows® version)
- Corel® WordPerfect® Office (with WordPerfect®, Quattro® Pro, Paradox, Corel® Presentations, and Corel® CENTRAL)
- Lotus® SmartSuite® (with WordPro®, Lotus® 1-2-3, Approach®, Freelance Graphics®, and Organizer®)

Which Type of Software Is Right for You?

The type of application software you choose depends on what you want it to do, how much you are willing to spend, and how easy the programs are to learn. It also depends on whether the software will work on your computer and how much space each program will take up on your hard drive. You might want to match the software you use at home with the programs you use at school so you can work on documents in both locations.

Most computers are sold with some application software installed. But a computer may not have the software you need. Your software needs may also change over time. Then you can consider upgrading your existing software or buying new programs to make your computer a more useful tool.

Demonstrate Your Knowledge

Critical Thinking

1. What type of application software do you think would be most difficult to learn? Why?

_____

_____

2. What kind of application software might you recommend to a friend who wants to create basic graphics, write reports, and create a budget? Why?

_____

_____

3. What questions should buyers answer before choosing application software?

_____

_____

Activities

1. Complete the T-chart below to identify advantages and disadvantages of office suites.

Advantages	Disadvantages
_____	_____
_____	_____
_____	_____
_____	_____
_____	_____
_____	_____
_____	_____
_____	_____

2. Find out which software applications are used on computers in your school office and library. Make a list, and identify each application as *stand-alone, integrated,* or *office suite.* If these computers use integrated programs or office suites, name the programs they include.

Obtaining Application Software

Objectives

- Explain why computer hardware and software must be compatible.
- Identify sources for obtaining application software.
- Summarize the best way to install or uninstall application software.
- Analyze how piracy affects makers and users of computer software.

🔑 Key Terms

- system requirement (p. 64)
- commercial software (p. 64)
- shareware (p. 65)
- freeware (p. 65)
- public domain software (p. 65)
- install (p. 65)
- uninstall (p. 66)
- software license (p. 66)

As You Read

Organizing Information Make an outline of the lesson. Use Roman numerals for main headings. Use capital letters for subheadings, and use numbers for supporting details.

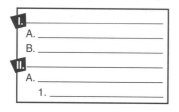

What's Online

In Lesson 5–2 of the iText, you will find more features and information for this lesson, including:

- Interactive tutorials
- As You Read worksheet
- Learn More interactivities
- Check Your Understanding interactive assessments
- Interactive lesson review

Minimum System Requirements

Each software program has minimum **system requirements.** The computer must meet the minimum hardware and software needs of the program for it to work properly.

To get the most from your computer, it is important to choose software that will work with the following:

- your type of computer (Macintosh® or PC compatible)
- microprocessor speed
- operating system (such as Linux®, Mac OS® X, or Windows® XP)
- available amount of memory (RAM)
- available hard drive space
- special equipment, such as a modem or CD-ROM drive

Obtaining Application Software

Some application software is already loaded on new computers. You can also obtain additional software in multiple forms.

Commercial Software Companies own the copyrights to the application software they sell to the public. This prevents you from legally copying it to sell it to others, giving it away, or sharing it. **Commercial software** is copyrighted software that you must buy before using it.

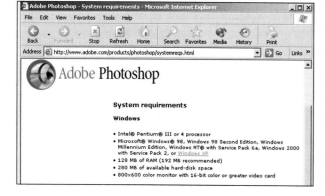

Figure 5.2.1 You can check a program's system requirements at the developer's Web site.

Shareware Copyrighted software that you can use on a try-before-you-buy basis is called **shareware**. If you decide to keep using it after that, you must pay a registration fee to the company. You are also allowed to copy shareware and give it to your friends. They, then, must follow the same process to acquire the software.

Freeware Some companies give away their copyrighted software for free. This is known as **freeware**. The companies allow users to install the program as long as they do not resell it to other people.

Public Domain Software On occasion, program authors allow you to use programs, share them, give them away, or even alter them to meet certain needs. This is called **public domain software**. Beware, the quality of these programs can vary widely, and they may contain more errors than other types of software.

Installing and Uninstalling Programs Application software must be **installed**, or prepared to run on a computer, before it can be used. You must copy it from a location such as a disk, a CD, or the Internet to the computer's hard drive.

Most programs come with an installation, or setup, program that prompts you to load the software onto the computer. Companies that make commercial software often provide printed or online guides, or telephone support, to help solve users' problems.

Technology @ Work

Shareware companies make money by collecting fees for the products they send out on a free trial basis.

Think *About* **It!**

Shareware has many advantages for its producers. Identify each benefit of shareware as either true (*T*) or false (*F*). Write your answer beside each item.

➤ A user might try shareware rather than buying a commercial program.

➤ Shareware companies do not have to pay for distribution.

➤ Users who do not like the product still have to pay for it.

Real-World Tech

Authoring Shareware California-based Tenadar Software develops adventure games and distributes them as shareware. To play the game more than once, you send the requested royalty to the copyright holders. Who are they? Tenadar employees are all between 10 and 12 years old. What started as a fifth-grade project has grown into a business of several employees offering a variety of computer games for the Macintosh®. The company's motto is "Great Software for Kids, by Kids."

If you were to create shareware, what might you choose to develop? Write your ideas below.

_____

_____

_____

To delete a program from the computer, you must run a special removal program to properly remove, or **uninstall,** it. Otherwise, parts of the program can remain on the computer and may interfere with its operation.

Using Software Legally

Buying copyrighted software usually permits the buyer to install and use that software on only one computer. This permission is contained in a document known as the **software license.** Users agree to the terms of the license, usually during the installation process.

Software Piracy People who copy copyrighted software to install on other computers, give away, or sell are guilty of copyright violation and stealing, called software piracy. Violating a copyright and pirating software are both morally wrong and illegal. These activities discourage the authors of good software from writing new and better programs because they may not get paid for their work. Pirated software cannot be registered, so users do not get the support services they may need.

Figure 5.2.2 Most software programs come with a license agreement, like the one shown here for Roxio, Inc.

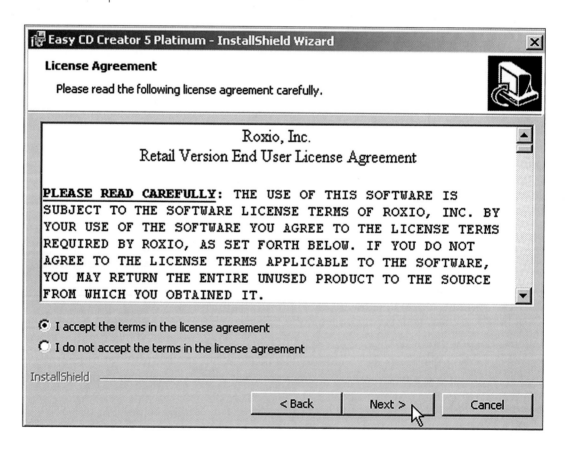

Demonstrate Your Knowledge

Critical Thinking

1. Why must computer hardware and software be compatible?

_____

_____

2. Why might public domain software have more errors than commercial software, shareware, or freeware?

_____

_____

3. How do copyright violations or software piracy affect computer companies and users?

_____

_____

Activities

1. Complete the sequence chart below to sequence the steps in acquiring shareware.

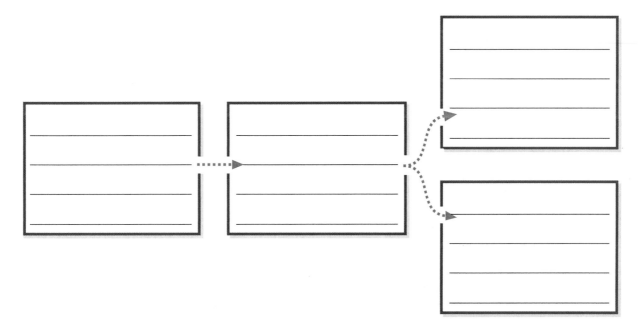

2. Make a class list of the programs installed on your classroom computers. List the minimum system requirements for each program. Compare software needs to your hardware. Write a paragraph explaining how effectively your programs can run on your computers.

Using Application Software

Objectives

- Describe how to launch a program.
- List common features of application software windows.
- Explain how to maximize and minimize a program window.
- Explain how to create, open, save, and close a file.
- Explain how to exit an application.

🔑 Key Terms

- launch (p. 68)
- maximize (p. 69)
- minimize (p. 69)
- title bar (p. 69)
- menu bar (p. 69)
- Help menu (p. 69)
- scroll (p. 70)

As You Read

Draw Conclusions Use a conclusion chart to help you understand how to use application software as you read.

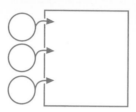

In Lesson 5-3 of the iText, you will find more features and information for this lesson, including:

- Interactive tutorials
- As You Read worksheet
- Learn More interactivities
- Check Your Understanding interactive assessments
- Interactive lesson review

Launching an Application

Most application software runs in your computer's operating system. Two popular operating systems are Mac OS® for the Apple Macintosh® or Microsoft® Windows for IBM-compatible computers. Your operating system and application software often have similar commands for starting and ending a program and for conducting basic tasks. This makes learning a new program fairly easy.

Starting a Program When a computer is turned on, it typically starts its operating system. You can then **launch**, or start, any application installed on the computer. You can launch an application in two ways:

- menu
- desktop icon

Menu In Windows®, clicking the Start button displays a list of programs installed on the computer.

Desktop Icon Desktop icons are on-screen symbols that stand for a computer function or program. Because they are shortcuts to programs, it is helpful to customize your PC or Macintosh® desktop to include icons for the programs you use most often.

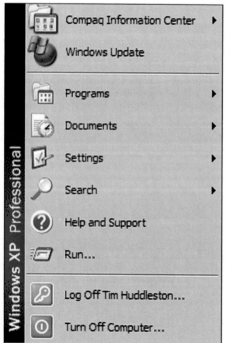

Figure 5.3.1 The Start menu from Windows XP Professional

Application Windows

A launched application appears in a frame called a window. You can work in any size window, but it is usually best to **maximize** the window, or make it as large as it can be. Sometimes you will want to use another program without closing the first one. You can **minimize** a program window, or make it as small as possible, so it remains out of the way while you use the other program. The largest portion of an application window is the space for your work. The rest of the window contains many features.

Title Bar The top row of an application window is called the **title bar.** The title bar shows the program's name and, in some cases, the name of the document you are working on.

Menu Bar A **menu bar** lists sets of commands. In Windows®, the menu bar usually is located below the title bar. On a Macintosh®, it appears at the top of the screen. You can click a menu's name to see its options. For example, clicking Help on the menu bar allows you to access options in the **Help menu.** This menu is a set of directions for program functions.

Figure 5.3.2 Many productivity applications share these basic features.

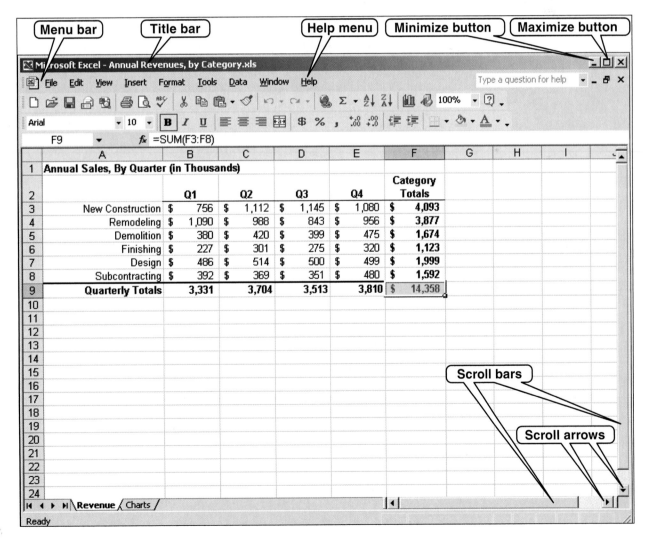

© Pearson Education, Inc.

Creating, Opening, Saving, and Closing

Application software lets you create new documents, save them for future use, or work on documents you have saved. You can close the application when you are done working. Most applications have a File menu, which includes these commands:

- New—creates a file into which you can enter data
- Open—finds a document that was previously saved as a disk file and displays it in a window
- Save—saves the document in the current window to a disk file
- Close—closes an open file
- Exit or Quit—closes the application and removes its window from the screen

Moving in the Application Window

Some tools allow you to **scroll,** or move from one part of a window to another. The scroll bars usually appear at the right side of the window and at the bottom. Boxes appear in these bars to show whether you are at the beginning or end of the file or somewhere in the middle. You can move from one place to another by either dragging these scroll boxes or clicking the scroll arrows at each end of the scroll bars.

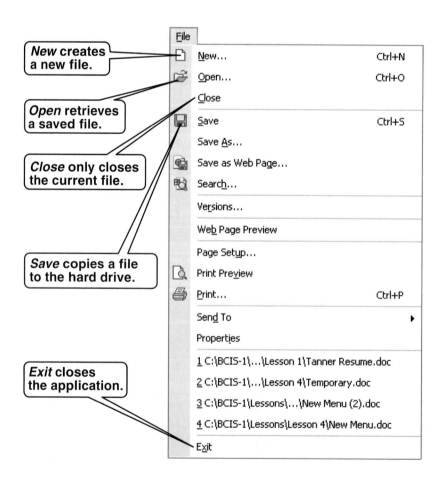

New creates a new file.

Open retrieves a saved file.

Close only closes the current file.

Save copies a file to the hard drive.

Exit closes the application.

© Pearson Education, Inc.

Demonstrate Your Knowledge

Critical Thinking

1. What is the purpose of the title bar and the menu bar?

_____

_____

2. What is one advantage of maximizing a window when using application software? Of minimizing a window?

_____

_____

3. Why do you think that it is important to save a file before you close it?

_____

_____

Activities

1. Complete the chart below by identifying four computer commands in the File menu and the purpose of each one.

Command	Purpose

2. Two popular operating systems are Microsoft® Windows® and the Mac OS®. Conduct online research to find information about an operating system called Linux®, and describe how it differs from Microsoft® Windows® and the Mac OS®.

Use the Vocabulary

Directions: *Match each vocabulary term in the left column with the correct definition in the right column. Write the appropriate letter next to the word or term.*

_____ **1.** personal information manager

_____ **2.** integrated software

_____ **3.** office suite

_____ **4.** shareware

_____ **5.** freeware

_____ **6.** public domain software

_____ **7.** uninstall

_____ **8.** maximize

_____ **9.** minimize

_____ **10.** scroll

a. software that you can try before purchasing

b. uncopyrighted software that is given away without cost

c. software that stores phone numbers and creates schedules

d. software that combines several different applications

e. to make a window as small as possible

f. to delete a program from the computer

g. software that combines several applications

h. move from one place in a window to another

i. to make a window as large as possible

j. copyrighted software that is given away without cost

Check Your Comprehension

Directions: *Circle the correct choice for each of the following.*

1. Which of the following items is NOT an example of application software?
 a. spreadsheet
 b. database
 c. operating system
 d. word processor

2. Which of the following types of application software combines the basic features of several applications?
 a. stand-alone program
 b. integrated software
 c. office suite
 d. personal information manager (PIM) program

3. Which of the following types of software must be purchased in advance?
 a. commercial software
 b. shareware
 c. freeware
 d. public domain software

4. Which of the following types of software is available on a try-before-you-buy basis?
 a. commercial software
 b. shareware
 c. freeware
 d. public domain software

5. Which of the following features allows the user to launch an application?
 a. Help menu
 b. menu bar
 c. title bar
 d. desktop icon

6. Which of the following tools allows the user to move from one part of a window to another?
 a. scroll arrows
 b. scroll icons
 c. scroll menu
 d. scroll file

Think Critically

Directions: *Answer the following questions on the lines provided.*

1. Why might a computer user choose to purchase an integrated software program instead of an office suite?

_____

_____

2. Why should you check a program's system requirements before purchasing it?

_____

_____

3. Why is it important to uninstall a program you no longer use?

_____

_____

4. What is the difference between the New and Open commands in the File menu?

_____

_____

5. Why does an application window include tools such as scroll bars, scroll boxes, and scroll arrows?

_____

_____

Extend Your Knowledge

Directions: *Choose one of the following projects. Complete the exercises on a separate sheet of paper.*

A. The Start menu often shows many different types of icons. Icons can represent applications, files, or file folders. Experiment with a Macintosh or Microsoft Windows operating system. Make a three-column chart of the icons that appear on the screen. Include a description of what happens when each icon is clicked, and identify what type of file or program the particular icon represents.

B. Several types of application software are listed in this chapter. They include word processors, spreadsheets, databases, presentation graphics, telecommunications, and personal information managers. Using the Internet or other resources, prepare a report that compares two types of application software that you may use based on their appropriateness, effectiveness, and efficiency. Share your reports with the class.

Word-Processing Basics

What Is Word Processing? In 1968, IBM first used the term *word processing*. The term described machines that could be used to type a document, remember the typist's keystrokes, and produce more than one copy. With this new tool, workers saved time.

That was just the beginning. Today's word-processing programs do much more. Suppose you were writing something by hand and made a mistake or changed your mind about what you wanted to say. If you were using a pen, you would probably cross out the words you wanted to change or brush on correction fluid. Doing that leaves the page messy, though. With word-processing software, you can change the text and still create neat pages. You can even save what you typed and use it again a day, a week, or even a year later.

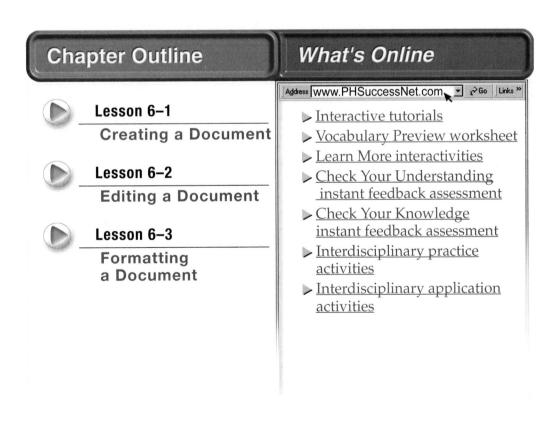

Chapter Outline

▶ **Lesson 6–1**
Creating a Document

▶ **Lesson 6–2**
Editing a Document

▶ **Lesson 6–3**
Formatting
a Document

What's Online

Address www.PHSuccessNet.com ▾ 🗘Go | Links »

▶ Interactive tutorials
▶ Vocabulary Preview worksheet
▶ Learn More interactivities
▶ Check Your Understanding
 instant feedback assessment
▶ Check Your Knowledge
 instant feedback assessment
▶ Interdisciplinary practice
 activities
▶ Interdisciplinary application
 activities

Creating a Document

Objectives

- List the four basic functions of word-processing programs.
- Name two tools used to navigate a word-processing document.
- Summarize four key features of word-processing programs.
- Identify three standards for word-processing documents.

As You Read

Organize Information Complete a spider map to help you organize basic facts about word processing as you read.

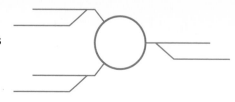

What's Online

In Lesson 6–1 of the iText, you will find more features and information for this lesson, including:

- Interactive tutorials
- As You Read worksheet
- Learn More interactivities
- Check Your Understanding interactive assessments
- Interactive lesson review

🔑 Key Terms

- word-processing program (p. 76)
- insertion point (p. 77)
- word wrap (p. 78)
- pagination (p. 78)
- AutoCorrect (p. 78)
- autosave (p. 78)

Functions of Word-Processing Programs

Word-processing programs are used for creating and printing text documents. These programs have four functions:

- writing—entering text and symbols into a document
- editing—revising or reorganizing the text
- formatting—changing how the text looks on the page
- printing—producing a printed copy

These tasks do not need to be done all at once or even in the order shown here. Whatever the order, these four functions are at the heart of word processing.

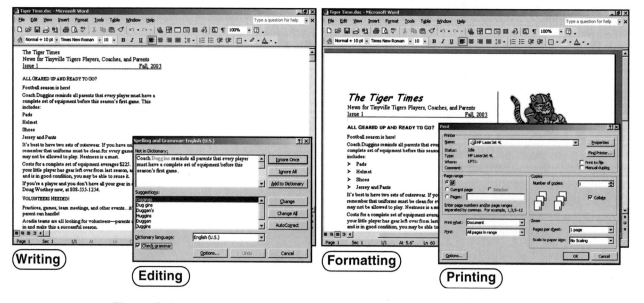

Figure 6.1.1 The four main functions of a word-processing program

Uses of Word Processing

Word-processing programs can be used to create almost any kind of printed document, such as letters, reports, and brochures. They can also be used to create calendars, return-address labels, and labels for homemade CDs. It is no surprise that word-processing software is the application that people use more than any other application.

Working With a Word-Processing Document

When you open a word-processing program, a new, blank document is created. It looks like a blank piece of paper on the screen. The program is ready for you to start writing. You can create another new document any time by clicking New on the Standard toolbar.

Every time you create a new document you need to save it. Click Save on the Standard toolbar or select the File menu and click Save. When the Save As dialog box opens, name your document.

Insertion Point The **insertion point** shows where the text you type will appear. It moves as you type.

Scrolling As you write, you might want to reread or change something you wrote earlier. That is made easy by scrolling—using the mouse or keyboard to move through the document.

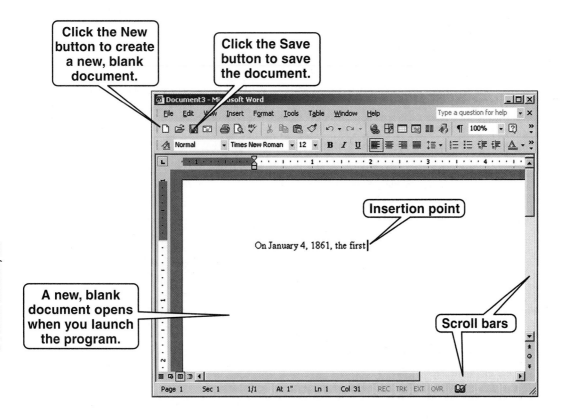

© Pearson Education, Inc.

Copy Editor Copy editors check documents for correct spelling, grammar, and consistency of style. Although some copy editors work on hard copy, or paper, many edit soft copy, or electronic files. Among the problems they look for are inconsistent or wrong formats, such as incorrect em dashes, en dashes and spacing, or unacceptable hyphenation generated by the word processor.

You can scroll up or down by using the mouse to click the scroll bar or drag the scroll box at the right of the document window. Some new mouse devices have scrolling wheels. You can also use the Up and Down arrow keys or the Page Up, Page Down, Home, and End keys to move around in the document.

Basic Features

Most word-processing programs have four basic features. They help you write, edit, and save your work.

- With **word wrap,** the program automatically starts a new line, or "wraps" the text, when the current line is full. If you wish, you can force text onto a new line by pressing Enter.
- When a page is full, the **pagination** feature automatically starts a new page. You can also force a new page by inserting a special character, called a page break.
- The **AutoCorrect** feature fixes common spelling mistakes as they are typed. You can turn off this feature or modify it to accept unusual words that you often use.
- The **autosave** feature protects you from losing work. It does so by automatically saving a document as often as you want. If the computer shuts down accidentally, you can retrieve the most recently saved version.

Standards for Word-Processing Documents

As you write, keep in mind three standards of style to make your work look professional.

- Two standards are met automatically by many programs. They change two hyphens (--) to an em dash (—). They also convert quotation marks to curly quotation marks, or "smart quotes."
- The other standard is not automatic—you have to remember to do it. This standard is to type one space, not two, between sentences.

Figure 6.1.3 Word wrap and pagination

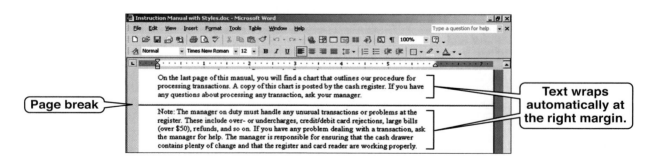

Demonstrate Your Knowledge

Critical Thinking

1. What is the purpose of the insertion point in a word-processing program?

   _____

   _____

2. How do you use a mouse to scroll through a document? How do you use the keyboard?

   _____

   _____

3. Of the three standards of word-processing style, which do you think puts more demands on the person using the program? Why?

   _____

   _____

Activities

1. Look at the chart below, which shows the steps that Shanique took while word processing a document. Complete the missing information by writing it in the spaces provided.

Step 1:	_____
Step 2:	Start writing the first paragraph.
Step 3:	Go to the File menu and select _____ to save her work.
Step 4:	_____
Step 5:	_____ the document by making changes.
Step 6:	_____
Step 7:	Go to the File menu and _____ to print the document.

2. Ask three people of different generations what kinds of documents they create with word-processing programs. What are the most typical uses? What are the most unusual ones? Which documents do you think will be used on the job in the future?

Lesson 6–2

Editing a Document

Objectives

- Explain how to identify document files in a list of files.
- Describe the benefits of selecting text.
- Contrast different editing tools, such as insert and overtype modes, the Cut and Copy commands, and the Undo and Redo commands.

As You Read

Identify Cause and Effect
Complete a cause-and-effect chart to help you identify what happens when word-processing functions are applied as you read.

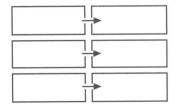

What's Online

In Lesson 6–2 of the iText, you will find more features and information for this lesson, including:

- Interactive tutorials
- As You Read worksheet
- Learn More interactivities
- Check Your Understanding interactive assessments
- Interactive lesson review

Key Terms

- insert mode (p. 80)
- overtype mode (p. 80)
- select text (p. 81)
- Clipboard (p. 81)

Opening a Document for Editing

Editing can take place at any time after you have created the document. To do so, you need to open the file you created so you can work on it again.

You can use a word-processing program's Open command to open a file, or you can use a file management program to find files on a disk. In Windows®, file names have extensions, such as .txt, .rtf, .doc, or .wpd, although these extensions may be hidden from view. On a Macintosh computer, documents are simply listed by file name.

Word-processing programs make editing easy. You can add words simply by typing them. You can delete characters by pressing the Delete or Backspace keys. Powerful features in these programs help you do even more.

Insert and Overtype

Word-processing programs offer two ways of entering text. They are called insert mode and overtype mode. When you work in **insert mode**, new characters are inserted between existing ones. This mode lets you add a new word to the middle of a sentence, for example.

In **overtype mode**, as you type new characters, they replace any characters in front of them. In other words, overtype mode lets you "type over" existing text. Be sure to select the typing mode you want or problems will occur.

The status bar at the bottom of the program window usually shows what mode the program is using. Programs let you switch from one mode to another using either the keyboard or the mouse. Some keyboards have an Insert key to do this, too.

© Pearson Education, Inc.

Selecting Text

Usually, people edit more than one character at a time. The **select text** feature lets you highlight anything from a word to a whole document. Then you can delete it, move it, copy it, or change its formatting.

To select text, simply drag the mouse over the text you want. Some programs also let you select text by using the keyboard. Selected text is highlighted on the screen; that is, it appears with a different background color.

Cutting, Copying, and Pasting

Two common reasons for selecting text are cutting and copying. Both actions place the text in the Clipboard.

The Clipboard The **Clipboard** stores cut or copied text while you work. Once you close the program or shut down the computer, items on the Clipboard are lost. Some programs store only one item at a time, so cutting or copying new text replaces what was held before. Some programs can hold many items on the Clipboard.

- The Cut command removes the selected text from a document and places it on the Clipboard.
- The Copy command places a duplicate of the selected text on the Clipboard.

The Cut and Copy commands can be found in the Edit menu. These commands also have icons on the Standard toolbar.

Technology @ Work

Businesses sometimes use text called *boilerplate.* This is text that is used exactly the same way in many places to make certain that wording or features stay consistent in the same document or in many documents.

Think *About* **It!**
Identify which word-processing action would be best for handling boilerplate. Underline the feature you think is most useful for this purpose in the list of options below.

- ➤ Copy and Paste
- ➤ Cut and Paste
- ➤ Select and Move
- ➤ Undo and Redo

Figure 6.2.1 Selecting text in a word-processing program

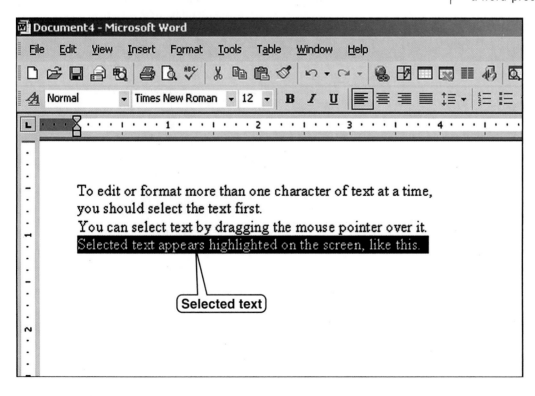

Think *About* **It!**

Think about what the Copy command does. Next to the items below, write *T* if you think the Copy command is useful. Write *F* if the Copy command is not useful.

- ▶ the delivery address for letters to different people
- ▶ the cook's name on the top of recipe cards
- ▶ the title of a CD in a list of CDs
- ▶ a paragraph to appear in two different letters

Figure 6.2.2 The Cut, Copy, and Paste commands

Pasting Use the Paste command to relocate items stored on the Clipboard. Simply position the insertion point where you want the text to reappear. Then, click the Paste icon on the Standard toolbar or choose Paste from the Edit menu. The cut or copied text appears where you want it.

Using Cut and Paste Moving a sentence from the middle of a paragraph to the beginning can be done by selecting and dragging it. You can use Cut and Paste to move that sentence farther—for example, to another page—or to move text or a graphic from one document to another. You can even open a new window, paste the text you cut from another document, and save the pasted text as a new document.

Using Copy and Paste Copying and pasting saves time when you need to repeat some text. You can also copy and paste to bring a graphic from one document into another.

Undoing and Redoing

Word-processing programs have commands that can undo or cancel an edit. If you delete a word by mistake, you can use the Undo command to put it back. Many programs also have a Redo command. You can use this feature to put a change back in effect after cancelling it with Undo.

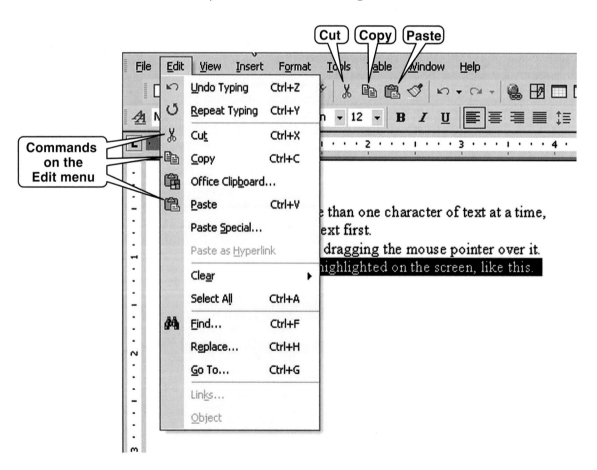

Demonstrate Your Knowledge

Critical Thinking

1. Give two examples of the file name extensions that could be opened as a document by a word processor in Windows. Why could the program open them?

_____

_____

2. In a word-processing document, what are three actions you can perform on selected text?

_____

_____

3. How do insert mode and overtype mode differ?

_____

_____

Activities

1. Complete the Venn diagram below. Write facts that are true about the Cut command in the area labeled *Cut*. Write facts that are true about the Copy command in the area labeled *Copy*. Write facts that are true about both in the area labeled *Cut and Copy*.

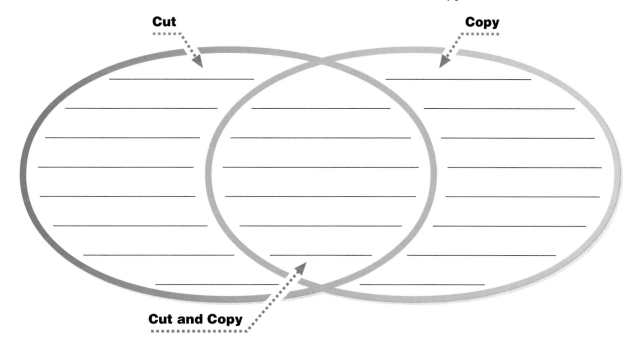

2. Choose a word-processing program. Find out what actions by the mouse and the keyboard can be used to move text from one place to another. Complete a chart to show your findings.

Formatting a Document

Objectives

- Explain what default formatting is.
- Identify four parts of any document that can be formatted.
- Summarize the advantages of dividing a document into sections for formatting.
- Compare portrait and landscape orientation.

As You Read

Summarize Complete a summary chart to help you identify different features that can be formatted as you read the lesson.

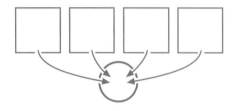

What's Online

In Lesson 6–3 of the iText, you will find more features and information for this lesson, including:

- Interactive tutorials
- As You Read worksheet
- Learn More interactivities
- Check Your Understanding interactive assessments
- Interactive lesson review

Key Terms

- default (p. 84)
- style (p. 85)
- section (p. 86)
- page formatting (p. 86)

Figure 6.3.1 Dialog boxes like these let you change all sorts of formatting options.

Appearance Is Important

A document's formatting—its appearance—is sometimes as important as its contents. This is why word-processing programs have so many tools to format documents.

Word-processing programs include many preset formats, called **defaults**. The program applies these formats automatically, unless you change them. For example, many word processors use Times New Roman as the default font, but you can use a different font whenever you want.

You can format four distinct parts of a document: characters, paragraphs, sections, and pages.

The Font dialog box lets you format individual characters or groups of characters.

The Paragraph dialog box lets you change spacing, indentations, and other features of a paragraph.

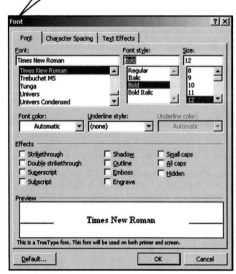

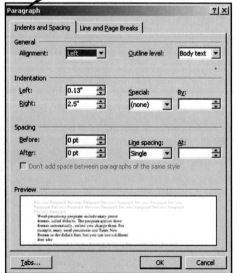

Formatting Characters

Character formatting lets you change the look of letters. Three primary formats are applied to characters:

- The font is the family of characters used. A font is a named set of characters that have the same appearance. Popular fonts are Times New Roman and Courier.
- Font size is the height of characters, measured in points. One point equals 1/72 inch.
- Font styles are characteristics such as boldface and italic.

Programs make it easy to format similar groups of characters the same way throughout a document. For instance, you can create a set of formatting characteristics, called a **style**, for all the subheadings in a document. When you apply that style to all the subheadings, you apply that group of formats in one step.

Formatting Paragraphs

A paragraph is any text that ends with a forced new line. Whenever you press Enter, you create a paragraph. You can change many paragraph formats, including:

- Alignment—the way a paragraph lines up between the page's left and right margins
- Line spacing—the amount of space between the lines of text in a paragraph
- Indentation—added space between a margin and the text
- Tabs—stops placed along a line. Pressing the Tab key moves the insertion point to the next stop. Tabs can be used to align text in tables or columns.

You can apply these paragraph formats through dialog boxes, but you also can apply some of them by using ruler settings. In Word, for example, you can create a tab stop simply by clicking the horizontal ruler at the point where the stop should appear. You can change a paragraph's indentations by dragging indent markers, which normally are found at each end of the ruler. Ruler settings apply only to the paragraph that contains the insertion point, or to selected paragraphs.

Formatting Sections

In some word processors, a **section** is part of a document that contains specific format settings. A document begins as one section, but it can be split into more than one. You can format each section in its own unique way.

Formatting Pages

Page formatting affects how and where text is positioned on the page. The main features in page formatting are:

• Paper size—Various sizes of paper can be used to create documents.

• Orientation—Text can be printed in one or two directions, or orientations. In portrait orientation, text is printed down the page's long edge, creating a page that is taller than it is wide. In landscape orientation, text is printed down the page's short edge, creating a page that is wider than it is tall.

• Margins—the space between the four paper edges and the text. This open space frames the page and can make the text easier to read.

• Headers and footers—special information placed at the top of the page—headers—or at the bottom—footers. These placeholders can show page numbers, the date, or the document's title.

• Graphics—drawings, photographs, or other images. Some graphics, like charts and graphs, are informative. Others are decorative. Many word-processing programs let you create or add graphics.

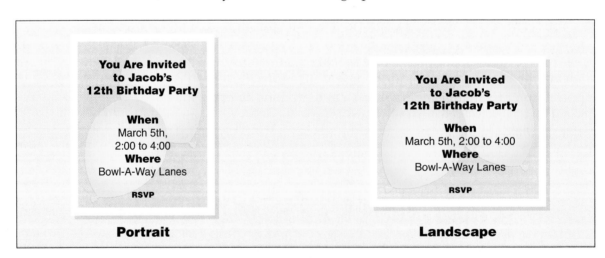

Figure 6.3.3 Word-processing programs let you print documents in portrait and landscape orientations.

Demonstrate Your Knowledge

Critical Thinking

1. What is a default format?

_____

_____

2. Why do you think you should save your work after making formatting changes?

_____

_____

3. Which kinds of documents would you print in portrait orientation, and which kinds would you print in landscape orientation?

_____

_____

_____

Activities

1. Suppose you are planning the format for an essay you are writing for school. From each pair of options below, choose the most appropriate option for formatting the essay's text. Circle your choices in each column of the T-chart.

Option 1	Option 2
a. 11-point type for the main text	**a.** 24-point type for the main text
b. all lines centered	**b.** all lines left-aligned
c. printing in landscape orientation	**c.** printing in portrait orientation
d. 8½" x 11" paper	**d.** 5½" x 8½" paper

2. Interview three adults who use word-processing programs on the job. Ask how they learned their skills. Discuss your findings with the class.

Use the Vocabulary

Directions: *Match each vocabulary term in the left column with the correct definition in the right column. Write the appropriate letter next to the word or term.*

_____ **1.** insertion point

_____ **2.** word wrap

_____ **3.** pagination

_____ **4.** AutoCorrect

_____ **5.** select text

_____ **6.** Clipboard

_____ **7.** default

_____ **8.** section

_____ **9.** page format

a. features that identify how and where text is positioned

b. a separate part of a document with its own formatting

c. area where cut or copied text is temporarily stored

d. fixes common spelling mistakes as they are typed

e. shows the place in a document where text will be added or deleted

f. automatically moves text to a new line

g. the automatic division of a document into pages

h. action made on a block of text before changing it

i. preset formats

Check Your Comprehension

Directions: *Complete each sentence with information from the chapter.*

1. The four functions of word processing are writing, editing, _____, and printing.

2. The_____ feature protects you from losing work because you forgot to save.

3. One standard of word processing is to have only one space after each _____.

4. Some programs add extra characters, called an _____, to a file name.

5. In _____ mode, you can replace existing characters by typing over them.

6. You can repeat a sentence in more than one location in the same document—or in other documents—by using the _____ and Paste commands.

7. Collections of formats called a _____ make sure that all elements of the same type have the same look.

8. One _____ equals 1/72 inch.

9. Indentation refers to the _____ between a margin and the text in a paragraph.

10. An example of a _____ is a page number that appears at the bottom of every page in a report.

Think Critically

Directions: *Answer the following questions on the lines provided.*

1. Why would you want to force a new page after creating the title page of a 20-page report?

   _____

   _____

2. Why is selecting text an important function in word processing?

   _____

   _____

3. Why are there both mouse and keyboard methods for performing actions such as selecting, cutting, copying, and pasting?

   _____

   _____

4. What is the difference between landscape and portrait orientation?

   _____

   _____

5. Why might a student type his or her name and the class period in the header of a homework assignment?

   _____

   _____

Extend Your Knowledge

Directions: *Choose one of the following projects. Complete the exercises on a separate sheet of paper.*

A. Open a word-processing program and type these directions in full. Add the heading *Formatting Sample* above the first line of text. Then do the following: (1) Copy your text and paste the copy below the first paragraph; (2) Format the text by changing fonts and type size; (3) Change the page to landscape orientation; (4) Add a header; and (5) Print your document. Remember to save your file.

B. Open a word-processing program. Choose one of the menus on the menu bar at the top of the program. Write the items listed on the menu. Choose two of those menu items. Look them up in the program's Help system. Take notes on what you read. Make a presentation to the class describing which actions result from choosing each menu item. Identify a way that someone could use both menu items.

Spreadsheet Basics

What Is a Spreadsheet? Suppose you wanted to keep track of all your grades in one of your classes so you could figure out your final average for the class. Spreadsheet programs are the perfect software for doing this kind of work.

Spreadsheets are set up like tables with information running across rows and down columns. You could enter your assignments in one vertical column. Then you could enter the grade or score you received on each assignment in the next column. The spreadsheet could add up all the scores and calculate your average. When an assignment is returned to you, you could add it to the spreadsheet, and your average would be updated automatically. Just think how long it would take you to do this if you did it by hand!

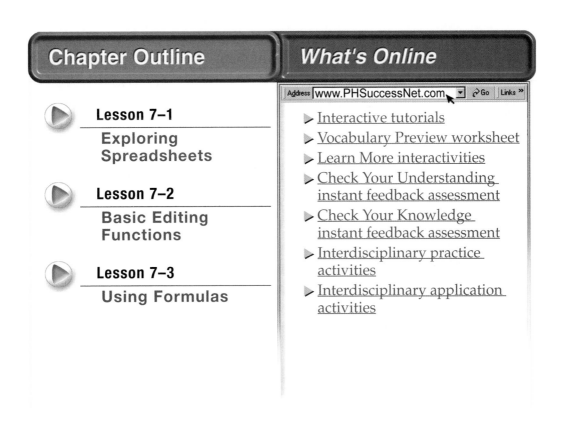

Chapter Outline

Lesson 7–1

Exploring
Spreadsheets

Lesson 7–2

Basic Editing
Functions

Lesson 7–3

Using Formulas

What's Online

Address www.PHSuccessNet.com ⌄ &Go Links »

- Interactive tutorials
- Vocabulary Preview worksheet
- Learn More interactivities
- Check Your Understanding instant feedback assessment
- Check Your Knowledge instant feedback assessment
- Interdisciplinary practice activities
- Interdisciplinary application activities

Exploring Spreadsheets

Objectives

- Explain the purpose of spreadsheet software.
- Identify and describe parts of a worksheet.
- Summarize key features of spreadsheet software.

As You Read

Organize Information Use a concept web to help you organize basic facts about spreadsheets as you read the lesson.

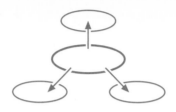

What's Online

In Lesson 7–1 of the iText, you will find more features and information for this lesson, including:

- Interactive tutorials
- As You Read worksheet
- Learn More interactivities
- Check Your Understanding interactive assessments
- Interactive lesson review

🔑 Key Terms

- spreadsheet (p. 92)
- worksheet (p. 92)
- cell (p. 92)
- cell address (p. 92)
- active cell (p. 93)
- formula (p. 94)
- function (p. 94)

Spreadsheet Basics

A **spreadsheet** is a program that processes information that is set up in tables. Spreadsheets can be used to:

- place numbers and text in easy-to-read rows and columns
- calculate numbers and show the result
- calculate new results when the numbers are changed
- create charts to display data

These features make spreadsheets perfect for tracking information that involves numbers. Suppose you work at a company that needs to decide what price to charge for a product. You can create a spreadsheet that shows how much profit your company will make by charging several different prices. The spreadsheet finds the results quickly. Those results can be used to set a price.

Understanding Worksheets When you use a spreadsheet program, your data goes into a special kind of document called a **worksheet,** a grid made of vertical columns and horizontal rows. Columns are labeled with letters, and rows are labeled with numbers.

Each column and row meets to make a box called a **cell.** Each cell in the grid is identified by a unique name—its **cell address.** The address is made simply by taking the letter of the column and the number of the row that meet to make the cell. For example, column C and row 3 create the cell address C3.

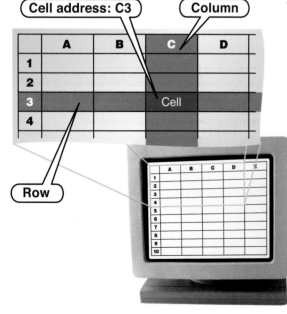

Figure 7.1.1 A worksheet includes rows and columns, which create a grid of cells that hold data.

© Pearson Education, Inc.

Parts of a Worksheet

Most worksheets look similar. The parts of a worksheet include:

Frame The frame forms the top and left borders of the worksheet. It includes the column and row headings.

Active Cell The **active cell** is the cell currently in use. A rectangle appears around this cell to highlight it and make it easy to spot.

Cell Identifier Located in the upper left corner, just above the frame, the cell identifier is an area that shows the cell address of the cell that is active.

Formula Bar The formula bar displays what you type. This data will be entered into the active cell when you are done. The formula bar is like a one-line word-processing program. Pressing Enter, Return, or an arrow key completes the entry and places the data in the cell.

Scroll Bars Scroll bars appear on the worksheet's right and bottom edges. You can click on the arrows or slide the scroll box to see another part of the worksheet.

Worksheet Tabs On the same line as the horizontal scroll bar are tabs that show the other worksheets that belong to the same spreadsheet file. If you click on one of these tabs, you switch to that worksheet.

Status Bar The status bar appears below the scroll bar at the very bottom of the worksheet. Messages from the program are displayed here.

**Did You Know?**

A spreadsheet can hold a great deal of information. Microsoft Excel, for instance, can hold:

- 256 columns
- 65,536 rows
- As many worksheets as your computer's memory can keep open

If you filled every column and row on just one worksheet, you would have filled 16,777,216 cells!

Figure 7.1.2 All spreadsheet programs share these basic features.

© Pearson Education, Inc.

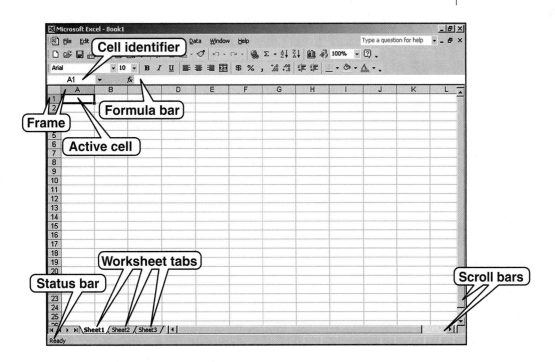

Working With a Spreadsheet

Spreadsheet programs share many features. You can perform many similar actions, regardless of the program.

Moving Around You can use the Home, End, Page Up, and Page Down keys, along with the scroll bars, to move large distances within the worksheet. You can use the Tab key to move one cell to the right or the arrow keys to move one cell at a time in any direction.

Selecting Cells and Entering Data To make a cell active, click on that cell. Then type to enter data in the cell. Data can be text, numbers, dates, or formulas.

Formulas **Formulas** are mathematical expressions, which sometimes link numbers in cells. A simple formula might add the numbers in two cells. The formula appears in the formula bar but not in the active cell. The active cell shows the result of the formula—in this case, the sum of the two numbers in the other cells. **Functions** are commonly used formulas built into the program that make it easier to write the formulas you need.

Formatting the Worksheet You can change the look of a worksheet in many ways. You can add or remove rows or columns or change their size. You can change the font or type size of the data. You can also add color, borders, or shading and change how the data is aligned in the cell.

Spotlight on...

DAN BRICKLIN

❝ *In terms of the success of VisiCalc . . . it is nice to be able to realize you've done something very worthwhile. . . . I feel that I've made a change in the world. That's a satisfaction that money can't buy.* ❞

Dan Bricklin
Software developer

When Dan Bricklin was a business school student in the late 1970s, he had to do his calculations for class on a calculator and then write them down. Bricklin wanted to develop a computer program that could calculate and display the work automatically. He and his friend Bob Frankston created such a program. They called it *VisiCalc*—short for visible calculator. It was the first computer spreadsheet. Although VisiCalc is not sold anymore, today's spreadsheets are all based on Bricklin's original idea.

Demonstrate Your Knowledge

Critical Thinking

1. Both spreadsheets and word processors can be used to make tables. Which kind of program would be more effective and efficient for making a budget for producing a movie? Why?

_____

_____

2. How are cells identified in a worksheet? Why does this method work for all cells?

_____

_____

3. What appears in a cell when you enter a formula in it?

_____

_____

Activities

1. Fill in the missing information about spreadsheets below by writing in the spaces provided.

All About Spreadsheets

Parts of a Worksheet	Function
Formula bar	displays what you type
Status bar	displays messages from the program

2. Find out how people use spreadsheets. Ask your teacher, the school office staff, or your parents to describe the spreadsheets they use. Make a list of your findings.

Basic Editing Functions

Objectives

- Compare and contrast values and labels in a worksheet.
- Describe ways to enter, edit, and format data in a worksheet.
- Use a spreadsheet to create a chart.
- Evaluate the benefit of printing options.

As You Read

Sequence Steps Use a sequence chart to help you sequence the steps in working with spreadsheets as you read the lesson.

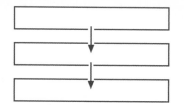

What's Online

In Lesson 7–2 of the iText, you will find more features and information for this lesson, including:

- Interactive tutorials
- As You Read worksheet
- Learn More interactivities
- Check Your Understanding interactive assessments
- Interactive lesson review

Key Terms

- value (p. 96)
- label (p. 96)
- AutoFill (p. 97)
- chart (p. 98)
- print area (p. 98)

Entering Data

In addition to formulas, you can enter three types of data in a worksheet: values, labels, and dates and times. The spreadsheet program identifies the data type entered and formats it.

Values A **value** is a number, such as a whole number, a fraction, or a decimal. Values are formatted to align to the right in a cell. If a value is too large for the width of the cell, you may see a set of symbols such as ###### or *******. You can change the column width so that the full number shows. Click the right edge of the column heading and drag it to the right.

Labels A **label** is text or a combination of numbers and text. Labels are typically used for headings or explanations. By default, labels are aligned to the left in a cell. Labels that are too wide will overlap into the next cell to the right—if that cell is empty. If that cell already has text, the long text in the first cell will appear cut off. Again, you can widen the column to show the entire label.

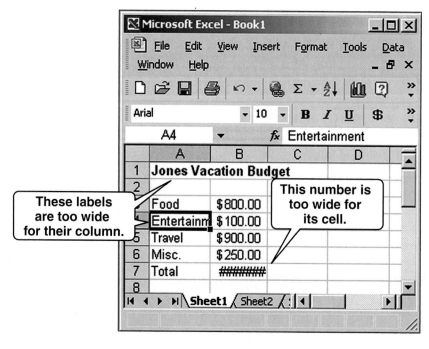

These labels are too wide for their column.

This number is too wide for its cell.

Figure 7.2.1 If a cell's contents don't fit, they may not display correctly.

© Pearson Education, Inc.

Dates and Times Data typed as dates or times are displayed in the format you choose. For example, November 1, 2005, can be typed as 11/01/05 or 01-Nov-05. Times can simply be typed as the hour and minute—07:45 or 12:52, for instance.

Filling Cells Easily

Certain kinds of data can be entered automatically by using the **AutoFill** feature. To use this feature, you usually have to type only the first item in the series. Then move the mouse to the lower right corner of the cell, where a small plus symbol, or arrow, appears. Drag that symbol to the right or down to highlight the cells you want filled and release the mouse. For example, you could enter 1/1/2005 in the first cell and then use AutoFill to enter the rest of the dates automatically.

Changing and Formatting Data

You can easily change data to correct an error or reflect new information in a spreadsheet.

Editing Cell Data To edit data, click the desired cell. Then click within the formula bar to place the insertion point where you want to make the change. Press Backspace or Delete to remove characters, or type to add them. Press Enter to place the edited information in the cell.

Moving or Copying Data To move information from one cell to another, select the cell and drag its contents to the new cell. You can also go to the Edit menu and select Copy or Cut. Click the new location and then go to the Edit menu and select Paste.

Removing Data To remove data, select the cell and press Delete to remove the data. You can also go to the Edit menu and select Delete. A dialog box will ask if you wish to delete the entire row or column or just those cells.

Formatting Data You can change the appearance of the data in the cells. You can show data in bold or italic type and change its type size. You can also change the format of numbers.

Many people use spreadsheets at home to track monthly income and expenses. They can set up a worksheet to show regular monthly costs. Then, they only need to copy and paste it on other blank worksheets to create budgets for other months.

Think *About* **It!**
Before you set up a budget, think about which expenses arise each month. Underline each item below that you think would be a regular monthly expense.

- ➢ housing payment
- ➢ vacation
- ➢ telephone
- ➢ holiday presents
- ➢ food
- ➢ magazine subscription

Figure 7.2.2 The steps for formatting data in spreadsheet programs vary slightly depending on the software you are using.

Program	Menu	Selection	Next step
Excel	Format	Cells	Select the Numbers tab and select the desired format from the dialog box.
Quattro Pro	Format	Selection	Select the Numeric Format tab and select the desired format from the dialog box.
AppleWorks	Format	Numbers	Select the desired format from the dialog box.

Physical education teachers in one school are taking advantage of the spreadsheet's ability to make graphs. They chart students' performance on basic fitness tests. Then they make graphs showing students' progress over time.

Think *About* It!

Think about other ways graphs could be used at school. Circle each item for which you think graphed test results would be useful.

- ▶ to show parents how well their children are doing
- ▶ to show students which skills they need to work on
- ▶ to compare students by athletic ability

Creating a Chart

With a spreadsheet program, you can create **charts,** which are also called graphs. Charts show data in ways that are visually more interesting than tables. Simply select the cells that have data you want to graph. Then choose the command for creating a chart.

Next, you select a type of chart. Bar charts compare different amounts, such as how many students there are in each grade in a school. Pie charts show how parts relate to the whole. For instance, a pie chart would show what percentage of all students are in each grade. Line charts show change over time, such as the number of students in a grade each year. Once you have chosen the type of chart to create, dialog boxes help you through the rest of the process. After you have made a chart, you can copy it and paste it into another document.

Saving and Printing a Worksheet

Saving and printing are both selected from the File menu. Some programs also have icons on the toolbar for these functions. It is always wise to save your work again before printing—just in case a glitch occurs and data is lost.

Most spreadsheets have special features for printing. For example, you can specify a portion of a worksheet called a **print area** before you instruct the program to print. This way you can choose to print only specific data. Headings for columns and rows normally only print on the first page, but you can choose to print the headings on every page.

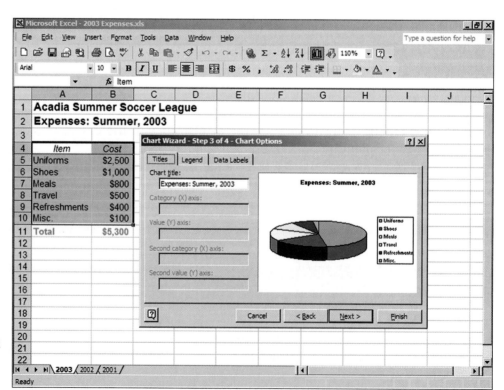

Figure 7.2.3 Creating a chart from data in a worksheet

© Pearson Education, Inc.

Demonstrate Your Knowledge

Critical Thinking

1. How do you enter data using the AutoFill feature?

_____

_____

2. Where in the spreadsheet do you edit data? What action confirms that the edit is done?

_____

_____

3. What is one instance in which you would use the print area option and another instance when you would not?

_____

_____

Activities

1. Complete the Venn diagram below. Write facts true only of values in the appropriate area. Write facts true only of labels in the appropriate area. Write facts true of both types of data in the area labeled *Both*.

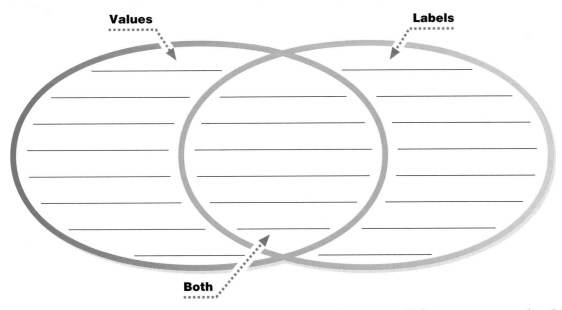

2. Open a spreadsheet and create a document. Use the AutoFill feature to enter the days of the week in the first column. In the next column, enter the following values: 8, 7, 8, 7, 8, 6, 7. These are the number of hours that Ivan slept each day in one week. Save the file. Use the program's chart-making feature to graph the data on a bar chart. Save the spreadsheet and print it.

Using Formulas

Objectives

- Construct a simple formula using one or more operators.
- Explain the importance of the order of evaluation.
- Evaluate the benefit of building formulas using cell references.
- Describe how to use the automatic summing function.

As You Read

Enter Information Use a concept web to help you enter formulas in a worksheet as you read the lesson.

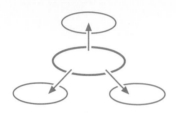

What's Online

In Lesson 7–3 of the iText, you will find more features and information for this lesson, including:

- Interactive tutorials
- As You Read worksheet
- Learn More interactivities
- Check Your Understanding interactive assessments
- Interactive lesson review

🔑 Key Terms

- order of evaluation (p. 101)
- cell reference (p. 102)

Entering Formulas in Worksheets

The power of a spreadsheet is its ability to use formulas to represent data in different cells.

Writing Formulas To write a formula, click the cell where you want the result of the formula to appear, and type the formula in the formula bar. You need to begin the formula with a symbol to signify that you are typing a formula. In Excel® and AppleWorks®, that symbol is an equal sign (=). In Quattro® Pro and Lotus® 1-2-3, formulas start with a plus (+) or minus (–) sign.

Simple Formulas Many formulas use the basic arithmetic operations of addition (+), subtraction (–), multiplication (*), and division (/). Another useful operation is exponentiation (^), in which the raised number tells how many times the normal sized number is used as a factor in multiplication. For instance, 2^2 is $2 * 2$; 2^3 is $2 * 2 * 2$.

Writing simple formulas is like writing a math problem. To add 5 and 2, you simply write =5+2 or +5+2 as the formula, depending on which program you are using. To divide 5 by 2, write the formula =5/2 or +5/2. When you are done writing the formula, press Enter. That completes the formula and places the result in the selected cell.

Figure 7.3.1 Entering a formula in a worksheet

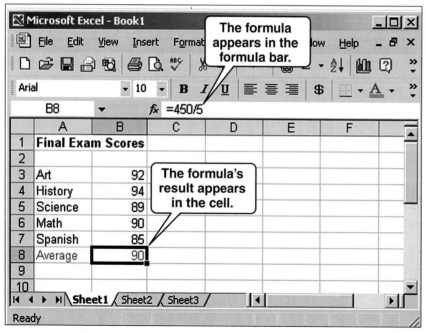

The formula appears in the formula bar.

The formula's result appears in the cell.

Complex Formulas You can write more complex formulas as well. Formulas can include many numbers, such as =1+2+3+4+5. They can also include more than one mathematical operation. For instance, suppose you owned a store that sold 50 copies of a game one month and 56 copies the next. You want to know by what percentage your sales of that game increased. You could find out by writing this formula: =(56–50)/50. In this formula, you subtract 50 from 56 to find the number of additional games you sold. Then you divide the result by 50, the number of games sold the first month, to find the percentage increase. The answer is .12, or 12 percent.

Working With Complex Formulas

Many formulas, like =(56–50)/50, have two or more operations. How does the program know which one to do first? It uses the **order of evaluation.** This rule tells the program to do the most important operation first. Then it does the others in order, from most to least important.

Ranking Operations Operations within parentheses are the most important. Exponentiation comes next, followed by multiplication or division, then addition or subtraction. Use the sentence, "Please excuse my dear Aunt Sally" to remember the order. The first letter of each word (P-E-M-D-A-S) matches the first letter of each operation in the right order.

Using Order of Evaluation Suppose you want to write an Excel formula to average the numbers 29, 34, and 27. The formula =(29+34+27)/3 is correct. The parentheses tell the program to add the three numbers first. The sum, 90, is then divided by 3 to find the average, which is 30.

The formula =29+34+27/3 is not correct. In this case, the program would first divide 27 by 3 because division is the more important operation. It would then add the result, 9, to 29 and 34 for an answer of 72.

Some formulas have more than one operation with the same importance, such as addition and subtraction. In this case, those operations are done in the order in which they appear from left to right.

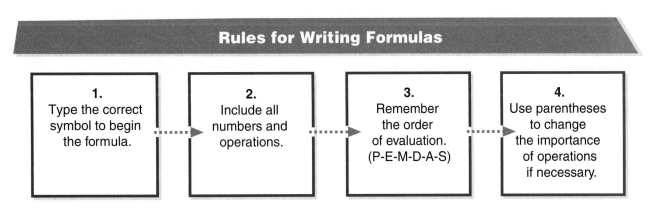

Rules for Writing Formulas

1.	2.	3.	4.
Type the correct symbol to begin the formula.	Include all numbers and operations.	Remember the order of evaluation. (P-E-M-D-A-S)	Use parentheses to change the importance of operations if necessary.

Career Corner

Statistician People who work with statistics, or facts expressed as numbers, are called statisticians. They study information about the number and ages of people in a population, the economy, the number of people who tune in to radio and television shows, and so on.

Statisticians rely heavily on computers, as the information they work with can be very complex. Spreadsheets are very useful for them because of their power to store and process numbers.

Using References, Not Values

The formulas discussed so far have used values. But formulas can also use **cell references,** or cell addresses. For example, suppose you wanted to multiply cell A1, with a value of 5, and cell B2, with a value of 3. Instead of =5*3, you can write =A1*B2. In fact, it is better to use cell references for the two reasons listed below.

Avoiding Errors You might accidentally type the wrong value and not realize it, as the formula does not always show in the cell. If you insert a cell reference, however, the formula will always use the correct value.

Reflecting Changes A value in a formula never changes. The formula =5*3 will always produce 15. But what if the value in cell A1 changes? The formula =5*3 will no longer correctly multiply A1 and B2. If you use a cell reference, the formula uses whatever value the cell has. If the cell value changes, so will the result calculated by the formula. By using cell references, you make sure that your worksheet remains up-to-date even if data changes.

Using a Function

Adding a column of numbers is a common task, so spreadsheet programs include a function named SUM, which performs addition. This function is typically shown on the toolbar by the symbol Σ. Simply select the cells you want to add and click that symbol. The total appears in the following row.

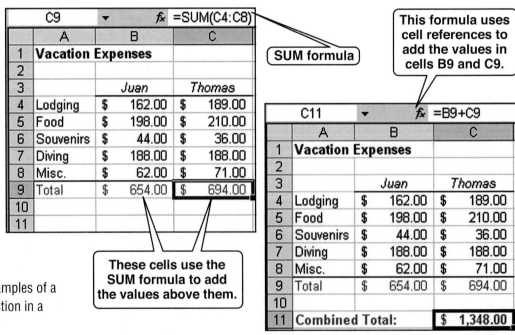

Figure 7.3.2 Examples of a formula and a function in a worksheet

© Pearson Education, Inc.

102 • Chapter 7

Demonstrate Your Knowledge

Critical Thinking

1. How does the order of evaluation affect the way formulas are calculated?

_____

_____

2. Why do you think it is better to use cell references than values when writing formulas?

_____

_____

3. What is the simplest way to add the following cells: B1, B2, B3, B4, and B5?

_____

_____

Activities

1. Operations that formulas are expected to carry out are shown in the left column of this chart. In the right column, write the formula as it should appear in a spreadsheet's entry line.

Operation	Formula
Multiply B1 and B2 and add B3.	_____
Divide C2 by the total of C4 and C5.	_____
Add D7 and D9 and then multiply by 4.	_____

2. Open a spreadsheet and create a worksheet. Type "January" in cell A1, and use AutoFill to enter the remaining months of the year through June in A6. Enter the following values in B1 through B6: 10, 12, 14, 15, 9, 12. Save the file. In cell C3, write a formula using cell references for finding the average of the values from B1 to B3. In C6, write a formula for finding the average of the values from B4 to B6. Save the spreadsheet and print it. Change the following values: B3 to 20, B4 to 9. Print the file again. Compare the numbers in C3 and C6 in the two printouts. On a separate piece of paper, explain why they change.

Use the Vocabulary

Directions: *Match each vocabulary term in the left column with the correct definition in the right column. Write the appropriate letter next to the word or term.*

_____ **1.** cell

_____ **2.** cell address

_____ **3.** active cell

_____ **4.** formula

_____ **5.** function

_____ **6.** value

_____ **7.** label

_____ **8.** AutoFill

_____ **9.** print area

_____ **10.** order of evaluation

a. rules followed for carrying out the order of more than one mathematical operation

b. mathematical expression that might link numbers in cells

c. part of a spreadsheet to which printing can be limited

d. place where a column and row meet

e. number in a cell

f. command used to automatically insert a series of data in a series of cells

g. highlighted cell in use, where data or a formula will be entered or edited

h. text or text and numbers in a cell

i. shortcut to a formula that is used frequently

j. identifies each individual cell

Check Your Comprehension

Directions: *Circle the correct choice for each of the following.*

1. Tables in spreadsheets are better than tables in word processors because they
- **a.** use numbers only.
- **b.** will have unchanging formats.
- **c.** can be easily updated.
- **d.** have accurate data.

2. All changes to values, labels, or formulas in a spreadsheet are made in the
- **a.** formula bar.
- **b.** cell.
- **c.** frame.
- **d.** function line.

3. Values, by default, are aligned
- **a.** to the left.
- **b.** to the right.
- **c.** centered in the cell.
- **d.** at the top of the cell.

4. How does an Excel® spreadsheet know that =10/12 is a formula and not the date October 12?
- **a.** The equal sign (=) signals it.
- **b.** The division (/) sign signals it.
- **c.** Dates cannot be shown that way.
- **d.** It would not know.

5. Operations are carried out in the following order:
- **a.** A-D-E-M-P-S
- **b.** M-D-E-P-S-A
- **c.** P-M-D-A-S-E
- **d.** P-E-M-D-A-S

6. It is best to write formulas using cell references so that a spreadsheet
- **a.** has no hidden information.
- **b.** has all correct values.
- **c.** can be updated easily.
- **d.** can be more easily graphed.

Think Critically

Directions: *Answer the following questions on the lines provided.*

1. How do values and labels differ in the way they treat data that is too wide for the cell?

_____

_____

2. If you were preparing a budget for a business, how would you indicate that the numbers represent dollar amounts in the worksheet?

_____

_____

3. In what situations do you think it would be useful to repeat column headings in a printed worksheet? Why?

_____

_____

4. What type of graph would be best for showing how much a child grew in inches over the years? Why?

_____

_____

5. Look at the formulas =B1/B2+B3 and =B1/(B2+B3). Would these formulas give the same result? Why or why not?

_____

_____

Extend Your Knowledge

Directions: *Choose one of the following projects. Complete the exercises on a separate sheet of paper.*

A. Open a spreadsheet program and create a new worksheet. Place the title "Video Store Sales" in cell A1. Use AutoFill to fill in the days of the week in cells A2 to A8. Enter the following values in cells B2 to B8: $10,000; $11,500; $13,000; $9,500; $12,000; $13,000; $8,000. Write a formula that places a total in B9. Create a chart that compares sales for each of the seven days. Save the file and print it.

B. Think of three ways spreadsheets could be used. Identify one use that is suitable for each of the following people: a 12-year-old student; a 35-year-old businesswoman; and a 70-year-old man. Describe each use and explain how it is suitable to the person's age. If possible, create one of the spreadsheets using fake data to show what it would look like.

chapter 8

Database Basics

© Pearson Education, Inc.

What Is a Database? What do the following things have in common: an address book, a telephone directory, a list of family birthdays, and a catalog of DVDs? For one thing, each can be stored in a **database,** or an organized collection of information. Databases can exist on paper or on a computer. Computerized databases can be huge, containing information on millions of items. A computerized database is an ideal tool for making use of huge amounts of existing data.

Databases make it easy to store, add, organize, and retrieve information. Suppose a worker has to find the account number for a customer. Imagine how much time that worker saves if he or she can find the information simply by typing the customer's name instead of searching through piles of paper!

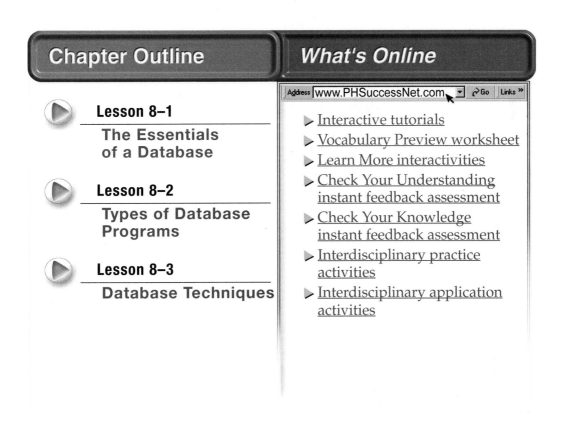

Chapter Outline

▶ **Lesson 8–1**
   The Essentials of a Database

▶ **Lesson 8–2**
   Types of Database Programs

▶ **Lesson 8–3**
   Database Techniques

What's Online

Address www.PHSuccessNet.com ▾ ⟳ Go Links »

▶ Interactive tutorials
▶ Vocabulary Preview worksheet
▶ Learn More interactivities
▶ Check Your Understanding instant feedback assessment
▶ Check Your Knowledge instant feedback assessment
▶ Interdisciplinary practice activities
▶ Interdisciplinary application activities

The Essentials of a Database

Objectives

- Describe the basic organization of a database.
- Summarize advantages to using database software.
- Define GIGO and explain how it relates to the quality of a database.

As You Read

Organize Information As you read the lesson, use a concept web to help you organize basic facts about databases.

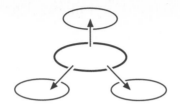

What's Online

In Lesson 8–1 of the iText, you will find more features and information for this lesson, including:

- Interactive tutorials
- As You Read worksheet
- Learn More interactivities
- Check Your Understanding interactive assessments
- Interactive lesson review

Key Terms

- database (p. 107)
- table (p. 108)
- record (p. 108)
- field (p. 108)
- data type (p. 108)
- garbage in, garbage out (GIGO) (p. 110)

Figure 8.1.1 Databases are made of tables, fields, and records.

Database Organization

What makes up a database? How is it organized? Picture a file cabinet. One drawer might hold information on a company's customers, and another might have data on the company's products. Within each drawer are folders. Each folder is dedicated to a particular person or product. Finally, each folder stores different bits of information about that person or product.

A computerized database is also structured in three parts:

- tables
- records
- fields

Tables A database has one or more tables, just as a file cabinet may have one or more drawers. Each **table** contains a collection of related data. Although databases can store data in one large table, it is more typical to divide databases into smaller tables. For example, your school's database might contain separate tables for students and for teachers and staff.

Records The data in each table is further split into smaller units that contain related information about one individual or item. Each of these units is called a **record.** For your school's database, each unit of information, or record, is about an individual student or teacher.

Fields Each separate piece of data that is stored in a record—a student's last name, first name, and so on—is called a **field.** Each field is set up so that only a certain type of information, called the **data type,** is permitted in that field. For example, a field for date of birth allows only dates to be entered.

© Pearson Education, Inc.

Advantages of a Database

While smaller databases might just as easily be kept on paper as on a computer, computerized databases make it easier to do the following:

Enter Information You can enter information neatly, quickly, and in an organized way with your keyboard and mouse.

Store Large Amounts of Information If you want to keep track of 20 or 30 phone numbers, you can easily use an address book. A computerized database, however, can hold thousands, or even millions, of telephone numbers.

Find Information Quickly A computerized database can save you time in finding information. It might take you only a minute or two to find a number in your personal address book, but a telephone directory on CD-ROM can help you find one of millions of phone numbers in even less time.

Organize Information in Different Ways Paper filing systems can limit your ability to arrange information. For example, should you organize your personal phone book by listing each person's phone number, cell phone number, or e-mail address first? With a computerized database, you can easily switch between these different methods.

Technology @ Home

A database is a useful tool for organizing information at home. For example, you can create a database to organize your CD or video game collection.

Think About It!

Fields are the groups of information that are included for every table in a computerized database. Circle each field below that you think would be useful for a database of your CDs.

- ▸ type of music
- ▸ artist
- ▸ movie title
- ▸ stars
- ▸ CD title
- ▸ director

Real-World Tech

Preserving Ancient Art Databases are often put to unexpected uses. Because databases can record and store large amounts of information, organizations have come up with creative ways to use them.

For example, at New Mexico State University, CD-ROMs store aerial views of 1,500-year-old American Indian rock art to preserve a natural art form that is vanishing due to erosion and vandalism.

How might you use a database to record information about the culture of your family or your community? Write your ideas below.

_____

_____

_____

Social Studies Many government agencies store personal information about people in databases.

You have legal rights to the information that pertains to you. If you find incorrect information, the agencies are required by law to amend your records.

Figure 8.1.2 Students can use databases to organize information gathered for research projects.

Update Information Database software makes it easy to change or update data. Think about adding a new name to your address book. It would be difficult to re-alphabetize the list if it existed only on paper. Think about how messy the book might look after just a few changes. With a computerized database, names and numbers can be added, deleted, or changed easily and quickly. After making these changes, you have an easy-to-read, updated version of the database.

It's All About the Data

Databases can be useful tools at home and at work. They also have many different uses at school. Administrators can use them to track student performance, payroll, and supplies. Teachers can use them to record students' test scores and attendance. Students can use them to organize their grades or search for information for a project.

However, databases are useful only if they are accurate. In other words, databases are only as good as the data they contain. The acronym *GIGO* explains this principle. **GIGO** is short for **"garbage in, garbage out."** It means that if the information placed in a database is wrong, anyone using that information will get the wrong results. When adding information to a database, it is very important to do so accurately and to check your entries.

Demonstrate Your Knowledge

Critical Thinking

1. How is a computerized database organized?

_____

_____

2. What are four advantages of a database?

_____

_____

3. What does *GIGO* mean? What significance does this principle have for databases?

_____

_____

Activities

1. List the parts of a database on the top lines below. Then, give examples of information to be included in a new database that an appliance-repair business was creating of its customers.

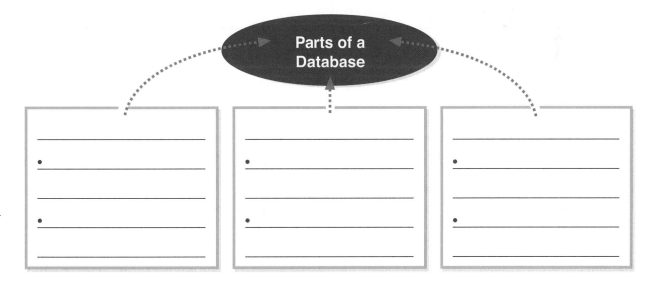

2. Conduct research to find out what databases are used in your school. Create a chart that shows the purpose of the databases, who uses them, and who has access to them.

Types of Database Programs

Objectives

- Summarize the purpose of a database management system.
- Compare and contrast types of database management programs.
- Evaluate the characteristics of a well-designed database.

As You Read

Outline As you read the lesson, use an outline to help identify types of database management systems and characteristics of good design.

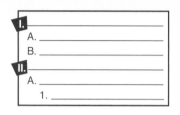

What's Online

In Lesson 8–2 of the iText, you will find more features and information for this lesson, including:

- Interactive tutorials
- As You Read worksheet
- Learn More interactivities
- Check Your Understanding interactive assessments
- Interactive lesson review

Key Terms

- database management system (DBMS) (p. 112)
- flat-file database (p. 112)
- sort (p. 112)
- relational database (p. 112)
- key field (p. 112)
- object-oriented database (p. 113)

Database Management Systems

A **database management system,** or **DBMS,** is software used to manage the storage, organization, processing, and retrieval of data in a database. There are several kinds of database management programs, including flat-file databases, relational databases, object-oriented databases, and multimedia databases.

Flat-File Databases A **flat-file database** allows you to work with data in only one table. A computerized address book is one example. In flat-file databases, records can be retrieved randomly. That is, you can look for just one name on a list. You can also retrieve an entire table and **sort** the data, or arrange it in a different order. You might sort to find all the people living in the same town, for example.

Flat-file databases have a limitation. The data in one table cannot be linked to the data in another table. That might not be a problem with a simple address book. However, many businesses and other large organizations use databases in more complex ways, and they need added flexibility.

Relational Databases A **relational database** can use data from several tables at the same time. This is because the tables are linked by a **key field,** a field that is found in each of the tables. A relational database is more complex than a flat-file database program. It also requires more skill to use and costs more. However, its greater power makes it more popular.

Think about a relational database a school might have. One table might hold all students' schedules. Another might have all their grades. Yet another table might include their addresses and phone numbers. All the tables can be linked by a key field: each student's name or student identification number. By using key fields, administrators can find data about a particular student from any available table.

© Pearson Education, Inc.

Businesses can link their relational databases by customer names and numbers. Companies use these databases for many purposes, including storing customer information, such as name, address, and telephone number; seeing where to ship goods the customer buys; issuing bills for purchases and receipts for payments made; and tracking what customers have bought over time and using that information to tailor ads and promotions.

Object-Oriented Databases Another type of DBMS is called an **object-oriented database.** These databases store objects, such as documents, video clips, and audio clips. Each object contains both that data and the program needed to display that data, including showing a graphic or playing a sound.

Object-oriented databases are not yet widely used. Some experts believe that they will replace relational databases in the future.

Multimedia Databases Traditional databases can store all kinds of text and numerical data. Today's computers also often deal with pictures, sounds, animation, or video clips. Multimedia professionals use databases to catalog media files, such as art, photographs, maps, video clips, and sound files. Media files themselves generally are not stored in databases because they are too large. Instead, a multimedia database serves as an index to all the separately stored files. Users can search through the index and then locate the particular file they want.

Spotlight on...

CHARLES W. BACHMAN

❝ *I received my first computer when I was in the army in 1943. Since then, I would never have dreamed where the industry would go. I believe that databases . . . will always be there because we need to maintain our inventory of information. I also believe that data communications is essential in tying the people of the world together.* ❞

Charles W. Bachman
Database Developer

Called "the father of database management," Charles W. Bachman is known for his work with database technology in the early 1960s. While working at General Electric, he developed the Integrated Data Store (IDS), the first successful database management system.

In 1973, Bachman received the highly regarded A. M. Turing Award for his outstanding contributions to database technology. After spending more than 40 years in the software development industry, Bachman reflects on the past and looks ahead to the future.

Figure 8.2.1 Protecting the database with a password

Well-Designed Databases

For databases to be effective, they need to be planned carefully. Following are three characteristics of good database design:

Ensuring Data Security The same features that make databases efficient tools make them vulnerable to invasions of privacy. Personal information can be misused. Requiring users to input a password before they can access data is one way of keeping a database secure.

Preserving Data Integrity The accuracy and validity of the information gives a database its data integrity. Errors make the database less accurate and less useful. Because many databases are bought and sold, it is almost impossible to delete or correct errors after they are initially made.

Avoiding Data Redundancy Repeating the same data in many tables wastes space by requiring a computer to store the same information more than once. It also increases the amount of work needed to update records because the data needs to be changed in more than one place. That, in turn, increases the chance of errors and slows down searches for data. Storing data in only one table and then linking the table to others enables the data to be used in various ways.

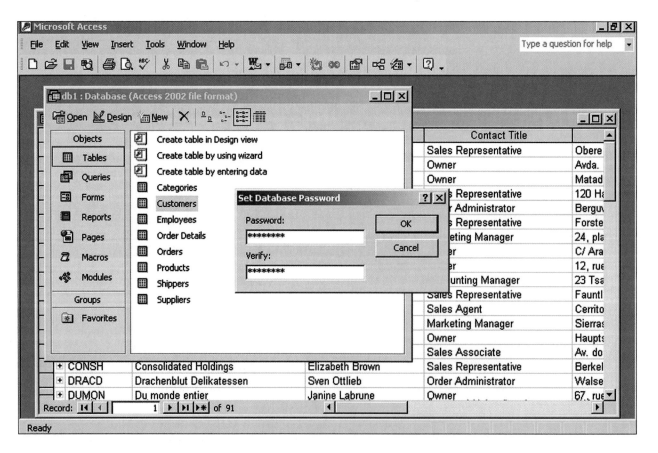

© Pearson Education, Inc.

Demonstrate Your Knowledge

Critical Thinking

1. What is one key advantage of a relational database over a flat-file database?

_____

_____

2. How do traditional databases and multimedia databases differ?

_____

_____

3. Which characteristics of a well-designed database do you think are most important to the creator of a customer database? Which are important to the customers represented in the database?

_____

_____

Activities

1. Complete the following Venn diagram to compare and contrast flat-file databases and relational databases.

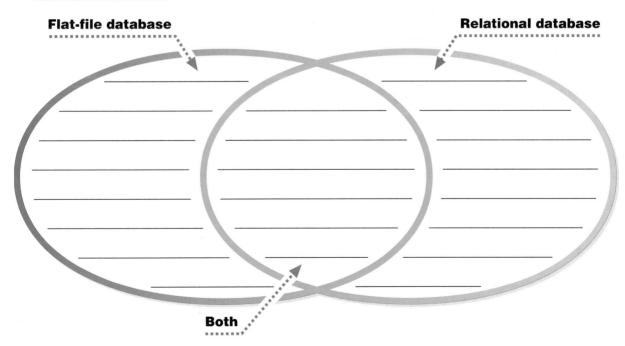

2. Suppose you are a media store owner who wants to create a database that includes video and audio clips of various artists. You also want your database to automatically open the software program needed to display the data. Research which kind of database you would select based on its quality, appropriateness, efficiency, and effectiveness for your business.

Database Techniques

Objectives

- Give examples of how to manage information in databases.
- Compare and contrast browsing, sorting, and querying data in a database.
- Describe the features of a report template.

As You Read

Summarize As you read the lesson, use a chart to help you summarize techniques for using databases effectively.

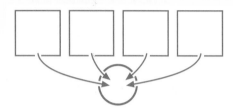

What's Online

In Lesson 8–3 of the iText, you will find more features and information for this lesson, including:

- Interactive tutorials
- As You Read worksheet
- Learn More interactivities
- Check Your Understanding interactive assessments
- Interactive lesson review

🔑 Key Terms

- information overload (p. 116)
- browse (p. 116)
- ascending order (p. 117)
- descending order (p. 117)
- report (p. 118)
- report template (p. 118)

Information Management

Computers can produce too much information, or **information overload.** Database creators can help manage data by:

- summarizing information so that database users are not overwhelmed by details
- including in reports only the data that meets specific information needs
- arranging data in a specific order so that it is easier to view and understand

Browsing Data

Putting data into a database is of little help if you cannot retrieve it when you need it. One way to find data is to **browse,** or look through, all the records. Databases can display data like a spreadsheet, with each record occupying a row and each field in a column. You can also display each record on a separate screen.

Each field occupies a column.

	Supplier ID	Company Name	Address	City
+	1	Exotic Liquids	49 Gilbert St.	London
+	2	New Orleans Cajun Delights	P.O. Box 78934	New Orleans
+	3	Grandma Kelly's Homestead	707 Oxford Rd.	Ann Arbor
+	4	Tokyo Traders	9-8 Sekimai	Tokyo
+	5	Cooperativa de Quesos 'Las Cabras'	Calle del Rosal 4	Oviedo
+	6	Mayumi's	92 Setsuko	Osaka
+	7	Pavlova, Ltd.	74 Rose St.	Melbourne
+	8	Specialty Biscuits, Ltd.	29 King's Way	Manchester
+	9	PB Knäckebröd AB	Kaloadagatan 13	Göteborg
+	10	Refrescos Americanas LTDA	Av. das Americanas 12.890	São Paulo
+	11	Heli Süßwaren GmbH & Co. KG	Tiergartenstraße 5	Berlin
+	12	Plutzer Lebensmittelgroßmärkte AG	Bogenallee 51	Frankfurt
+	13	Nord-Ost-Fisch Handelsgesellschaft	Frahmredder 112a	Cuxhaven
+	14	Formaggi Fortini s.r.l.	Viale Dante, 75	Ravenna
+	15	Norske Meierier	Hatlevegen 5	Sandvika

Record: 1 of 29

Navigation buttons **Scroll bars**

Figure 8.3.1 Navigation buttons allow users to move quickly through a large database table.

Many database programs provide keyboard commands and other tools, such as scroll bars and navigation buttons, that help users browse quickly through records. You can also limit the browsing so that the program displays only certain records and fields. This can greatly reduce the time it takes to locate or review specific records.

Sorting Data

Another way to save time is to sort the data. Sorting lets you locate information quickly.

Types of Sorting Databases can sort data in one of three ways:
- Alphabetical sorting of letters and symbols
- Numerical sorting of numbers and values
- Chronological sorting of dates and times

Data can be sorted in **ascending order,** in which values increase, such as A, B, C or 1, 2, 3. It can also be sorted the opposite way, in **descending order.** In this order, values decrease. Letters are listed C, B, and A, and numbers are sorted 3, 2, and 1.

Single and Multiple Sorts The easiest kind of sort uses a single field, such as name. Databases can also sort data using more than one field, such as last name and first name. When two records are identical in the first field, they are sorted again based on the next field. In this case, a database would list "Williams, Serena" before "Williams, Venus."

Technology @ School

School databases contain such information as students' names, classes, health records, teachers' names, grades, and standardized test scores.

Think About It!

Think about how such data might be organized. Circle each field below that you think could be usefully sorted in ascending order.

- names of all students in a course
- addresses
- courses offered
- telephone numbers
- student ID numbers
- teachers' names

Figure 8.3.2 Sorting lets you organize data so it best suits your needs.

ID No.	Last Name	Birthday
1	Rodriquez	10-13-89
2	Goldstein	06-03-88
3	Smith	05-15-88
4	Hernandez	11-01-87
5	Abdullah	04-21-89
6	Chung	01-03-87

Sort by ID Number

ID No.	Last Name	Birthday
5	Abdullah	04-21-89
6	Chung	01-03-87
2	Goldstein	06-03-88
4	Hernandez	11-01-87
1	Rodriquez	10-13-89
3	Smith	05-15-88

Sort by Last Name

ID No.	Last Name	Birthday
1	Rodriquez	10-13-89
5	Abdullah	04-21-89
2	Goldstein	06-03-88
3	Smith	05-15-88
4	Hernandez	11-01-87
6	Chung	01-03-87

Sort by Birthday

Technology @ Work

Querying Data

Databases can speed up the process of browsing information by finding only records that match specific criteria. A query is a user-created direction that tells the database to find specific records.

Creating Reports

A benefit that database software has over paper databases is the ease with which reports can be created. A **report** is an ordered list of selected records and fields in an easy-to-read format. Reports can display data in columns, as labels, or as single records. Reports are usually printed on paper.

To generate a report, the database software uses the appropriate data currently in its tables. If you print the same report at a later time, it might contain different data reflecting whatever changes were made when the database was updated.

Designing a Report Template In most databases, users design a **report template,** a pattern that controls how data will be displayed. This template typically has several main features:

- a report header that appears at the beginning of a report, such as the report title
- a report footer that appears at the end of a report, such as summary totals or averages
- a page header that appears at the top of each page, such as field headings
- a page footer that appears at the bottom of each page, such as the date the report was printed and the page number
- the arrangement of the data that you want the report to include

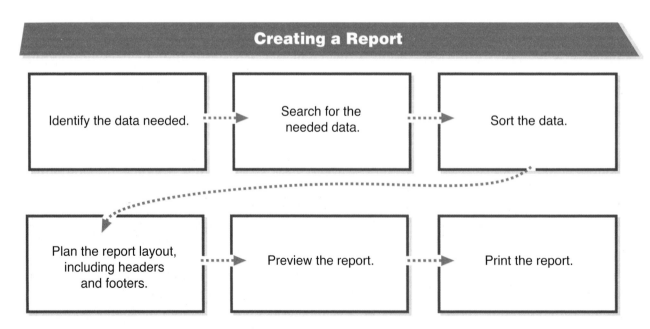

Creating a Report

Identify the data needed. → Search for the needed data. → Sort the data. → Plan the report layout, including headers and footers. → Preview the report. → Print the report.

Demonstrate Your Knowledge

Critical Thinking

1. What is one way that databases can reduce information overload?

_____

_____

2. How do browsing, sorting, and querying in a database differ?

_____

_____

3. Which report feature appears at the top of a report? Which appears at the top of every page? Which contains the data that will be included in the report?

_____

_____

Activities

1. Complete the following chart to compare browsing and querying data in a database.

Comparing Browsing and Querying

Characteristic	Browsing	Querying
How carried out		
Action performed by		
Relative speed		

2. Create an employee database with the following fields: Employee name, Date of employment, Job title, Weekly salary, Vacation days allowed. Using invented names, create records for ten employees and complete each field with fictitious, but relevant, information. Then create a report, using rows and columns, that includes employee names and weekly salaries. Sort the data in ascending order by employee name. Print your report and save the database.

Use the Vocabulary

Directions: *Match each vocabulary term in the left column with the correct definition in the right column. Write the appropriate letter next to the word or term.*

_____ **1.** database
_____ **2.** record
_____ **3.** field
_____ **4.** data type
_____ **5.** GIGO
_____ **6.** flat-file database
_____ **7.** database management system
_____ **8.** relational database
_____ **9.** key field
_____ **10.** ascending order

a. smallest part of a database; holds an individual piece of data

b. phrase that stresses the importance of inputting accurate data

c. examples are A, B, C and 1, 2, 3

d. organized collection of information stored on computer

e. database that allows you to work with data in only one table

f. part of a database that holds data about a particular person or item

g. software used to manage the storage, organization, processing, and retrieval of data in a database

h. database in which shared key fields link data among tables

i. limited kind of information that can be entered into a field

j. element that links tables

Check Your Comprehension

Directions: *Complete each sentence with information from the chapter.*

1. Some databases have only one _____, but others can hold several, each containing a set of related data.

2. Database programs are superior to paper databases in part because the information can be _____ in different ways.

3. GIGO is a reminder that a database is of poorer quality if the _____ is not accurate.

4. The kind of database that stores and opens programs for images, video clips, and audio clips is an _____.

5. A multimedia database is similar to a book _____.

6. Protecting sensitive data by requiring users to input a _____ is one way to aim for data security.

7. Data _____ is usually undesirable because it wastes space and introduces the possibility of errors.

8. One way that databases can be used to reduce information overload is to _____ information so that users are not overwhelmed by details.

9. Dates and times are sorted in _____ order.

10. You can create multiple _____ to tailor the reports generated from a database.

Think Critically

Directions: *Answer the following questions on the lines provided.*

1. Suppose you wanted to create a database of your school's DVD collection. What fields might you include?

_____

_____

2. Based on efficiency, which kind of database software would you choose to create a database in which you needed to link information? Why?

_____

_____

3. What can you do to try to ensure the accuracy of the data you enter into a database?

_____

_____

4. If having a lot of information is useful, why is information overload a problem?

_____

_____

5. Suppose you were creating a report listing the books in a library. What headers and footers might you design for the report?

_____

_____

Extend Your Knowledge

Directions: *Choose one of the following projects. Complete the exercises on a separate sheet of paper.*

A. Select a magazine in your school library and create a database of the articles featured in that issue. Include such fields as author, title, topic, and starting page number. Add another field for date of the issue, and add some records from another issue of the same magazine. Create a report that displays the data you input. After printing your report, find another way of presenting the data and print that report. Save your database.

B. In small groups, make an appointment to visit a local business. Interview the owner or a key employee about the databases that the business uses. Find out what tables, records, and fields the databases have. Ask how the databases are used. Prepare a brief report summarizing your findings. Present it to the class.

chapter
9

Graphics
Basics

What Is a Graphic? In day-to-day speech, people use the word *graphic* to refer to any visual image or object. A family photo, a road map, and a stick figure drawn on a chalkboard are all examples of graphics.

When people talk about a computer **graphic**, they usually are referring to an image. Images include drawings, painted backgrounds, and photographs. Computer graphics can be displayed in a variety of ways. They can appear on the screen as a background, or they can be placed into a document to add color and information. Thus, in the broadest sense of the term, *computer graphic* could refer to anything that can be seen on the computer screen.

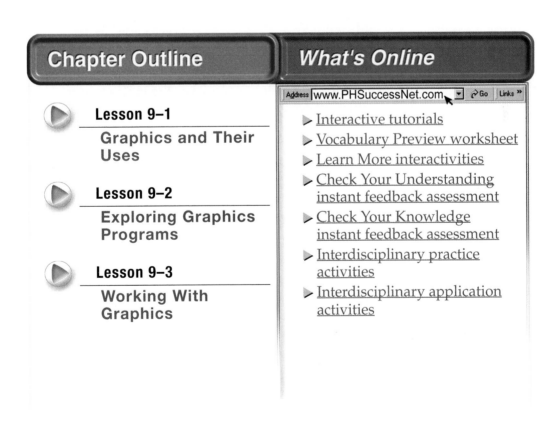

Chapter Outline

Lesson 9–1
Graphics and Their Uses

Lesson 9–2
Exploring Graphics Programs

Lesson 9–3
Working With Graphics

What's Online

Address www.PHSuccessNet.com | Go | Links »

- Interactive tutorials
- Vocabulary Preview worksheet
- Learn More interactivities
- Check Your Understanding instant feedback assessment
- Check Your Knowledge instant feedback assessment
- Interdisciplinary practice activities
- Interdisciplinary application activities

Graphics and Their Uses

Objectives

- Identify two different types of graphics and explain the differences between them.
- List the advantages of each type of graphic.
- Differentiate between draw and paint programs.

As You Read

Compare and Contrast As you read this lesson, use a Venn diagram to show the similarities and differences between bitmapped graphics and vector graphics.

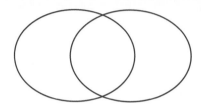

What's Online

In Lesson 9–1 of the iText, you will find more features and information for this lesson, including:

- Interactive tutorials
- As You Read worksheet
- Learn More interactivities
- Check Your Understanding interactive assessments
- Interactive lesson review

Key Terms

- graphic (p. 123)
- bitmapped graphic (p. 124)
- pixel (p. 124)
- vector graphic (p. 125)
- resolution (p. 125)
- paint program (p. 126)
- draw program (p. 126)
- image editor (p. 126)

Types of Graphics

There are hundreds of different uses for computer graphics. However, graphics fall into only two categories:

- bitmapped graphics
- vector graphics

Bitmapped Graphics A **bitmapped graphic,** or bitmap, is an image formed by a pattern of dots. Imagine a sheet of graph paper with each of its squares filled in with a certain color to make a picture. If seen from far enough away, the picture will look clear, and the squares won't be noticed. But up close, you can see the individual squares of the graph paper.

Bitmapped graphics are composed of tiny dots of different colors. Each single point in the image is a **pixel,** short for "picture element." The smaller the pixels in the image, the smoother it will look. The more colors in the image, the brighter and sharper the image will look.

Some common bitmapped file formats include:

- Graphics Interchange Format (GIF)
- Joint Photographic Experts Group (JPG)
- Portable Network Graphics (PNG)
- Windows Bitmap (BMP)

Some formats are used for images on Web pages, while others are used for icons and images in the operating system. These same abbreviations are used as the file extensions. A file ending in *.gif,* for example, is in the GIF file format.

Bitmaps are preferred for some types of images. They often are used for photos or images that require backgrounds.

Vector Graphics A **vector graphic** is an image that is created using paths or lines. A vector image tells the computer where a line starts and where it ends. It allows the computer to figure out how to connect the two points. The lines can form shapes, which may be filled with a color or pattern.

Encapsulated PostScript, or EPS, is one of several formats commonly used for vector art. EPS files contain the information that a printer needs in order to print a graphic correctly. The information is combined with a small sketch of what the graphic should look like. The sketch inside an EPS file allows you to preview an image on-screen. This way, you can be sure the image is correct before printing it.

Size, Resolution, and Dots Per Inch

Two basic qualities affect how every bitmapped image will appear. Size, the height and width of the graphic, is normally measured either in pixels or in inches. **Resolution** tells how many pixels are in a certain piece of an image. Resolution also determines the quality of the computer image. Resolution is usually measured in dots per inch, or dpi. An image that is 1 inch square at 72 dpi will contain a total of 5,184 pixels (72 x 72). Generally, the higher the resolution, the sharper the image will look.

Vector graphics are created using lines or paths rather than pixels. Thus, the number of dots per inch is not a concern when changing the size of vector graphics. If a bitmapped image is enlarged to twice its normal size, it will look fuzzy and jagged. A vector image can be enlarged to any size and keep its quality.

Students in different countries e-mail pictures from their everyday lives to one another. The pictures help students understand what life is like in a different culture.

Think *About* **It!**
Circle the number that correctly shows the number of pixels in a 1 inch by 1 inch picture at 150 dpi.

➤ 2,500 pixels
➤ 10,000 pixels
➤ 22,500 pixels

Figure 9.1.1 When viewed on the screen, vector graphics look sharper than bitmapped graphics.

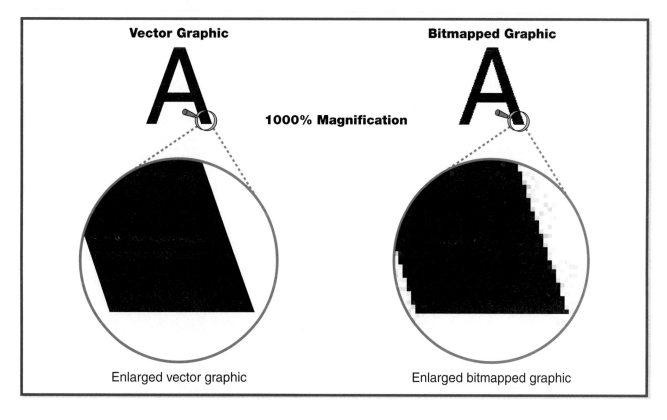

Vector Graphic   Bitmapped Graphic

1000% Magnification

Enlarged vector graphic   Enlarged bitmapped graphic

Graphics Programs

Different programs allow you to create, edit, and view different graphic file types. Choosing the right program depends on which type of graphic you are working with and what your needs are.

Paint Programs A **paint program** allows you to create a new bitmapped image. Paint programs also allow you to open a bitmapped image, view it on-screen, and make changes to it.

Draw Programs A program that allows you to create and edit vector images is called a **draw program.** Since draw programs focus on vector images, they make editing easy. You can change the size of an image or add color to it.

Basic draw programs, such as the one in Microsoft® Word®, allow you to perform simple drawing tasks. More complex programs, such as Adobe® Illustrator® and CorelDRAW®, allow you to do more but require more time to learn.

Image Editors An advanced paint program is called an **image editor.** Image editors are designed for editing bitmapped images. They are also often used for adding special effects to photographs. Adobe® Photoshop® and Adobe® Photodelux® are examples of popular image editors.

Spotlight on...

PIXAR STUDIOS

You may have never heard the name *Pixar,* but you've probably heard of their animated films. *Toy Story* and *Monsters, Inc.* are just two examples of their work. These films were created using computers.

Pixar films are known for their realistic cartoon characters. Some aspects of creating these characters involved technology similar to the draw and paint programs and image editors discussed in this lesson.

After final drawings or clay models of the characters were approved, 3-D models were designed on computers. Next, designers considered movements and expressions. They looked at photos of live actors in various positions and with different expressions to get an idea of how each figure should move. Animators then used Pixar's animation software to make the images come to life with movements and expressions.

© Pearson Education, Inc.

Demonstrate Your Knowledge

Critical Thinking

1. How do bitmapped graphics and vector graphics differ?

_____

_____

2. If you want to enlarge a graphic to three times its size, should you start with a bitmapped or a vector image? Why?

_____

_____

Activities

1. Complete the following spider map showing the functions of paint programs, draw programs, and image editors.

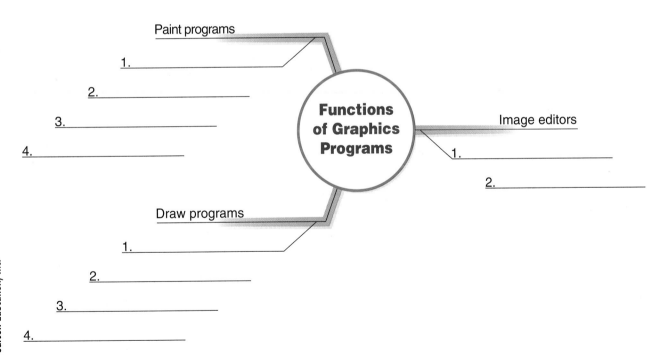

2. Research a company that works with graphics. Find out what types of graphics they use, the programs they use, and what they do with the images. Write a one-page report that details your findings.

Exploring Graphics Programs

Objectives

- Identify the main sections of a graphics application window.
- List the different tools available in paint and draw programs.
- Determine when to use the tools in a paint or draw program.

As You Read

Summarize Information Make a table that lists tools used in paint and draw programs on the left. On the right, include the type of program(s) each tool is used in.

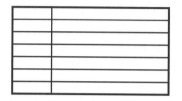

What's Online

In Lesson 9–2 of the iText, you will find more features and information for this lesson, including:

- Interactive tutorials
- As You Read worksheet
- Learn More interactivities
- Check Your Understanding interactive assessments
- Interactive lesson review

🔑 Key Terms

- workspace (p. 128)
- color palette (p. 128)
- Eyedropper (p. 129)
- Selection tool (p. 130)
- graphics tablet (p. 130)
- stylus (p. 130)

Exploring the Application Window

Paint and draw programs vary from one to another, but most include a workspace, toolbars, and color palettes.

Workspace Most of the screen is devoted to the **workspace,** the blank, white area which contains the graphic. This area is sometimes called the drawing area.

Toolbars A toolbar is a bar across the top or down the side of a window. It contains icons that link to the program's tools. By clicking an icon, you can create, edit, add, or remove information within the graphic. Toolbars usually appear, or are docked, on the edges of the screen. They also can be moved around, or floated, to fit your preferences.

Color Palettes The display of color options in paint and draw programs is called the **color palette.** These options allow you to choose colors for an image. Most programs also allow you to change the color palette.

Figure 9.2.1 Paint and draw programs share several basic tools, such as a workspace, toolbars, and color palettes.

Paint Program Tools

In paint programs, the following tools are used to place and remove color in the workspace.

Pencil The Pencil tool is used for freehand drawing. Clicking and dragging this tool across the workspace leaves a trail of the selected color. This tool is used to draw fine details but only the color or thickness of the line drawn can be changed.

Brush The Brush tool works like the Pencil tool, but it makes a broader stroke of color. Often, the shape of the brush can be changed to create different shapes of colors. For instance, the brush can be large and square or small and circular.

Line and Shape The Line tool allows you to draw a line and use the toolbar to change its color and width. Various shapes, such as rectangles and ovals, also can be drawn using tools on the toolbar. Shape tools allow you to create shapes in three different forms: Outline, Filled With Outline, and Filled Without Outline.

Eyedropper The **Eyedropper** tool allows you to work with a specific color from an image. You place the eyedropper over the desired color in an image and click. That color becomes the selected color and can be used elsewhere in the image.

Eraser The Eraser tool removes color from an image. It is used by clicking the tool and dragging the eraser across the image. The area touched with the eraser becomes the background color.

Connections

Science The eyedropper has been used in science for years. One of its purposes is to collect or test small quantities of liquids or chemicals.

First, the eyedropper is squeezed to suction in a liquid. Then, pressure on the dropper is relieved to let go of the liquid.

The concept is similar when working with graphics. The eyedropper tool "suctions" in a color and then releases it into the image.

Figure 9.2.2 Some tools are commonly found in Paint programs. The toolbar shown here is from Paint Shop Pro.

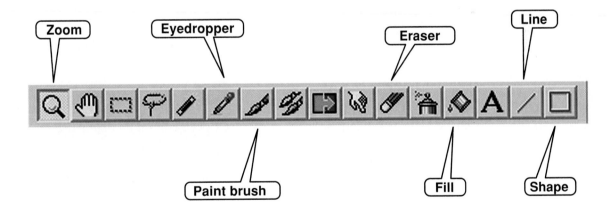

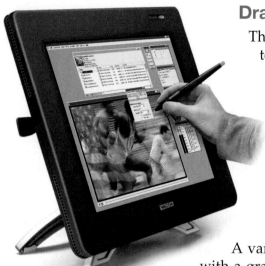

Draw Program Tools

The Line and Shape tools in draw programs are similar to those in paint programs, but with one important difference. In a draw program, you can change an image's lines and shapes without changing nearby ones. In paint programs, it is hard to change one part of an image without altering other parts that are close to it. A **Selection tool** allows you to select a portion of an image to be enlarged, moved, or edited.

Interacting With the Program

A variety of different input tools allow you to work easily with a graphics program. A mouse is used to select part of an image or to activate tools on the toolbar. By dragging, releasing, or double-clicking the mouse, a tool's function is performed.

A **graphics tablet** is a piece of hardware used for drawing. The user moves a **stylus,** or pointing device, over the drawing surface. The tablet senses the movement of the stylus and moves the cursor on-screen. As the cursor moves, it creates on the screen the image that is being drawn on the tablet.

Figure 9.2.3 A stylus is a pointing device that is often used when working with a graphics tablet.

Real-World Tech

Using Graphics Tools The tools in paint and draw programs have many uses. As you might expect, they often are used by newspaper and magazine publishers. What you might not expect is that students your age are using them, too. For example, at Centennial Middle School in Boulder, Colorado, students publish an online newspaper called *The Vocal Point*. To create and edit the images in the newspaper, students rely on graphics programs.

How might you use draw and paint programs at school? Write your ideas below.

_____

_____

Demonstrate Your Knowledge

Critical Thinking

1. What are the three main sections of a graphics application window? How does each function?

_____

_____

2. Identify the two categories of tools used in draw programs, and explain what each does.

_____

_____

Activities

1. Complete the following chart showing how using the tools of a paint program causes the computer to respond.

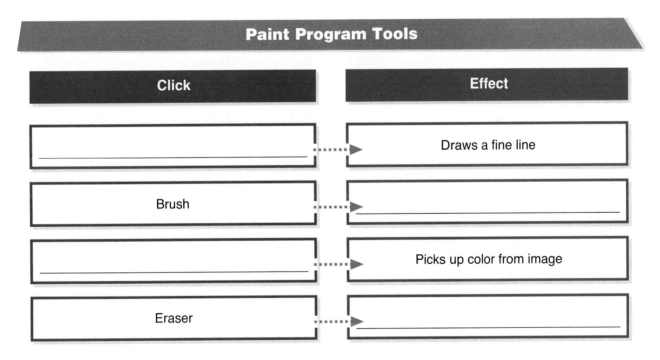

Paint Program Tools

Click	Effect
_____	Draws a fine line
Brush	_____
_____	Picks up color from image
Eraser	_____

2. Open a draw program and find out how the Line, Shape, and Selection tools work. Draw a simple image, such as a house. Then, use various tools to add detail. After you apply each function, print a copy of the image to show how it changed.

Working With Graphics

Objectives

- Explain how to modify an image with special effects.
- Compare the processes for combining vector or bitmapped graphics.
- Explain how to work with clip art.
- Describe how graphics can be converted from one format to another.

As You Read

Organize Information As you read this lesson, make an outline. Use Roman numerals for main headings. Use capital letters for subheadings, and use numbers for supporting details.

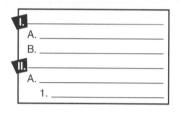

What's Online

In Lesson 9–3 of the iText, you will find more features and information for this lesson, including:

- Interactive tutorials
- As You Read worksheet
- Learn More interactivities
- Check Your Understanding interactive assessments
- Interactive lesson review

🔑 Key Terms

- import (p. 132)
- export (p. 132)
- group (p. 133)
- ungroup (p. 133)
- layer (p. 133)
- clip art (p. 134)
- trace (p. 134)

Adding Effects to Graphics

To create a new graphic, start with a blank workspace. If you are creating the graphic in a paint program, use the paint tools to add color and form to the image. If you are creating the graphic in a draw program, use the Line and Shape tools to add information to the image.

Special effects can be used to modify an image. Flipping an image turns it upside down. Mirroring the image makes it flip from left to right, as if it were being viewed in a mirror. Stretching makes the image appear longer in one direction than the other, as if it were drawn on a sheet of rubber that was stretched out. Skewing tilts the image horizontally or vertically.

Inverting reverses the colors in the graphic. In a black-and-white graphic, all the white dots will turn black, and all the black will turn white. In a color graphic, each color will change to its "opposite" color. For example, yellow will become dark blue.

Combining Images

Bringing information, such as a graphic, into a file from another file is called **importing.** Once imported, the image can then be modified or expanded.

Exporting is when data is formatted so it can be used in another application. This means that the program you are working in must be able to translate its own language to the language another program understands.

Different processes are used to combine vector images or bitmapped images. These processes are known as:

- grouping, for combining vector graphics
- layering, for combining bitmapped graphics

Grouping Images In a vector graphic, different items can be placed together. **Grouping** is the process of combining separate images into one image. Once the images are grouped, they can be moved or resized as a single unit. To group images, select all of the desired items and then select the Group command. **Ungrouping** is the process of separating combined images into individual images. To ungroup an image, select a grouped image and then select the Ungroup command.

Layering Images Bitmapped graphics use layers, or stacks of information, to create a graphic. A powerful process known as **layering** stacks each level of an image on top of another. Imagine three or four sheets of wax paper, each with a different part of a drawing. When all of them are stacked, the complete picture is visible. Although the layers are stacked, you can still edit them separately. Any changes you make only affect the layer you touch.

The default layer is the background. You can add or delete layers as needed. The layer you're working with is usually highlighted in a color. You can hide a layer you're not using to see other parts of the image more easily.

You can use the Edit menu to import graphics from one application to another. This is done by saving information from one application onto your clipboard. Next, you use the clipboard to bring the information into another application.

Think *About* **It!**
Circle the menu that contains the clipboard.

➤ File
➤ Edit
➤ View
➤ Insert

Layers palette

Combined layers

Figure 9.3.1 Layering works by breaking an image into separate parts and stacking them.

© Pearson Education, Inc.

Career Corner

Graphic Artist A graphic artist creates the design and layout of different products, such as advertisements, brochures, Web sites, and CD-ROMs. They design or acquire images and choose and edit text features to communicate a message.

An art degree, courses in graphic arts or design, and recent experience using related software are important qualifications for this career.

Figure 9.3.2 Vector clip art may look sharper than bitmapped clip art and can be edited like any vector graphic.

Working With Clip Art

It is not always necessary to create an image from scratch. Instead, **clip art**—artwork that has already been created that you can download—can be used as a starting point.

Bitmapped Clip Art Clip art in a bitmapped format (such as GIF, JPG, or PNG) can be imported into a paint document. The art then can be edited like any other bitmapped graphic.

Vector Clip Art Vector art can be imported in a draw program and modified. If the image is complex, it can be ungrouped. Its individual parts can then be edited or moved.

Converting Graphics

Sometimes it is necessary to convert a graphics file into a different type of file, such as from JPG format to GIF format. This need often arises when a graphics program cannot read a file in its current format. Then the file must be converted into a format the program can use while keeping it as a bitmapped file or vector file. File conversion is also required if you want to change a vector graphic to a bitmapped graphic, or vice versa.

Vector-to-Bitmapped Graphics Vector graphics are based on lines and fills rather than pixels. The lines and fills must be changed to pixels before the image can be edited in a paint program.

Bitmapped-to-Vector Graphics Bitmapped graphics are based on pixels, not lines, and converting them to vectors requires a special process called **tracing.** Tracing requires special software and can be complicated when an image has a lot of color and detail.

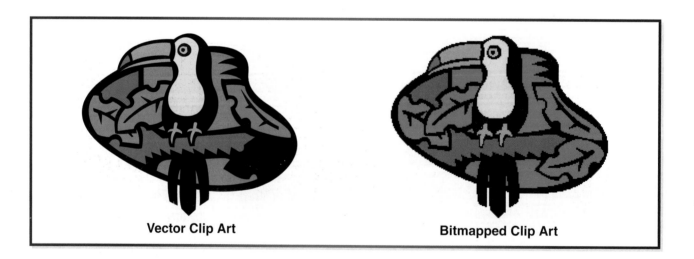

Vector Clip Art   Bitmapped Clip Art

Demonstrate Your Knowledge

Critical Thinking

1. Describe the processes of importing and exporting graphics.

_____

_____

2. What steps are taken to convert a vector graphic to a bitmapped graphic, and a bitmapped graphic to a vector graphic?

_____

_____

Activities

1. Complete the following chart on the concept of layering.

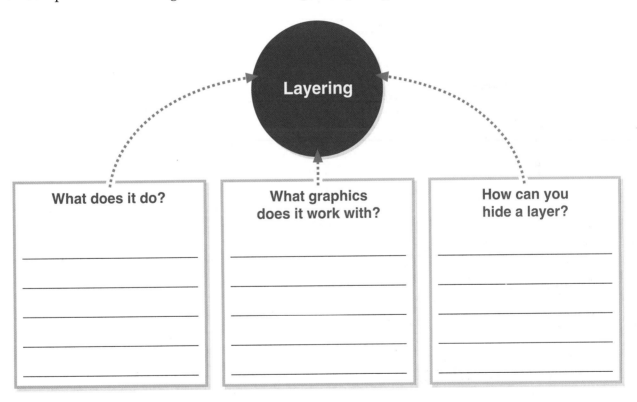

2. Use clip art to create two birthday cards for friends. One card should include a vector graphic and the other a bitmapped graphic. Then, show your teacher the cards.

Use the Vocabulary

Directions: *Match each vocabulary term in the left column with the correct definition in the right column. Write the appropriate letter next to the word or term.*

_____ **1.** bitmapped graphic

_____ **2.** vector graphic

_____ **3.** resolution

_____ **4.** paint program

_____ **5.** color palette

_____ **6.** Eyedropper

_____ **7.** graphics tablet

_____ **8.** import

_____ **9.** layer

_____ **10.** clip art

a. the number of pixels in a certain image that affects its visual quality

b. images that can be downloaded for use in a graphics program

c. images created using lines or paths

d. tool that captures and uses color from one portion of an image in another

e. input device for creating graphics

f. stacks of information on top of one another to form a more complete image

g. image created using pixels, or series of dots

h. allows you to modify bitmapped graphics

i. brings information into a file from another file

j. the display of color options in paint and draw programs

Check Your Comprehension

Directions: *Complete each sentence with information from the chapter.*

1. Sets of dots that make up an image are called _____.

2. A _____ allows you to create and edit vector graphics.

3. Advanced paint programs that allow you to edit and add effects to a bitmapped graphic are _____.

4. The area of the screen where images are created and edited is the _____.

5. The set of color options in a particular paint or draw program shown in small boxes on the screen is called the _____.

6. In a draw program, a _____ allows you to pick a certain portion of an image to work on.

7. A common input device in a graphics program is the _____.

8. The process of formatting data so that it can be used in another application is _____.

9. Combining separate images to form a single image is called _____.

10. The process of converting pixels to lines or paths is known as _____.

Think Critically

Directions: *Answer the following questions on the lines provided.*

1. What are two differences between a bitmapped graphic and a vector graphic?

_____

_____

2. When editing graphics, why is it important to consider the file format in which an image is created?

_____

_____

3. How do toolbars in draw and paint programs help you to edit and add effects to images?

_____

_____

4. Why are exporting and importing important functions for working with graphics?

_____

_____

5. How are layering and grouping similar? How are they different?

_____

_____

_____

Extend Your Knowledge

Directions: *Choose one of the following projects. Complete the exercises on a separate sheet of paper.*

A. When working with graphics, there are few limits to the projects you can make. Some projects can even be funny! Create a comic strip using vector or bitmapped graphics. You may create your own images or edit clip art. Your comic strip should have at least four frames. Be sure to use the different tools and colors in the program. Print your strip to show to the class.

B. Newspapers and magazines often use graphics to capture the readers' attention or to make a point. Find three graphics (including photos with special effects) in newspapers or magazines. Next, create a three-column chart. On the chart, paste each image, identify each source and page number, and categorize the graphic as bitmapped or vector. Present your findings to the class.

chapter
10
Presentation Basics

What Are Presentations?

Every day, presentations are shown on overhead screens in classrooms and at meetings. They help people teach ideas, sell products, and share information with others.

Before computers, creating a professional presentation took a lot of time and involved many people. First, an artist would create graphics. Next, the graphics and wording would be organized for logical flow and visual appeal. Then, this information was transferred onto transparencies or slides.

Now, thanks to presentation software, many people create presentations more quickly. Knowing how to use presentation software is an important skill in today's world.

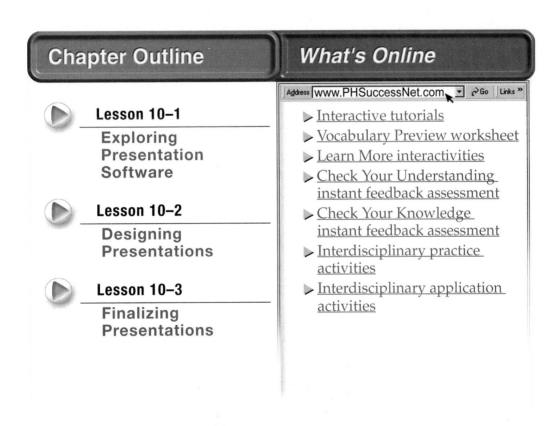

Chapter Outline

Lesson 10–1
Exploring Presentation Software

Lesson 10–2
Designing Presentations

Lesson 10–3
Finalizing Presentations

What's Online

Address www.PHSuccessNet.com Go Links »

- Interactive tutorials
- Vocabulary Preview worksheet
- Learn More interactivities
- Check Your Understanding instant feedback assessment
- Check Your Knowledge instant feedback assessment
- Interdisciplinary practice activities
- Interdisciplinary application activities

Exploring Presentation Software

Objectives

- Identify the benefits of presentation software.
- Identify three options for creating a new presentation.
- Describe six views in PowerPoint.

As You Read

Organize Information Use a concept web to help you organize ways to create and view presentations as you read.

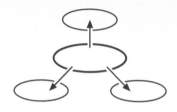

Key Terms

- presentation software (p. 140)
- slide (p. 140)
- wizard (p.140)
- AutoContent wizard (p. 140)
- template (p. 140)
- Outline view (p. 142)
- Normal view (p. 142)
- Slide Sorter view (p. 142)
- Notes Page view (p. 142)
- Slide Show view (p. 142)

Introducing Presentation Software

Presentation software allows you to organize and display information visually so it can be viewed by a group of people. In most cases, this information—called a presentation—consists of both graphics and text. Information in a presentation is organized into separate pages in an order the audience can follow easily. Each page is called a **slide.** Each slide can contain one or more main points. Information about each main point is organized into a list of short, easy-to-read key points. Programs such as Microsoft® PowerPoint® and Corel® Presentations™ are designed specifically to make presentations.

Creating a New Presentation

The most common presentation software is Microsoft® PowerPoint®. It allows three options for creating a new presentation:

- AutoContent wizard
- template
- blank presentation

AutoContent Wizard A **wizard** is a series of dialog boxes that guides you through a step-by-step procedure. The **AutoContent wizard** provides the steps for creating a presentation. It asks questions about the goals and purpose of your presentation. Once its questions are answered, the wizard creates a format for the presentation. To complete the presentation, you enter the words and images into the wizard's format.

Template Work on a presentation also may begin by selecting a **template,** or a preformatted version of a certain type of document. After choosing a template, you type in your information. You can also change the look and feel of the template by adjusting its settings.

Blank Presentation This option starts by providing a plain blank slide. While this option may require more work than the other choices, it does have benefits. For instance, since many schools and businesses use PowerPoint®, the templates included in this program may be familiar to others. You can create a new presentation from scratch to make your work more original by selecting your own color scheme, art, fonts, and other design elements.

Exploring Presentation Views

After you select the format for a presentation, work on the content can begin. One of the differences between a presentation graphics program and other application software is its ability to view a document in a variety of ways. Each view has its own strength. Depending on which version of PowerPoint® you use, you may be able to choose from these views, among others:

- Outline view
- Slide view
- Normal view
- Slide Sorter view
- Notes Page view
- Slide Show view

New screen-reading programs can make working on a computer easier for people who are blind or have poor vision.

- Job Access With Speech, or JAWS, uses your computer's sound to read aloud what is displayed on the screen.

- Hal Screen Reader also converts what is on the screen to sound. It can be used with PowerPoint® and even Braille text.

Figure 10.1.1 Creating a PowerPoint® presentation with the AutoContent wizard

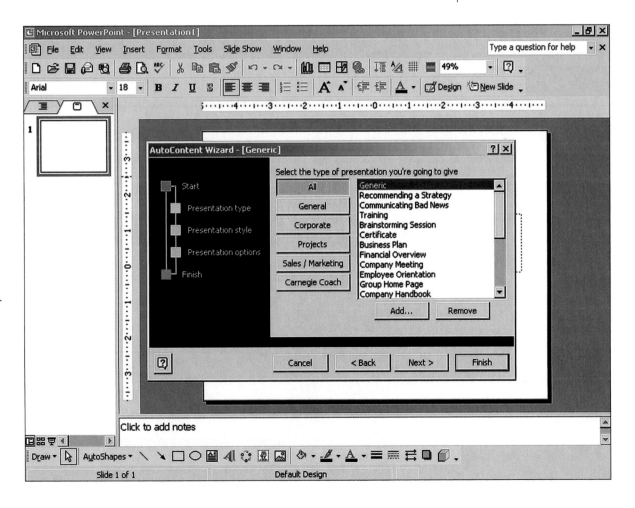

© Pearson Education, Inc.

At work, employees may be asked to make presentations to inform others about company policies, to show the results of the company's latest research, or to sell a new product.

Think *About* **It!**
Using the right view in presentation software can make creating a presentation a little bit easier. Circle the views that would help you organize your slides.

- Outline view
- Slide view
- Normal view
- Slide Sorter view
- Notes Page view
- Slide Show view

Figure 10.1.2 Slide Sorter view (left) and Normal view (right) in Microsoft® PowerPoint® 2002

Outline View To display a presentation's text in an outline, use **Outline View.** It is handy for improving the structure of complex presentations. Selecting an item in the outline generally displays the slide for that item. Text can also be edited in this view.

Slide View and Normal View Text and graphics can be added, removed, or edited in Slide view, a basic layout in some versions of PowerPoint®, or in Normal view. (Different versions of the program provide different views.) **Normal view** splits the screen to show a Slide view and an Outline view.

Slide Sorter View **Slide Sorter view** displays all of the slides in a presentation. In this view, you see thumbnail (miniature) versions of the slides. This view allows you to change the order of the slides by dragging them to different locations.

Notes Page View Another view, known as **Notes Page view,** uses part of the screen to display a slide. The rest of the screen shows a text box. You can jot down notes in the text box to use during a presentation or to print as handouts. Notes do not appear in the presentation that is shown to the audience.

Slide Show View The primary on-screen method of previewing and displaying slides during a presentation is called **Slide Show view.** Slides are displayed one after another, in order. A slide-show presentation can be set to automatically switch slides or to wait until you switch the slides yourself.

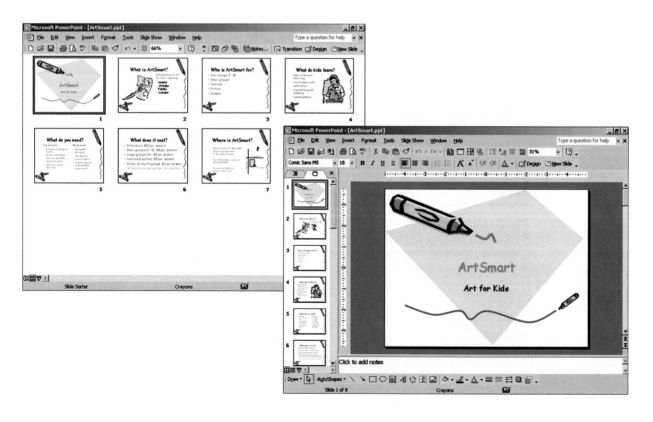

Demonstrate Your Knowledge

Critical Thinking

1. What are three ways to create a presentation in PowerPoint®, and how do they differ?

_____

_____

_____

2. What advantage does presentation software have over other application software?

_____

_____

3. Which view do you think is best for organizing and timing a presentation? Explain.

_____

_____

Activities

1. Complete the following cause-and-effect chart to show the effect of applying different PowerPoint® views.

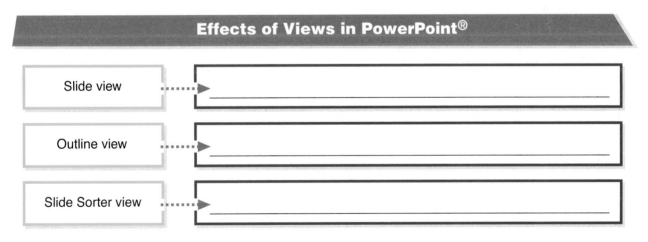

Effects of Views in PowerPoint®

Slide view ┈┈▶ _____

Outline view ┈┈▶ _____

Slide Sorter view ┈┈▶ _____

2. Use presentation software to design a presentation about the various views in a software program. Present your slides to the class, and explain which views you found most useful.

Designing Presentations

Objectives

- Explain how placeholders are used in presentation software.
- Identify five steps in designing presentations.
- Summarize techniques for creating effective presentations.

As You Read

Sequence Information Use a sequence chart to help you order steps for creating presentations as you read.

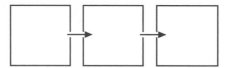

What's Online

In Lesson 10–2 of the iText, you will find more features and information for this lesson, including:

- Interactive tutorials
- As You Read worksheet
- Learn More interactivities
- Check Your Understanding interactive assessments
- Interactive lesson review

🔑 Key Terms

- placeholder (p. 144)
- AutoShapes (p. 144)
- animation (p. 144)
- Clip Art Gallery (p. 144)

Adding Data to Presentations

When you create a new slide in a presentation program, you are prompted to choose a slide layout. A **placeholder** is an area within a slide layout designed to hold data such as text or pictures. For instance, a layout might contain a box that asks you to add a title. Click (or, in some programs, double-click) the box and begin typing. The program automatically formats the text to fit the area with a preselected font and alignment.

Adding Drawings Presentation programs often contain a drawing toolbar—a list of basic drawing tools accessed through icons. PowerPoint® drawing tools also include a large list of ready-to-use shapes, called **AutoShapes.** The list includes banners, arrows, borders, frames, and more.

You do not need a placeholder to create a drawing. Select the desired tool and use it in a blank area of the workspace.

Adding Animation and Sound A multimedia presentation combines text and graphics with sound and animation. Both sound and **animation,** or moving images, are inserted by a special menu command. In some versions of PowerPoint, this command is in the **Clip Art Gallery** or Clip Art Organizer, a collection of ready-to-use images and sound.

Figure 10.2.1 This dialog box lets you find a piece of clip art, or another kind of image, to add to a PowerPoint® slide.

© Pearson Education, Inc.

Designing Presentations

Following these five steps will help you plan and design an effective presentation.

1. Decide How Your Slides Will Be Formatted   To begin designing a presentation, choose an option for creating it. Choose either a blank presentation, the AutoContent wizard, or a template. If none of the templates is exactly what you want, select the one that is closest. You can change much of its graphic content, format, and text. Graphics can be resized or deleted. Placeholders can be added, removed, or resized as well.

2. Choose the Slide Layout Every slide in a presentation can be formatted in a preset layout. These layouts already have placeholders in position. This allows text and graphics to be added immediately. Some examples of slide layouts include bulleted lists, tables, grids, and flowcharts. Since each slide in a presentation can have a different layout, select a layout for each new slide you add.

3. Work With Placeholders Each placeholder is designed to be filled with data. The data can be text, such as a bulleted list. It can also be a graphic, such as a pie chart or a photo. Placeholders make work easier because they recognize the type of information to be placed. For instance, selecting a text placeholder will change the cursor to the Text tool. Selecting a picture placeholder will bring up a prompt asking which image to place. Placeholder prompts guide you and are overwritten, or replaced, when you type new text.

Some teachers use interactive multimedia software to help them teach. This software allows students to control the pace of the instruction.

Think *About* **It!**
Using interactive multimedia in the classroom has advantages and disadvantages. Circle each item that could present a disadvantage for schools.

- ▶ expensive
- ▶ uses images
- ▶ uses sounds
- ▶ only some subjects available

Figure 10.2.2 Choosing a slide layout in Microsoft® PowerPoint® 2002

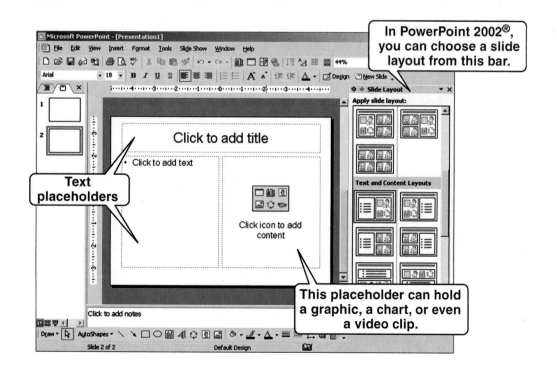

Career Corner

4. Insert Graphics and Sound   Make your presentations come to life. Use sound, video, clip art, drawing tools, or imported images to support or illustrate a slide's text.

5. View and Organize the Presentation   Once information has been added to the slides, preview the entire presentation using the Slide Show view. Make any changes to the order of the slides in Slide Sorter view. Typos and text changes can be handled in Outline view or Normal view.

Creating Effective Presentations

Use the following guidelines to help you create an effective presentation:

- Your slide presentation does not have to include every detail. Just the most important, basic facts should appear.
- Adding too many different media, such as unnecessary graphics, sound, and animation, can distract the audience from your main message. They also take up a lot of file space, which may slow down your presentation.
- Finally, remember to only use features that will help your audience learn what it needs to know.

Figure 10.2.3
Inserting a clip art image into a slide

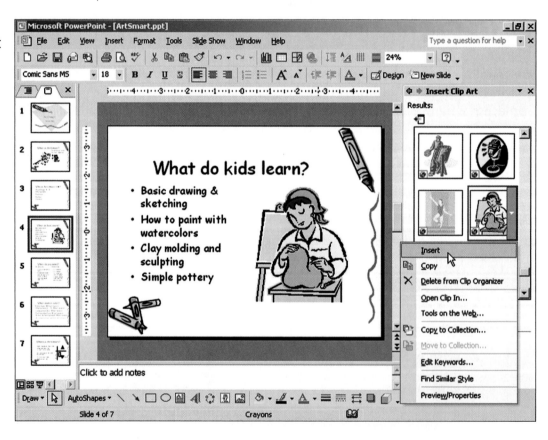

Demonstrate Your Knowledge

Critical Thinking

1. What is the purpose of placeholders in presentation software?

_____

_____

2. Which best enhances a presentation—text, graphics, sound, or animation? Why?

_____

_____

3. What recommendations might you make for creating an effective slide presentation?

_____

_____

Activities

1. Complete the following chart on the advantages and disadvantages of adding images and sound to presentations.

Advantages	Disadvantages
_____	_____
_____	_____
_____	_____
_____	_____
_____	_____
_____	_____
_____	_____
_____	_____

2. Design and create a multimedia tour of your school. In addition to text, add two of the following to your slides: graphics, sound, video, or animation. Share your presentation with your class. Then analyze the most and least effective elements.

Finalizing Presentations

Objectives

- Summarize seven tips for finalizing effective presentations.
- Identify options for displaying final presentations.

As You Read

Organize Information Use a main idea/detail chart to help you create useful presentations as you read.

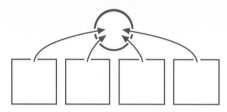

What's Online

In Lesson 10–3 of the iText, you will find more features and information for this lesson, including:

- Interactive tutorials
- As You Read worksheet
- Learn More interactivities
- Check Your Understanding interactive assessments
- Interactive lesson review

Key Terms

- transparency (p. 150)
- on-screen presentation (p. 150)

Finalizing Effective Presentations

Apply these seven tips to make your presentation more effective.

One Idea Per Slide Avoid crowding data onto a slide. Make as many slides as needed to present important information clearly.

Keep It Simple Remember, people will be listening to your speech while viewing your slides. Use simple words to make key points. Include clear transitions from one topic to another.

Display Key Facts Your slides should serve as an outline for the audience. Your speech will fill in the gaps in that outline. Displaying too much information can make a presentation hard to follow.

Mix It Up Vary the format of your slides to help keep people interested in your presentation. For instance, switch between lists that appear on the right-hand and left-hand sides of your slides. An occasional photo or animation can add examples or details to a presentation.

Figure 10.3.1 In a well-designed presentation, each slide explains one key point or answers one key question.

© Pearson Education, Inc.

Use Color Cautiously It is best to include only a few colors on your slides. Also, be sure the colors are pleasing to the eye. For instance, bright pink lettering on a bright blue background might make people look away from—rather than at—the information on a slide.

Watch the Fonts Do not use more than two fonts on a single slide. This helps prevent a presentation from becoming too distracting to read. Also, be sure to use fonts that fit the tone. A presentation about the Civil War, for example, would not use fonts that seem playful or humorous.

Make It Readable Many templates come with a dark background. If one of these backgrounds is used, choose readable font and color combinations. Check that your text and images are readable from the back of the room so your presentation can be viewed by your entire audience.

Displaying Presentations

Now that you have created your slides, how will your audience view your presentation? There are a number of options for displaying the finished product. Choose the best method to meet the needs of your audience and the difficulty of the material. Some choices include:

- transparencies
- on-screen presentations
- Internet viewing
- audience handouts

Technology@Home

Before giving a presentation, test it with an audience such as friends and family.

Think *About* **It!**
Ask your test audience to point out slides that were hard to see or to understand. Underline items that are items for concern on presentation slides.

- ► text too small
- ► animation
- ► detailed information given
- ► many colors used

Spotlight on...

DISTANCE LEARNING

Can you imagine creating presentations to show people who live hundreds of miles away? Distance learning teaches people at remote, or off-site, locations from the teacher. These students aren't seated together in a single classroom. Companies that develop distance-learning materials must create presentations students understand. It also means these presentations must keep students' interest.

Distance learning is on the rise. It was once used only by the

U.S. military to train troops stationed overseas. The method is now used by schools and businesses. As the technology for delivering online lessons improves, presentations used to teach these materials should improve, too.

Transparencies For an audience of fewer than 50 people, slides can be printed on **transparencies.** These are see-through sheets of acetate that are laser-printed and shown on an overhead projector. Teachers sometimes use overhead transparencies in their classrooms. Transparencies have limitations. For example, large groups may not see the information clearly, and animation cannot be used.

On-screen Presentations Sometimes two or three people can comfortably gather around a single computer to view a slide-show presentation. In other cases, large groups may view a presentation on an overhead or television monitor, a presentation projector, or a "jumbo" screen. This is called an **on-screen presentation,** or a screen display of the slides. Presentation software can advance the slides automatically, or you can change them yourself.

Internet Viewing If the audience is in a remote place, the presentation can be exported for use on a Web site. The user can then view the slide show at any time through a Web browser. This method is useful for long-distance education. Group size is not an issue, and interactivity and animation are both possible presentation features.

Audience Handouts You can help your audience remember important information by providing audience handouts. These handouts may be printouts of your slides or a summary of your main ideas. Handouts are especially helpful when presenting difficult information.

Figure 10.3.2 No matter how you present your slides, they should be clearly visible to everyone in the audience.

Demonstrate Your Knowledge

Critical Thinking

1. When creating presentation slides, what should you keep in mind about your choice of colors?

_____

_____

2. Why does the size of the audience affect what type of presentation should be used?

_____

_____

3. Which presentation display would be most effective for a presentation to your class? Why?

_____

_____

Activities

1. Complete the following chart by supplying examples of each type of audience.

Presentation Display Options	Examples of Best Audience
On-screen presentations	
Transparencies	
Audience handouts	
Internet viewing	

2. As a class, create a multimedia presentation of your community. Divide into groups to research community topics, such as the school system, housing, and businesses. Assign tasks to groups such as preparing text, audio, video, and graphics for the presentation. Follow the presentation tips and choose the best display options suggested in this lesson. Then, share your project with your local Chamber of Commerce.

Use the Vocabulary

Directions: *Match each vocabulary term in the left column with the correct definition in the right column. Write the appropriate letter next to the word or term.*

_____ 1. presentation software
_____ 2. slide
_____ 3. wizard
_____ 4. template
_____ 5. Slide Show view
_____ 6. placeholder
_____ 7. AutoShapes
_____ 8. animation
_____ 9. transparency
_____ 10. on-screen presentation

a. preformatted version of a certain type of document
b. list of ready-to-use drawing tools
c. presentation viewed on a computer monitor
d. single page in a presentation
e. creates and displays visual information
f. printed sheets viewed on an overhead projector
g. area in a presentation that holds data
h. can automatically show a presentation in the correct order
i. images that show movement
j. a series of dialog boxes that provides a step-by-step guide

Check Your Comprehension

Directions: *Complete each sentence with information from the chapter.*

1. Graphics designed using _____ usually are accompanied by text.

2. Using Outline view can improve the _____ of your presentation.

3. The _____ view provides information that only the presenter can see during a presentation.

4. An on-screen method of previewing a presentation's slides is called the _____.

5. Animation can be added to some PowerPoint® presentations using the _____.

6. Bulleted lists, flowcharts, and grids can be included in a slide's _____.

7. You can create a multimedia presentation with _____.

8. In a presentation, only the most _____ should be included on slides, not everything you plan to say.

9. When presenting information on difficult subjects, you may want to consider providing _____ for the audience.

10. If giving a presentation to an audience that is far away, you can _____ your presentation to be viewed on a Web site.

Think Critically

Directions: *Answer the following questions on the lines provided.*

1. Which option for creating a new presentation works best for you? Explain.

_____

_____

2. What are disadvantages to adding clip art to PowerPoint® presentations?

_____

_____

3. Why is it important to limit each slide in a presentation to a main concept or idea?

_____

_____

4. Why is it important to preview your presentation from the back of the room?

_____

_____

5. Which of the seven tips for finalizing effective presentations was the most meaningful to you? Why?

_____

_____

_____

Extend Your Knowledge

Directions: *Choose one of the following projects. Complete the exercises on a separate sheet of paper.*

A. In addition to PowerPoint®, other software is available to create professional-looking presentations. Conduct research online or in software catalogs to find one other presentation program. Create a Venn diagram to compare and contrast the features of this program to those of PowerPoint®.

B. Work in small groups, one for each of the PowerPoint® presentation views described in this chapter. In the groups, create text slides in your assigned view to summarize this chapter. Give your presentation to the class, and discuss the effectiveness of each view.

chapter
11
Multimedia Basics

© Pearson Education, Inc.

Different Media Offer Powerful Choices For centuries, people have shared their thoughts and ideas by speaking, drawing pictures, or using written words. When you talk or write words on paper, you use one medium, or means of expressing information. Today, however, computers allow people to use many different media (the plural of *medium*) at the same time.

When you play a video game, watch a movie, or visit a Web site, you see many kinds of media, such as text, graphics, audio, video, and animation. A few years ago, it took expensive equipment and a lot of experience to combine these different media. Today, ordinary PCs and inexpensive software tools allow anyone to create entertaining and useful presentations or programs, using any combination of media they choose.

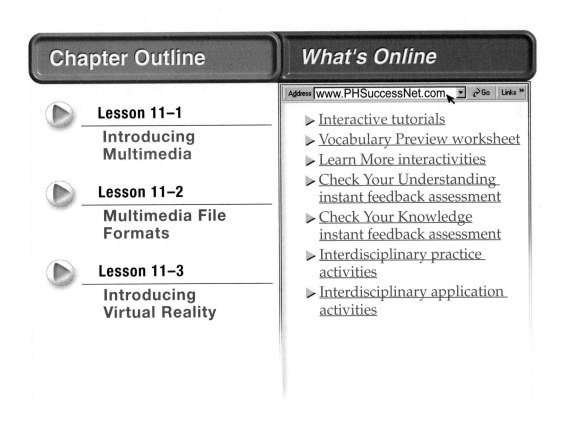

Chapter Outline

▶ **Lesson 11–1**
Introducing Multimedia

▶ **Lesson 11–2**
Multimedia File Formats

▶ **Lesson 11–3**
Introducing Virtual Reality

What's Online

Address www.PHSuccessNet.com ⟳ Go Links »

➤ Interactive tutorials
➤ Vocabulary Preview worksheet
➤ Learn More interactivities
➤ Check Your Understanding instant feedback assessment
➤ Check Your Knowledge instant feedback assessment
➤ Interdisciplinary practice activities
➤ Interdisciplinary application activities

Introducing Multimedia

Objectives

- Define *multimedia* and compare multimedia and interactive multimedia.

- Explain how multimedia is used in various fields.

- Identify tools used to produce multimedia presentations.

As You Read

Organize Information Use a main idea/detail chart to help you identify details about multimedia applications as you read.

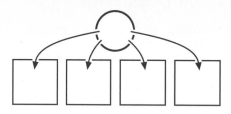

What's Online

In Lesson 11–1 of the iText, you will find more features and information for this lesson, including:

- Interactive tutorials
- As You Read worksheet
- Learn More interactivities
- Check Your Understanding interactive assessments
- Interactive lesson review

🔑 Key Terms

- multimedia (p. 156)
- interactive multimedia (p. 156)
- sound card (p. 158)
- video capture board (p. 158)
- video editor (p. 158)
- frame rate (p. 158)

Defining Multimedia

A medium is one way to communicate information or express ideas. Talking is a medium, as is writing or drawing. Different media can be combined together in many ways. An animated cartoon, for example, combines moving graphics (one medium) with sound and music (other media). This is what is meant by the term **multimedia**—combining different media to express information or ideas. A multimedia event can include text, graphics, sound, video, and animation.

Because multimedia can take so many forms and be used in so many ways, terms such as *event* or *experience* are often used to describe it. A multimedia event can be many things. Movies and television programs are common examples, but so is a lecture where the speaker displays slides or uses a chalkboard. Many kinds of computer programs use multimedia, from games to encyclopedias.

Not all examples of multimedia, however, are interactive. **Interactive multimedia** allow the user to make choices about what is displayed. Computer and video games, educational computer software, and some Web sites—which let you decide what you see and how you interact with the information—are all examples of interactive multimedia.

To be interactive, a multimedia event must provide more than audio or video. It must also give the user a way to control the action. In an interactive program, you make choices that determine what happens next. Think of a video game that lets you direct a character through a series of passages and then go back again. A multimedia encyclopedia provides navigation tools that let you jump to any topic you like, play audio or video clips, open Web pages, and view other kinds of content whenever you want.

Using Multimedia

Multimedia applications are widely used today in business, education, and entertainment.

Business Multimedia technologies help businesses communicate with their customers and employees. Many corporate Web sites, for example, use sound, video, or animation to demonstrate products to customers.

Businesses also use multimedia to train employees. For example, many companies create custom multimedia programs that workers can access via CD-ROM or a network. These programs use audio and video to demonstrate products and explain procedures. These programs can be interactive, which allows workers to jump to different areas of the content at will or take tests that provide feedback about their knowledge.

Education Multimedia can make learning more fun for students and provides extra tools for teachers. Interactive software can teach lessons, present quizzes, and give students immediate feedback to help them see how well they are doing.

Multimedia programs offer audio and video to enhance learning in ways that printed text alone cannot. For instance, instructional software may use audio to teach languages. Multimedia encyclopedias can play video clips from historical events.

Entertainment Video and computer games are multimedia programs. Flight simulators use rapidly changing graphics and sound to put the player "inside the cockpit" of a plane. Action games use realistic graphics and color to create the experience. But interactivity is what gives these games their true appeal. Using a game controller or keyboard, you can direct the action from start to finish. As you make choices about what action to take, you determine what the program will do next.

Technology @ School

The sales catalogs that are sent to schools these days don't just include books. They also offer a large number of multimedia programs that can be used in teaching various subjects.

Think *About* **It!**

Think about what benefits a school might gain from purchasing multimedia programs. Circle the items below that name a benefit.

- easier material
- providing immediate feedback to students
- capturing students' attention
- making an actual teacher unnecessary
- matching students' learning styles to material (whether they learn best through sight or sound)

© Pearson Education, Inc.

Figure 11.1.1 Many schools and libraries use multimedia programs to teach all kinds of subjects to people of all ages.

Camera Operator The people who operate the cameras that record movies, television shows, and other multimedia events are creative people, but they are also knowledgeable about the equipment they use and able to adapt to rapidly changing technology.

Camera operation is a competitive field, but it is expected to grow as multimedia applications expand in many areas. Interested candidates should take related courses in college or at a vocational institute and try to get experience working in related fields.

Creating Multimedia

Special tools are needed to create multimedia presentations. Some produce sound while others produce video and animation.

Sound Card A **sound card** is a special expansion board that allows the computer to input, edit, and output sounds. Audio—whether voices, music, or sound effects—is entered into the computer through the input jacks on the sound card. Once audio is captured on the computer's hard drive, you can edit and work with it. You can then play it through the computer's speakers or headphones, or save it to a disc. You can also send it to another audio device using the sound card's output jack. Full-featured cards even include optical inputs and outputs for digital sound and special software for mixing sound.

Video Capture Board Video signals, such as those from television programs or movies, have to be converted into a format that computers understand. This is done with a **video capture board,** a special card that plugs into a computer. You can transfer video to the capture board from camcorders, VCRs, digital cameras, and other sources.

Video Editor After video and audio are saved to the computer's hard drive, you can combine them in new ways. You do this work with a video editor. A **video editor** is a program that allows you to cut and paste sound and video segments and change the order in which segments appear. Video editors also allow you to define the **frame rate,** or how many still images are displayed in one second, and specify the speed at which video should be displayed.

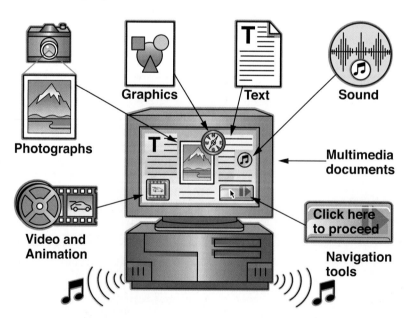

Figure 11.1.2 Today's multimedia products use several kinds of data, from simple text to sound to video.

Demonstrate Your Knowledge

Critical Thinking

1. Why is television an example of multimedia? What would make a television show an example of interactive multimedia?

   _____

   _____

2. Suppose you are asked to review an educational CD-ROM on U.S. geography. What features might you expect the program to offer?

   _____

   _____

3. Why do you think sound cards and video capture boards are essential multimedia development tools?

   _____

   _____

Activities

1. Complete the following chart to identify the uses of three types of multimedia tools.

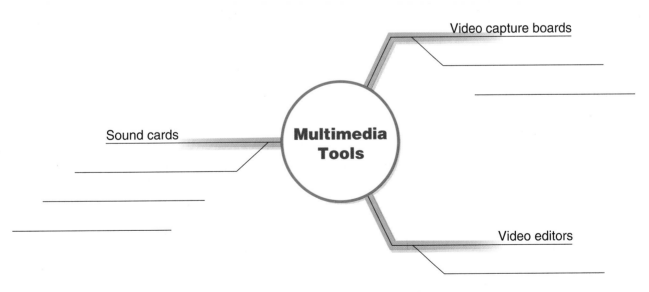

2. Research two multimedia encyclopedias on CD-ROM at the library or in the school media center. Choose a topic you are studying in one of your classes and look up this topic in both encyclopedias. Compare the content and the multimedia features of the two resources. Present your findings in a chart, and then provide a conclusion about which program makes better use of multimedia resources.

Lesson 11–2

Multimedia File Formats

Objectives

- Identify video file formats.
- Summarize audio file formats and the platforms on which they run.
- Explain popular formats used to flow multimedia across networks or the Internet.

As You Read

Outline Information Use an outline to help you understand multimedia tools as you read.

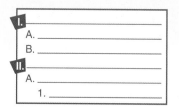

What's Online

In Lesson 11–2 of the iText, you will find more features and information for this lesson, including:

- Interactive tutorials
- As You Read worksheet
- Learn More interactivities
- Check Your Understanding interactive assessments
- Interactive lesson review

Key Terms

- encoder (p. 161)
- synthesize (p. 161)

Video File Formats

Multimedia can combine text, audio, graphics, video, and animation. To do such complicated work, designers choose from a number of file formats, each suited for a specific task.

MPEG MPEG is a family of formats developed by the Moving Picture Experts Group. Web sites and CD-based products commonly use MPEG to display video such as movie clips, animations, and recorded television broadcasts. MPEG files offer full-motion video; thus, they give a very realistic effect. In fact, the quality of a basic MPEG file is only slightly lower than that of a VCR recording.

MPEG-2 improves on the basic MPEG format and can be stored in a much smaller file. The quality of the video is as high as a television set can display, and the audio is CD-quality. MPEG-2 video is the format used in DVDs.

QuickTime® Designed by Apple® Computer, QuickTime® is the basic file format for showing animation and video on Macintosh computers. QuickTime® videos also can be viewed on Windows® computers, but a special player must first be installed. The QuickTime® format is often used for high-quality movie trailers shown on Web sites. It is also used for the video feeds from Web sites that provide news and weather information.

AVI Audio Video Interleave, or AVI, is another name for Microsoft® Video for Windows® format. Some AVI videos are not of the best quality, but they can be played on any Windows® computer. Many businesses create their multimedia in AVI format to tap into the huge market of Windows® users.

© Pearson Education, Inc.

Audio File Formats

While formats like MPEG, QuickTime®, and AVI capture both pictures and sound, other formats can be the best choice when sound quality is a priority.

MP3 MPEG audio layer 3 (MP3) files are very common today, thanks to the ease of downloading music from the Internet. The MP3 format takes a large audio file and makes it very small. It does this using regular compression methods and also by removing data from the music file that the human ear cannot hear. This results in a much smaller file, with little or no loss of sound quality.

WMA WMA is the music format of Microsoft®. It stands for Windows Media Audio®.

AU AU, or audio, is the standard format for audio files for the UNIX operating system.

WAV The waveform audio (WAV) format is built into the Microsoft Windows operating system. WAV files can be played on almost any computer system. WAV and WMA files can be converted into MP3 files using a hardware device or special software programs called **encoders** that convert the files from one format to another.

MIDI Musical Instrument Digital Interface, or MIDI, is a standard that allows a computer to control a musical instrument. MIDI sounds are **synthesized.** This means that sounds imitative of musical instruments are generated by the computer when they are played; no actual recorded sound is stored in the file.

Did You Know?

It is a crime to create a duplicate tape, CD, or DVD and then sell it for profit. This type of piracy, called intellectual piracy, is theft because the original artists and producers do not make the money they deserve from their work.

The international community is cooperating in stamping out intellectual piracy. In 2002, for example, officials in the Philippines destroyed two million pirated CDs and tapes!

Figure 11.2.1 Multimedia players let you play many kinds of media on your PC. Here, Windows Media® Player is being used to listen to an audio CD.

Technology @ Work

Have you heard of elevator music—that soothing music that plays in the background in elevators, hallways, and offices? Well, how about elevator multimedia?

Think *About* **It!**

Think about the kinds of multimedia productions that might be appropriate in public places. Circle each statement below that identifies a usable idea.

> an online multimedia news service

> a dramatic short story

> illustrated readings of poems

> a pattern of colors and shapes "matching" music

> a series of violent action scenes

Multimedia Players for the Internet

Several players are commonly used to play finished multimedia content on the Internet. Other players are used to develop multimedia content.

Windows Media®, QuickTime®, and RealOne Players

These three players are very popular for playing streaming audio and video—that is, content that is broadcast in a continuous feed from Web sites. They are also useful for playing content from some disc-based multimedia products.

All of these players can handle a wide variety of audio and video formats, although each one has its own unique format. You can use any of these players to listen to music broadcast by online radio stations, watch news and weather reports, check out movie trailers and music videos, and enjoy many other kinds of multimedia content. Many people have all three of these players installed on their computer.

Flash™ and Shockwave® Players Multimedia developers can use special file programs called Shockwave® and Flash™ to create interactive multimedia content, such as animated games. These programs can accept user input, use high-quality audio and graphics, and are very small so they can be downloaded quickly from a Web site or disk. To view content created in these programs you need the Flash™ Player and the Shockwave® Player, both of which are free.

Spotlight on...

GEORGE HARRISON

❝ *It is the first complete album of synthesized music by a major rock star, and the antithesis [direct opposite] of the rigid pop sound that put the Beatles in the spotlight: 100 percent synthesizer, no beats, no songs.* ❞

Greg Cahill
Reviewer, Metroactive Music

That quotation is from a tribute written after the death of George Harrison in 2002. Harrison is best known as a member of the Beatles, the music sensation of the 1960s and 1970s. But Harrison was a musical innovator in his own right. His 1969 release *Electronic Sound*, for example, led to more experimentation by other musicians and, ultimately, to the rave generation of music.

© Pearson Education, Inc.

Demonstrate Your Knowledge

Critical Thinking

1. Suppose a racing-bike manufacturer wants to feature a short video of new bicycle frames on its Web site. What advantage does the AVI format offer? Disadvantage?

   _____

   _____

2. Why might you want to use an encoder to convert a WAV file to an MP3 file?

   _____

   _____

3. What do people gain by having the Flash™ Player or the Shockwave® Player?

   _____

   _____

Activities

1. Complete the following chart to summarize details about multimedia file formats.

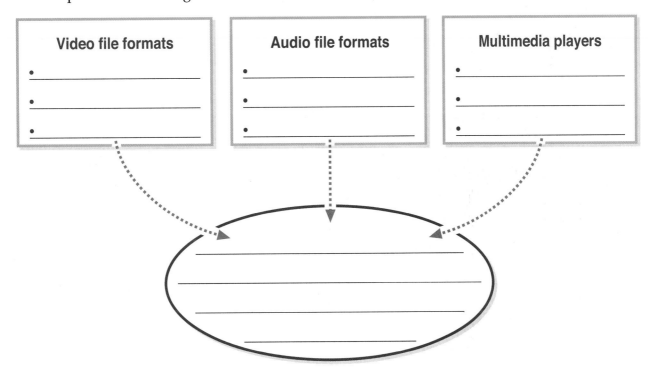

2. Work with a partner. Conduct a keyword search to locate Web sites that describe the features of one of the multimedia formats discussed in this lesson.

Introducing Virtual Reality

Objectives

- Explain what virtual reality is and describe some methods of presenting it.
- Identify uses of virtual reality.
- Discuss computer and video games.

As You Read

Organize Information Use a concept web to help you organize details about virtual reality as you read.

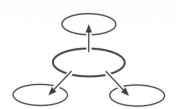

What's Online

In Lesson 11–3 of the iText, you will find more features and information for this lesson, including:

- Interactive tutorials
- As You Read worksheet
- Learn More interactivities
- Check Your Understanding interactive assessments
- Interactive lesson review

Key Terms

- virtual reality (VR) (p. 164)
- head-mounted display (HMD) (p. 164)
- Cave Automatic Virtual Environment (CAVE) (p. 165)
- Virtual Reality Modeling Language (VRML) (p. 165)
- simulation (p. 166)

Forms of Virtual Reality

The term **virtual reality,** or **VR,** is used to describe three-dimensional, computer-generated environments that you can explore by using special hardware and software. Such environments simulate spaces of various kinds, such as the flight deck of an airliner or the interior of a fantastic palace. But the purpose of all VR environments is the same: to let users explore every aspect of space, moving in any direction, just as if that space was real.

Sophisticated hardware and software are needed to create large-scale, detailed VR environments. Users can explore such environments in several different ways.

HMD A **head-mounted display,** or **HMD,** is usually a helmet or a set of goggles that wraps around the head, blocking out light. A tiny computer monitor is located in front of each eye. Using these two separate monitors gives the illusion of three dimensions. HMDs often have headphones to provide audio to the user.

In advanced HMDs, tiny sensors can tell when the user's head tilts in any direction. The image on the monitors then shifts accordingly, in order to create a convincing illusion of being part of the action, rather than a spectator of it.

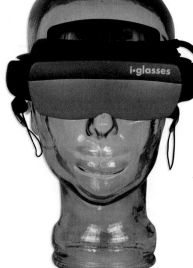

Figure 11.3.1 A head-mounted display is a portable, relatively inexpensive way to experience virtual reality.

CAVE The **Cave Automatic Virtual Environment,** or **CAVE,** is an expensive and advanced form of VR. Images of a virtual world are projected on the walls of a room. Visitors wear special goggles that create the illusion of three dimensions. The result is so realistic and so convincing that most "explorers" cannot tell where reality ends and virtual reality begins without reaching out and touching something.

In many CAVEs, users wear special gloves (called data gloves) or hold special wands, either of which can detect hand movements. These devices allow users to interact with objects in the virtual world, by opening doors, for example, or picking up the pieces in a virtual chess game.

Virtual Worlds Online To create virtual worlds on the Internet, programmers use a language called **Virtual Reality Modeling Language,** or **VRML.** VRML allows programmers to describe objects that appear in the virtual world. The objects can be shapes, buildings, landscapes, or characters.

To view VRML Web pages, you may need to download and install a special plug-in for your browser. You could then, for example, visit the Rossetti Archives, a collection of paintings by nineteenth-century painter Dante Gabriel Rossetti. The Rossetti Archives exist only online, as a virtual reality gallery. You visit the gallery through your Web browser, which lets you "walk" through the three-dimensional virtual museum. As you move about, you can even look at the paintings from different angles.

Connections

Science Many educators believe virtual reality is having a major impact on science classrooms. Students can now "visit" and explore various ecosystems—take a stroll in a rain forest, for example, or shiver on the Alaskan tundra. Students studying anatomy can get a 3-D view of the respiratory system, the digestive system, and so on. Students opposed to dissecting animals can cut apart a virtual frog, making that experiment less distasteful.

Real-World Tech

Strolling Through Comet Tails A new virtual reality deep vision display wall at Boston University will let students and professors stroll through comet tails, walk through the sun's weather, observe an earthquake, and study how air flows around airplanes. Two IBM supercomputers and 24 projectors fill a 15 x 8-foot screen with a high-resolution stereo image. The images change as the visitors move through the room.

What other phenomena could usefully be explored in a room like this? Write your ideas below.

_____

_____

Practical Applications of Virtual Reality

Virtual reality has become very useful for **simulations.** Simulations are virtual reality programs that mimic a specific place, job, or function. Virtual reality is used in many design and architectural businesses. It is also used in the military to train fighter pilots and combat soldiers without the risks of live training. In medicine, virtual reality is used to simulate complex surgery for training surgeons without using actual patients.

Computer and Video Games

The first electronic games displayed only simple, two-dimensional images with limited sounds. Today, because of virtual reality, you can choose from hundreds of games with detailed graphics, lifelike characters, and realistic environments.

Computer Games Today's PCs, with their fast processors, powerful sound and graphics cards, and large displays, let you get the most from your games. Games for PCs usually come on compact discs.

Game Consoles A game console is a device that uses a television to display a game. You interact with the game by using one or more controls, which are connected to the console. Consoles use games that are full-fledged computer programs. But, unlike computers, consoles are dedicated to game playing.

Online Games Many PC games are available on the Internet. Multiplayer versions of these games allow multiple players to compete in real time, and keep score. To participate, you need a new model game console or a PC with multimedia features and a fast Internet connection.

Station.com

Figure 11.3.2 Using virtual reality techniques, game developers can create lifelike characters and environments.

© Pearson Education, Inc.

Demonstrate Your Knowledge

Critical Thinking

1. Why do CAVEs present virtual reality environments better than HMDs?

_____

_____

2. Why might an architect use virtual reality, instead of two-dimensional drawings, to present a design to a client?

_____

_____

3. Why do you think some people might prefer game consoles to multiplayer online gaming?

_____

_____

Activities

1. Complete the following chart to show the effects of virtual reality tools.

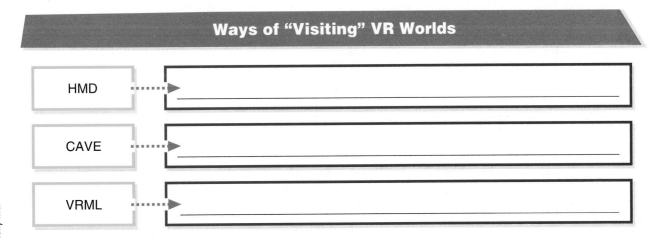

Ways of "Visiting" VR Worlds

HMD	_____
CAVE	_____
VRML	_____

2. Locate the Rossetti Archives online and tour the gallery. Compare the experience to any museum you have visited in person. How are they alike? How are they different?

Use the Vocabulary

Directions: *Match each vocabulary term in the left column with the correct definition in the right column. Write the appropriate letter next to the word or term.*

_____ **1.** multimedia
_____ **2.** video capture board
_____ **3.** video editor
_____ **4.** frame rate
_____ **5.** encoder
_____ **6.** synthesize
_____ **7.** virtual reality
_____ **8.** head-mounted display
_____ **9.** CAVE
_____ **10.** simulation

a. computer program that mimics a specific place, job, or function

b. very realistic form of virtual reality that is displayed in a room

c. hardware that lets a computer work with video data

d. software that changes a WAV file into MP3 format

e. using more than one medium to express information or ideas

f. program that lets users manipulate sound and video

g. realistic, but simulated, 3-D world

h. number of still images displayed in one second

i. helmet or goggles used to display a virtual reality environment

j. the process in which a computer generates sounds

Check Your Comprehension

Directions: *Circle the correct choice for each of the following.*

1. What kind of multimedia lets users make choices about the direction a program may take?
   a. graphic multimedia
   b. animated multimedia
   c. interactive multimedia
   d. technical multimedia

2. What hardware allows a computer to imput, edit, and output audio?
   a. a sound card
   b. a video editor
   c. AU
   d. 3-D

3. Which audio file format does a computer use to produce synthesized sounds?
   a. CAVE
   b. CD-ROM
   c. MIDI
   d. AVI

4. Which of the following file formats allows you to view interactive multimedia games on your computer?
   a. MPEG-2
   b. Shockwave®
   c. video capture board
   d. Net video

5. Where are the monitors in an HMD located?
   a. on the wall
   b. in a helmet or a set of goggles
   c. in a room
   d. online

6. Which of the following would NOT be a good choice for a simulation?
   a. gallbladder operation
   b. driver education
   c. space mission
   d. study-skills class

© Pearson Education, Inc.

Think Critically

Directions: *Answer the following questions on the lines provided.*

1. For what purpose might a business want to hire a computer specialist who knows QuickTime® and AVI?

2. What equipment and software would you need to develop your own multiplayer online game?

3. What two file formats are commonly used for interactive games found on Web sites?

4. Why is a virtual reality simulation used to train fighter pilots an example of interactive multimedia?

5. What is an example of how an electronic textbook might make use of VR technology?

Extend Your Knowledge

Directions: *Choose one of the following projects. Complete the exercises on a separate sheet of paper.*

A. In groups of four students, choose a topic you are studying in language arts, social studies, science, math, art, or music. Plan a two-minute multimedia presentation on that topic that includes at least one example of each of these media: audio, video, text, and graphics. Assign one medium to each member to complete. Use groupware or collaborative software to review one another's work. Then, use a video editor to combine the pieces into a smooth, logical sequence.

B. Electronic games can be a lot of fun, but some people believe that youngsters spend too much time playing them. Conduct online or library research to identify some specific objections that people have to these games. Then, debate the pros and cons of electronic games, using your research and your own gaming experiences as resources. Which argument was the most persuasive? Why?

chapter 12

Communications Basics

Why Are Telephones Valuable? Think of how important the telephone is to you. You call friends and relatives all the time. They could be across the street or across the country. In either case, technology makes your conversation possible and keeps it crisp and clear.

The telephone system provides valuable services to businesses, communities, and schools. If you need medicine, for example, your doctor might call in the prescription to the drugstore. If your school wants people to know about a school play, the drama teacher might fax a press release to the local newspaper.

Do you want to browse the Internet? Send e-mail or a fax? Chat with a friend through your computer? All these forms of communication rely on telephone networks.

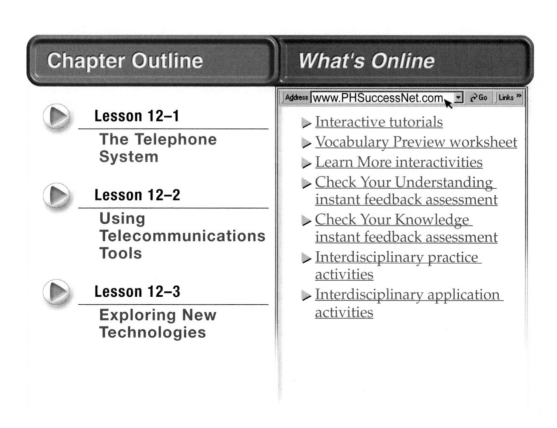

Chapter Outline

▶ **Lesson 12–1**

The Telephone System

▶ **Lesson 12–2**

Using Telecommunications Tools

▶ **Lesson 12–3**

Exploring New Technologies

What's Online

Address www.PHSuccessNet.com ⟳Go Links »

▶ Interactive tutorials
▶ Vocabulary Preview worksheet
▶ Learn More interactivities
▶ Check Your Understanding instant feedback assessment
▶ Check Your Knowledge instant feedback assessment
▶ Interdisciplinary practice activities
▶ Interdisciplinary application activities

© Pearson Education, Inc.

The Telephone System

Objectives

- Explain how local and long-distance telephone calls are made.
- Compare and contrast analog and digital connections.
- Identify the technologies that handle telephone calls.

As You Read

Organize Information Use a spider map to help you organize ways in which the telephone system operates as you read.

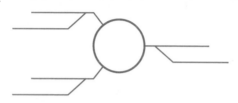

What's Online

In Lesson 12–1 of the iText, you will find more features and information for this lesson, including:

- Interactive tutorials
- As You Read worksheet
- Learn More interactivities
- Check Your Understanding interactive assessments
- Interactive lesson review

🔑 Key Terms

- telecommunications (p. 172)
- local loop (p. 173)
- analog (p. 173)
- digital (p. 173)
- twisted pair (p. 174)
- fiber-optic cable (p. 174)
- infrared (p. 174)
- microwave (p. 174)

Communicating by Telephone

The first telephone message was sent in 1876 over a line connecting two rooms. Eventually telephone cables were connected to a central office. Operators in the office could connect calls to anyone on the network. Today's equipment can connect telephones anywhere in the world.

Telecommunications Formats Sending information over a telephone network is called **telecommunications.** Telecommunications has grown due to the demand for instant communication. Today, people use many forms of telecommunications to rapidly relay information:

- telephones
- cell phones
- pagers
- e-mail
- Internet
- fax machines

Public Switched Telephone Network Phone calls are made through the Public Switched Telephone Network (PSTN). This network forms a circuit between the caller's telephone and another telephone. Even if the circuit is long and complicated, the quality of the sound sent through the system is generally good.

Figure 12.1.1 Today, telephones are so common and easy to use that we take them for granted.

Making Telephone Calls

In the past, one company provided all the telephone services in the United States. Today, people choose a long-distance company and, in some areas, a local telephone company.

Local Calls   People subscribe to a local telephone company to use the PSTN. This company provides directly wired services between the homes and businesses that belong to the local network. Within your neighborhood, telephones connect to a common network for telephone service. This common network, called the **local loop,** connects to the phone company's central office. Much of the local loop is an analog system. An **analog** system sends electrical signals that carry voice and other sounds.

Long-Distance Calls   Outside the local loop, the long-distance telephone system today is mostly digital. **Digital** connections use computer code and can carry voice, data, and video on a single line. When you dial a long-distance number, computers figure out how to complete your call. To connect analog and digital networks, special equipment changes analog signals into digital signals.

Contrasting Analog and Digital Communications   People often confuse the terms "analog" and "digital" when they are talking about communications or computers. The difference is important but easy to understand. In analog communications, sounds (such as a person's voice, music, or some other kind of sound) are transmitted as waves. Analog sound waves change shape and strength rapidly. In digital communications, sounds are converted into binary data (a series of 1s and 0s), just like other kinds of computer data.

To travel across great distances, either with or without wires, analog waves and digital data must be carried by a signal. When wires are used, a weak electrical signal may act as the carrier. In wireless communications, high-frequency radio waves are often used as the carrier.

Parts of a Telephone Number

1	214	555	7804
Long Distance	**Area Code**	**Prefix**	**Line Number**
Finds the country code (1 is the code for the United States.)	Finds a geographic area (214 is the code for Dallas, Texas.)	Finds a local-rate area	Finds a specific phone line

© Pearson Education, Inc.

The Wired—and the Wireless—World

Wires connect the phone jack in your wall to an interface box outside. Outside wires may be above or below ground. Wires also connect your local loop with distant places.

Twisted Pair At first, the entire telephone system depended on twisted pair technology. **Twisted pair** refers to a pair of copper wires that are twisted together to reduce interference, or outside noise. In the United States today, most homes and business buildings still have twisted pair wiring.

Fiber-Optic Cables **Fiber-optic cables** are strands of fiberglass that transmit digital data by pulses of light. These cables can carry large quantities of information. They work faster and more efficiently than copper wires.

Wireless Wireless communication frees users from traditional telephone lines. Messages are sent on radio or infrared signals. **Infrared** signals are light waves that cannot be seen by the human eye. Cell phones, for example, use radio signals.

Before fiber-optic cables, high-frequency radio waves called **microwave** signals were used to relay long-distance telecommunications. Microwaves are broadcast from repeater tower to repeater tower in a straight line.

Satellites orbiting Earth also transfer voice and data. Satellites provide an efficient means to handle large amounts of phone calls and data.

 Spotlight on...

BELL LABS

In the 1960s, New Jersey-based Bell Labs could not keep up with the number of telephone calls it received. Bell Labs decided to attempt using computers, instead of mechanical equipment, to monitor the company's incoming calls. The computers would automatically adjust the acceptance rate of the calls based on the quantity received by the system.

Developing electronic switching systems helped Bell Labs offer many new services to

its customers. Although the number of calls made to Bell Labs (today, part of Lucent Technologies) continues to grow, the basic principles of the system developed more than 30 years ago remain.

Demonstrate Your Knowledge

Critical Thinking

1. What happens to connect a local telephone call?

_____

_____

2. How do analog and digital communication systems differ?

_____

_____

3. What advantages does wireless communication offer over traditional phone lines?

_____

_____

Activities

1. Complete the following sequence chart to show how a long-distance telephone call is received by another telephone.

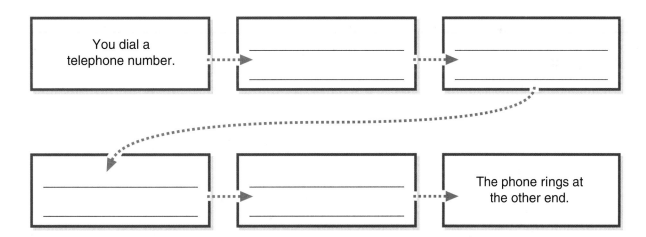

2. What role does the telephone play in your personal life? Work as a class to make a list of the purposes of the telephone in your lives.

Using Telecommunications Tools

Objectives

- Sequence the steps in a modem transmission.
- Explain how fax machines operate.
- Summarize how modems and fax machines have changed the ways people communicate.

As You Read

Compare and Contrast Use a Venn diagram to help you compare and contrast modems and fax machines as you read.

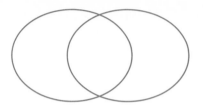

What's Online

In Lesson 12-2 of the iText, you will find more features and information for this lesson, including:

- Interactive tutorials
- As You Read worksheet
- Learn More interactivities
- Check Your Understanding interactive assessments
- Interactive lesson review

Key Terms

- modem (p. 176)
- modulation (p. 176)
- demodulation (p. 176)
- bits per second (bps) (p. 177)
- fax machine (p. 178)
- fax modem (p. 178)

Using Modems

Many computers use phone lines to connect to the Internet. Your computer is a digital device. The local loop that connects you to the telephone system, however, is analog. How do digital and analog signals work together? Modems make it possible.

How Modems Work A **modem** is a device that allows a computer to transmit data through telephone lines to other computers. Any kind of digital data can be sent—pictures, audio, or video. When you use the Internet, your computer uses a modem to connect to other computers.

The word *modem* actually names the work the device does: modulation and demodulation. Through **modulation,** the modem changes the digital signal of the computer to the analog sounds used by telephones. Then, the data can travel over the telephone wires. When the data arrives at its destination, the receiving modem changes the analog signals back to digital. This process is called **demodulation.** As a digital signal, the data is understandable to the receiving computer.

Figure 12.2.1 A 56K modem, like the one shown here, is a hardware device that enables your PC to send and receive data through a standard telephone line.

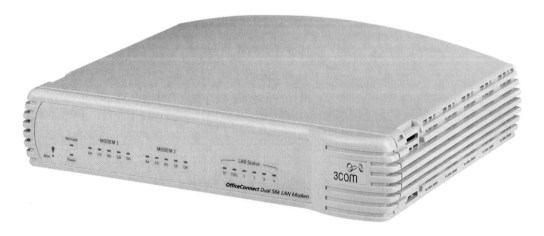

© Pearson Education, Inc.

When you direct your computer to connect to the Internet, the modem changes the digital command into an analog signal. When you visit a Web site, the text and images you see are changed from digital to analog signals to get to your computer. Then, your modem changes the signals back to digital to make the text and images visible on your screen.

Kinds of Modems A modem is a separate piece of equipment that can be housed inside or outside a computer. An external modem is connected by a special cable to a computer. A wire connects the modem to the telephone line. When the computer needs to send data, it connects to the modem. The external modem then connects to the telephone network through the telephone line.

An internal modem is placed inside a computer. A telephone line connects the modem directly to the telephone system—no extra cable is needed.

Modem Speed Modem speed is measured in bits per second. **Bits per second**, or **bps,** is the amount of data that can be sent in one second. In the early days of modems, only 300 bps could be transmitted. Today, modems have the ability to transmit 56,600 bps—nearly 200 times more information per second than the early modems.

The Arts Can a fax machine create art? Artist and lecturer Margaret Turner of Australia thinks so.

To demonstrate a connection between human emotions and computers, Margaret borrowed handkerchiefs—plain and fancy, white and patterned. The handkerchief represented a human element becoming art through an electronic medium.

She scanned the handkerchiefs into a computer and manipulated the images. Then, she faxed the resulting images to a gallery for a special exhibit called "Electric Hankie."

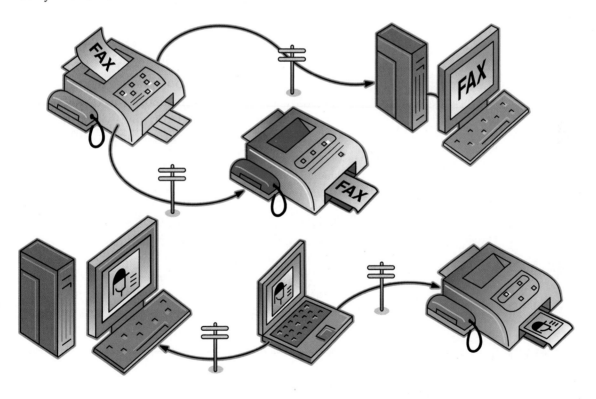

Figure 12.2.2 Fax machines and fax modems can send and receive documents to one another using standard telephone lines.

© Pearson Education, Inc.

Technology @ Work

Many stores now use special scanners at the checkout counters. These scanners read the Universal Product Code on a package and record the product and price on the sales receipt.

Think *About* It!

Think about the advantages store scanners offer. Next to each item below, write *T* if it identifies an advantage and *F* if it does not.

▶ Price changes can be entered in a central computer rather than stickered on a package.

▶ The computer prevents clerks from entering mistakes.

▶ The computer tracks the number of products sold.

▶ The computer cuts down on the need for employees.

Sending Faxes

Even without a computer, you can send printed messages over phone lines. A facsimile machine, or **fax machine,** is a device that allows you to send pages of information to another fax machine anywhere in the world. Fax machines can send hand-written documents, printed text, pictures, blueprints, or anything else on a page.

How Fax Machines Work As a document enters a fax machine, a sensor scans it. The data becomes a digital signal. An internal modem in the fax machine then changes the digital signal to an analog signal. The receiving fax machine accepts the analog signal, changes it back to digital, and prints a copy of the original document.

How Fax Modems Work A **fax modem** is a computer modem that is able to send and receive faxes. Built-in technology lets it communicate with fax machines and other fax modems.

If your computer has a fax modem, software can translate any document on your computer into an image the fax modem can understand. The fax modem dials the number of the receiving fax machine and begins the transmission. The receiving fax machine accepts the analog signal and converts the tones into a digital signal. A copy of the original document is transmitted to the receiver's computer.

How Scanners Work To send something sketched or printed on paper using a fax modem, you will need a scanner to translate the document into a digital format. A scanner is a device that reads information on paper as a digital signal. Once stored in the computer, a scanned document can be sent over telephone lines to other computers or fax machines.

Impact of Fax Transmissions Modems and fax machines have broadened how people communicate using telephone lines. Modems allow computers to connect to the Internet, other computers, and business networks. Fax machines and fax modems let people send contracts, news items, and other printed documents to businesses, schools, and homes.

Figure 12.2.3 In business, fax machines have become nearly as important as telephones and computers.

© Pearson Education, Inc.

Demonstrate Your Knowledge

Critical Thinking

1. What steps make the digital-analog-digital connection that lets one computer send a message to another?

_____

_____

2. How does a fax machine work?

_____

_____

3. What business problems do scanners solve?

_____

_____

Activities

1. Complete the concept web below to review the functions of a modem.

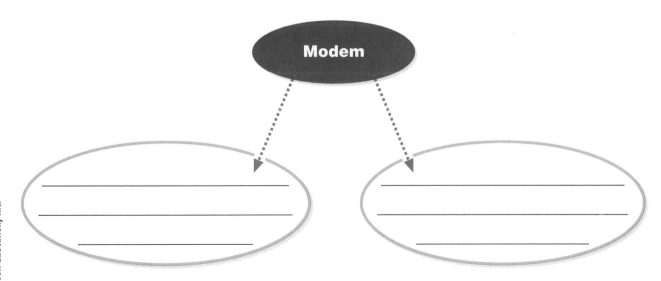

2. Observe someone scanning a document into a computer as you outline each step in the process. Then, ask if you can scan a document to practice the steps.

Exploring New Technologies

Objectives

- Explain the importance of bandwidth.
- Identify alternatives to analog systems.
- Predict advances in telecommunications.

As You Read

Organize Information Use a chart to help you identify various new technologies as you read.

What's Online

In Lesson 12–3 of the iText, you will find more features and information for this lesson, including:

- Interactive tutorials
- As You Read worksheet
- Learn More interactivities
- Check Your Understanding interactive assessments
- Interactive lesson review

Key Terms

- bandwidth (p. 180)
- broadband (p. 181)

Introducing Bandwidth

People always want faster, better, and less expensive telecommunications choices. Some improvements are limited, however, by the twisted pair copper wiring that exists in many homes and businesses in the United States. That wiring, in fact, is called the "last mile problem"—the last mile between the local analog connection and the digital superhighway. Telephone, cable, and computer companies are working on ways around the problem, but it is a very expensive problem to fix. Because of cost, major changes likely will not take place anytime soon.

Understanding Bandwidth **Bandwidth** is the amount of data a modem can send and receive through any network connection. The more bandwidth a modem has, the faster the connection. For example, a typical modem can transmit 56,600 bits per second (56.6 Kbps), while older modems could send only 14,400 bits per second (14.4 Kbps).

Connecting With ISDN One connection method that provides more bandwidth is ISDN service. ISDN stands for *Integrated Services Digital Network*. Offered by phone companies, this digital telephone service allows users to send data and voice over copper telephone wires more quickly.

An ISDN line is actually two separate phone connections. Each line has its own phone number. When the two connections are used at once for computer data, the bandwidth can measure up to 144 Kbps—more than double the speed of a typical modem. When a phone call comes in, the service automatically cuts back to 64 Kbps to answer the incoming call.

Figure 12.3.1 To use ISDN service, you need a special modem like this one.

© Pearson Education, Inc.

An ISDN connection requires a special ISDN adapter, sometimes called a digital modem. The adapter uses a digital signal rather than the telephone's analog signal.

ISDN and Bandwidth   While ISDN seems to offer a huge increase in bandwidth, it may not be enough. Imagine several people on different computers connecting to the Internet to visit Web pages, participate in video meetings, or send e-mail. These users need a lot of bandwidth and might benefit from services that transmit data faster than an ISDN line can.

Working With Broadband Transmission

Broadband is the general term for all high-speed digital connections that transmit at least 1.5 megabits per second (Mbps). Broadband transmission does not include ISDN or analog modems. Several broadband technologies already are available, and more are on the drawing board. This high transmission speed is required for videoconferencing, video-on-demand, and digital television services.

DSL   Digital Subscriber Line, or DSL, uses the same copper wires telephones use. However, it transmits data in digital form rather than analog. DSL allows for very fast connections to the Internet and features an "always-on" connection. There is one drawback to DSL: A user must be within a few miles of a local telephone switching station for a connection to be made.

Technology@ School

With all the ways that schools use technology these days, they need a lot of bandwidth to send and receive information electronically.

Think *About* **It!**
Think about who in your school might benefit from increased bandwidth. Circle the tasks below that would use bandwidth.

- students participating in a class teleconference
- a teacher researching Mars
- a librarian helping a student find a book
- a counselor checking student records
- a principal answering e-mail

Figure 12.3.2 In a video-conference, users in different locations transmit and receive audio, video, and computer data in real time. This kind of activity requires a great deal of bandwidth.

© Pearson Education, Inc.

Sales and Service Technician
Cable and satellite companies hire many sales and service technicians. These employees sell broadband services to customers and try to get current customers to upgrade their existing service. They also install and test the equipment.

Experience with technology is desirable, as is hands-on training specific to this industry. As more homes accept cable and satellite offerings, the need for sales and service technicians will grow to meet the demand.

Different companies offer DSL at different levels of service and price. Because of wiring limitations, most DSL subscribers receive data faster than they can send it. Thus, while DSL subscribers can receive Web pages, e-mail, and file downloads very quickly, DSL is not the best choice for sending large data files.

SONET Telephone companies that offer DSL and other Internet connection methods rely on a digital network called SONET. SONET stands for *Synchronous Optical Network*. It uses fiber optics to provide faster connections and greater bandwidth—52 Mbps to 1 Gbps (gigabits per second) or faster!

Cable and Digital Satellite Connections Some cable and digital television companies offer high-speed connections, too. Signals travel through the same cable or satellite that brings in television signals. The computer is connected to the cable service through a cable modem. Satellite television companies offer a similar service, but signals are received by the customer's satellite dish rather than through the customer's cable television company.

The Future of Bandwidth

The demand for bandwidth is growing. People want increased bandwidth for video-on-demand, meetings via the Internet, and Web-based learning. Thus, telephone and other high-tech companies continue to look for new ways to improve telecommunications services and data transmission.

Real-World Tech

Making Communication Possible It's not just governments and huge companies that put communications satellites into orbit. Students are doing it, too.

In 2001, for example, six students at the U.S. Naval Academy built a satellite with equipment anybody could buy: A tape measure was used as the antenna, and 24 AA batteries provided the power. Both a sailor in the Atlantic Ocean and some hikers in New Zealand used signals from the students' satellite to contact family at home.

How might students fund the cost of their experiments? Write your ideas below.

_____

_____

_____

Demonstrate Your Knowledge

Critical Thinking

1. What are the benefits of increased bandwidth?

_____

_____

2. How do telephone, cable television, and satellite television companies compare and contrast in the ways they offer Internet services to homes?

_____

_____

3. Which advance in telecommunications do you think will have the greatest impact on your future? Why?

_____

_____

Activities

1. Complete the following chart to compare and contrast regular twisted pair wiring to an ISDN line.

Twisted Pair Wiring	ISDN Line

2. Contact your local telephone company, a cable service provider, and a satellite provider. Find out about options for increasing bandwidth and telecommunications service in your area now and in the future. Record your findings in a three-column chart.

Use the Vocabulary

Directions: *Match each vocabulary term in the left column with the correct definition in the right column. Write the appropriate letter next to the word or term.*

_____ **1.** telecommunications

_____ **2.** analog

_____ **3.** digital

_____ **4.** fiber-optic cable

_____ **5.** microwave

_____ **6.** modulation

_____ **7.** demodulation

_____ **8.** bits per second

_____ **9.** bandwidth

_____ **10.** broadband

a. the measure of how much data can be sent through a network connection

b. system using computer code to carry different kinds of data

c. changing digital signals to analog

d. system using electrical signals that match the human voice and other sounds

e. high-frequency radio waves that carry data

f. strand of fiberglass that transmits data by pulses of light

g. using a telephone network to send information

h. high-speed digital connection of at least 1.5 Mbps

i. measurement of the speed at which data can be sent in one second

j. changing analog signals to digital

Check Your Comprehension

Directions: *Complete each sentence with information from the chapter.*

1. The _____ consists of the local loop and long-distance lines that handle data and voice communications.

2. The _____ part of your telephone number identifies the area of the country you live in.

3. In the long-distance telephone system, _____ largely have replaced twisted pair copper wire.

4. Radio and infrared signals make _____ communication possible.

5. If you have an _____ in your computer, you do not need a separate modem to connect to the Internet.

6. If you have a _____ in your computer, you do not need a fax machine to send faxes.

7. You could copy a printed page into your computer if you connected a _____ to your computer.

8. With _____ , your family could have two telephone lines and gain faster Internet connection.

9. *DSL* stands for _____.

10. The demand for _____ will continue to grow.

Think Critically

Directions: *Answer the following questions on the lines provided.*

1. Why is a modem needed to access the Internet?

_____

_____

2. Why is faxing an order to a company an example of telecommunications in action?

_____

_____

3. How have modems and fax machines changed the ways society communicates?

_____

_____

4. What challenges do you think telecommunications companies face in the near future?

_____

_____

5. Why might it be important for a home-office computer to have Internet service that offers a lot of bandwidth?

_____

_____

Extend Your Knowledge

Directions: *Choose one of the following projects. Complete the exercises on a separate sheet of paper.*

A. With the growing number of cell phones and computers that must be connected to phone lines, telephone companies must assign more telephone numbers. Sometimes they even need more area codes. Contact your local telephone company to find out how many telephone numbers can be assigned to a given area code and when the phone company anticipates assigning the next new area code. Present your findings to the class.

B. In a small group, choose a text or image to send. On a computer equipped with a scanner and a fax modem, scan the data into the computer and fax it to the designated computer. Retrieve the fax and print the scanned image. Then, compare the quality of the original to the scanned image and the fax. Summarize your findings about the quality of the output devices you analyzed.

chapter

13 Networking Basics

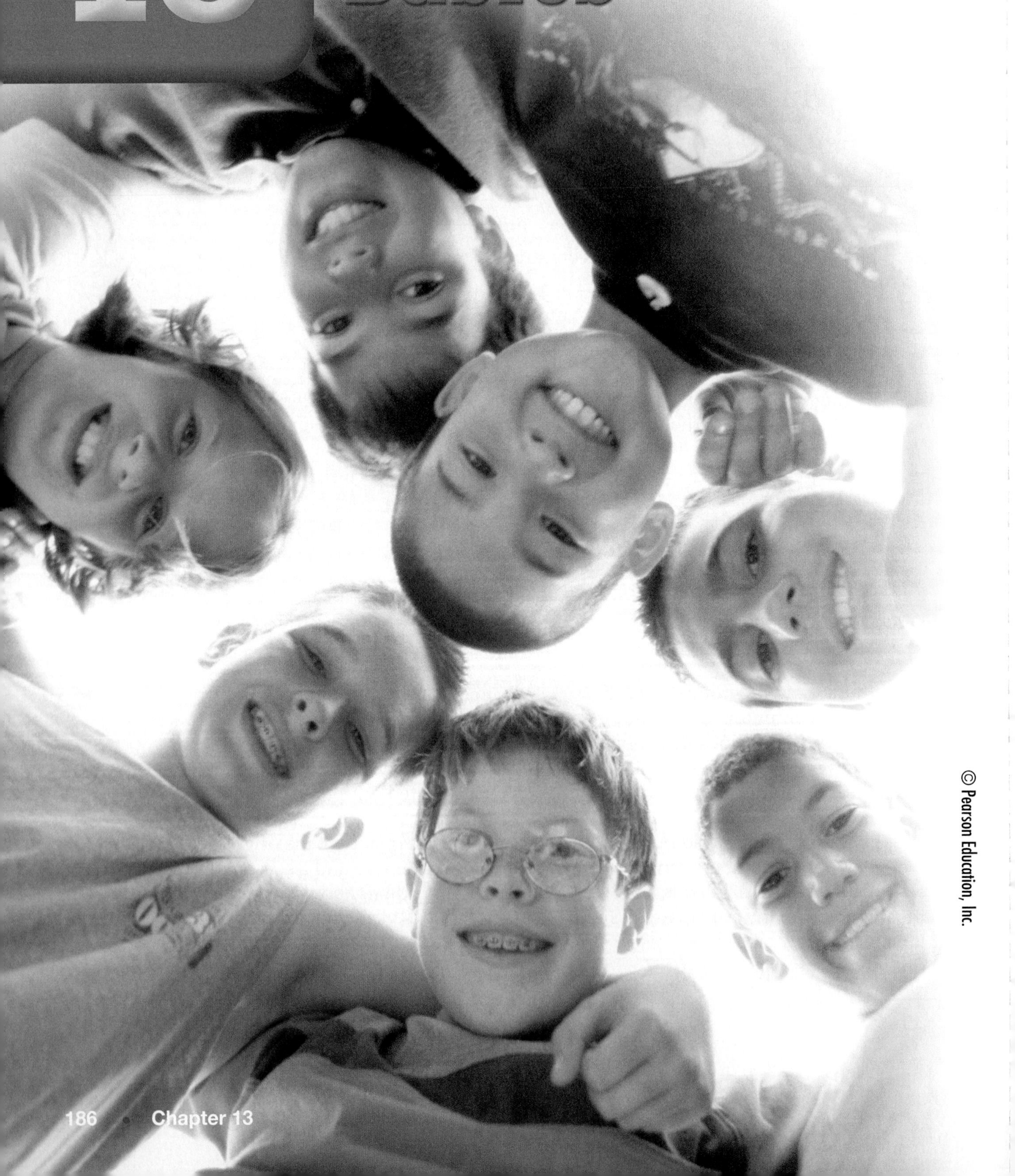

What Is a Computer Network? Imagine that you and your friends want to publish a school newspaper. Some of you will be writers. Others will be photographers and artists. Some will be editors, and some will work on page layout. All of you will work on different computers in different parts of your school.

Sometimes writers and photographers need to work together. So do text and layout editors. A computer network allows all the people involved in a project to communicate with one another from their own computers. With a network, all of their work can be put together easily.

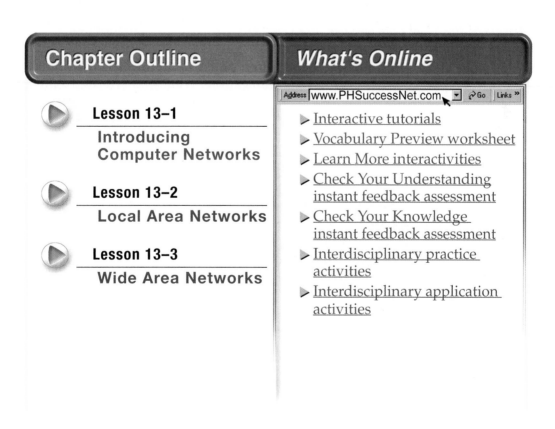

Chapter Outline

▶ **Lesson 13–1**
Introducing
Computer Networks

▶ **Lesson 13–2**
Local Area Networks

▶ **Lesson 13–3**
Wide Area Networks

What's Online

Address www.PHSuccessNet.com ⟳ Go Links »

▶ Interactive tutorials
▶ Vocabulary Preview worksheet
▶ Learn More interactivities
▶ Check Your Understanding instant feedback assessment
▶ Check Your Knowledge instant feedback assessment
▶ Interdisciplinary practice activities
▶ Interdisciplinary application activities

Introducing Computer Networks

Objectives

- Explain what a computer network is.
- List commonly used network media.
- Identify three key benefits of using a network.

As You Read

Organize Information Complete a chart to help you identify the details that support the main idea of the lesson.

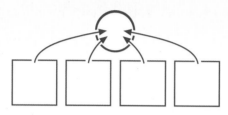

What's Online

In Lesson 13–1 of the iText, you will find more features and information for this lesson, including:

- Interactive tutorials
- As You Read worksheet
- Learn More interactivities
- Check Your Understanding interactive assessments
- Interactive lesson review

Key Terms

- network (p. 188)
- physical media (p. 188)
- network interface card (NIC) (p. 188)
- workstation (p. 189)
- node (p. 189)
- terminal (p. 189)
- protocol (p. 190)

Introducing Networks

If your family owns two computers, can they both use the same printer? They can if your computers are networked.

A computer **network** is two or more computers connected to one another to share resources. Networks allow users to access files and programs. They also let users share printers and other equipment. They allow people to work together, too. If you've ever used the Internet, you have used a computer network.

Physical Media Various ways of connecting computers can be accomplished through **physical media.** The medium can be any type of telecommunications connector: twisted pair telephone lines, coaxial cable, fiber-optic cable, or a microwave, radio, or infrared system.

Working together, the network media and the computers determine how much data can be sent through the connector. Wireless networks usually aren't as fast as wired networks.

Network Interface Cards Some computers are designed with the ability to connect to networks. Others need a **network interface card,** or **NIC,** which handles the flow of data to and from the computer in both wired and wireless networks. If the network is put together by actual cables, those cables connect to the NIC. NICs often have a light that blinks green and amber to alert you to activity it's experiencing.

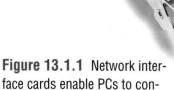

Figure 13.1.1 Network interface cards enable PCs to connect to a network.

© Pearson Education, Inc.

Organizing Users

If you have more than one computer at home, you probably identify them by each user's name—your computer, Mom's computer, and so on. In businesses, schools, and other organizations, a network is organized into workstations, each with its own name and address. In both home and larger networks, pieces of equipment connected together must be able to understand one another.

Network Members   A **workstation** is a computer connected to a computer network. It is often set up with the same operating system, applications, and access to resources as the other computers in the network. Workstations are where individuals do their day-to-day work.

In a large network, a workstation is also called a **node** by the people who take care of the network. A node is anything connected to the network—a workstation, a printer, a fax machine, or any other piece of equipment.

Network Alternative   Sometimes network users work at a **terminal,** which usually includes a keyboard, a monitor, and a mouse. A terminal can feel as if the computer is local, but it's not. Users are actually sharing time on a central computer, with their own work displayed on their terminal's monitor. (This kind of network is sometimes called a timesharing system.)

Terminals can save on the cost of purchasing workstations. They are also useful in situations with limited need for a workstation, such as a public computer in a library.

© Pearson Education, Inc.

Figure 13.1.2 Networks enable many people to use the same data, programs, and hardware at one time.

Speaking the Language

If you spoke only English and your neighbor spoke only Spanish, you might have a tough time communicating. On a computer network, the same idea applies. Computers on a network must all speak the same language.

Imagine a sneaker factory. The factory needs a way to update the salespeople on the number and styles of shoes available. And the salespeople need a way to place orders for the factory to make certain sneakers. The company's network allows the factory workers and the salespeople to exchange data very quickly. It is network protocols that allow the salespeople's computers to communicate with the factory's computers.

Setting Rules   A **protocol** sets a standard format for data and rules for handling it. It's the language computers speak on a network. There are many different protocols available to use on networks. For computers to speak with one another, they must use the same protocol.

Seeing Benefits   Computer networks provide hardware benefits because they let people share hardware. Networks also provide software benefits because they let people share programs and data. And they provide people benefits because they let people work together in new and exciting ways.

Physical media connect the network, but they're not enough by themselves. Protocols make sure that the links among hardware, software, and people actually work.

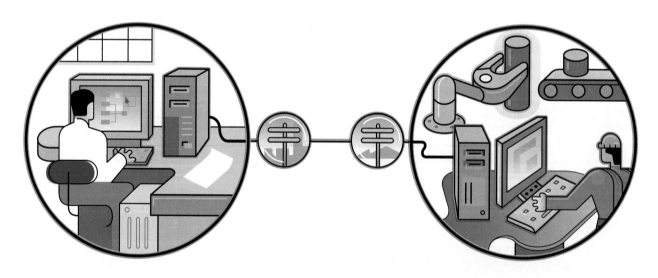

Figure 13.1.3 Computers in different locations can communicate as long as they use the same network protocols.

Demonstrate Your Knowledge

Critical Thinking

1. What do the physical media and the network interface card do for a network?

_____

_____

2. What is the difference between a workstation and a node?

_____

_____

3. Why must a network be ruled by a protocol?

_____

_____

Activities

1. Complete the Venn diagram below to compare and contrast a network and a timesharing system.

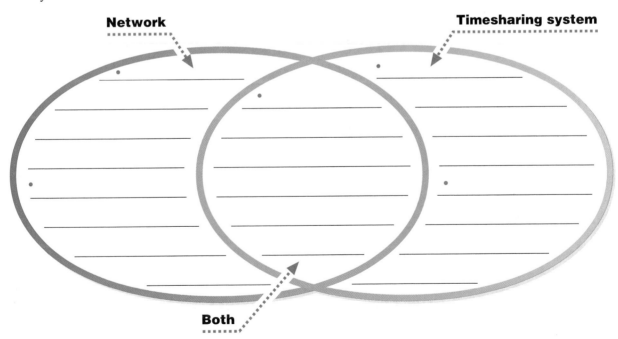

2. List the advantages of networking computers at home, even if the home has only two computers and peripherals.

Local Area Networks

Objectives

- Describe how local area networks work.
- Define how local area networks allow information sharing.
- Compare peer-to-peer and client/server networks.

As You Read

Organize Information Complete a concept web to help you organize the basics of networking as you read the lesson.

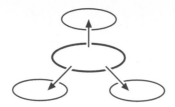

What's Online

In Lesson 13–2 of the iText, you will find more features and information for this lesson, including:

- Interactive tutorials
- As You Read worksheet
- Learn More interactivities
- Check Your Understanding interactive assessments
- Interactive lesson review

🔑 Key Terms

- local area network (LAN) (p. 192)
- file sharing (p. 192)
- collaborative software (p. 192)
- peer-to-peer network (P2PN) (p. 192)
- client/server network (p. 194)
- client (p. 194)
- file server (p. 194)
- network operating system (NOS) (p. 194)

Introducing LANs

A school lab with its ten computers networked together is an example of a **local area network,** or **LAN.** A LAN is a network in which all the workstations and other equipment are near one another. LANs can be set up in any defined area, such as a home, a school, an office building, or even a cluster of shops.

A LAN can have just a few or several hundred users. Small or large, a LAN lets its members share equipment and information. There are three key ways to share information: sharing files, using collaborative software, and sharing peripherals.

Sharing Files Through a computer's operating system, people connected to a LAN can participate in **file sharing.** File sharing is making files available to more than one user on the network.

Using Collaborative Software **Collaborative software** enables the network to help people work together more closely. With collaborative software, users can share calendars, work on a document together, or even hold meetings through the network. Collaborative software is also called groupware.

Sharing Peripherals In addition to sharing files and software, a LAN allows users to share peripherals, such as printers, fax machines, or any other equipment.

Using a Peer-to-Peer Network

Your peers are your equals. In a **peer-to-peer network (P2PN),** all the computers are equals. Peer-to-peer networks are usually small, made up of two to ten computers.

Sharing Files In a P2PN, each user decides whether any files on his or her computer will be shared. You can share the files with your neighbor, a few of your neighbors, or everyone on the network. The reverse is true, too. Other workstations may have files you'd like to access through the network—and you can if you have permission.

Creating a P2PN A P2PN is an easy network to create, since all of the workstations are equals. The operating system of each computer typically has built-in file-sharing abilities. The workstations are connected to each other through the network cable. In some systems, the network cables all connect to a central device called a hub. A hub handles the flow of traffic from computer to computer.

Evaluating P2PNs A peer-to-peer network is ideal for small offices and homes. In a large business, however, peer-to-peer networking has some drawbacks:

- Security problems can arise.
- Data can be hard to back up.
- With many users, file sharing can become difficult.
- Finding shared files can be difficult.
- Managing resources can be complicated.

These problems arise because resources are scattered across many computers. If one computer fails or is turned off, its resources are no longer available to the network.

Technology @ Work

Shared files and databases are extremely useful in many office situations. If the office is networked, any employee on the network can access the data.

Think *About* It!
Think about what information might be useful at a magazine publishing house. Underline ONLY the databases below that you think should be networked for any employee to access.

- a collection of photographs of famous people
- a list of employees' salaries
- a directory of all the subscribers and their addresses
- a dictionary and a thesaurus
- a series of notes on recent historical events

Spotlight on...

COOLTOWN @ SCHOOL

" *Cooltown @ school is helping us bring to life a vision in which students, teachers, parents, and administrators have access to the resources they need to create a personalized, self-empowering educational experience.* "

Dr. Jim Parsley
Superintendent,
Vancouver School District

Cooltown @ school is a joint effort of the Hewlett-Packard Company and the Vancouver School District in Vancouver, Washington. It hopes to turn an educational network into a personalized educational experience for each student and family.

Vancouver will be using its network to set up family support centers linked to the schools, to personalize instruction for each student. Each student will be able to use technology to participate in that instruction.

More and more families who own at least two computers are deciding to network their homes.

Think *About* **It!**

Before networking a home, think about what you will need. Circle each item below that you think would be needed to set up a home network.

➤ a file server

➤ a network interface card for each computer

➤ a wire or the right equipment for a wireless connection

➤ a network operating system

Using a Client/Server Network

Large businesses usually use a **client/server network.** With this system, one powerful computer provides information and management services to the workstation computers, the **clients.** You use client/server networks whenever you send e-mail, use the Internet, chat, and play games online. Your computer is the client.

Creating a Client/Server Network The main computer in a client/server system is called the **file server** or the server. It contains the network operating system, other programs, and large data files. The **network operating system,** or **NOS**, manages and secures the entire network. It controls access, permissions, and all aspects of network use.

Evaluating a Client/Server Network For a large office, file servers are better than peer-to-peer networks, for several reasons:

• They offer a central location for files.
• Data is easy to back up and easy to recover.
• Servers are faster than workstations.
• Servers usually are powered on.
• Security is easier to maintain.

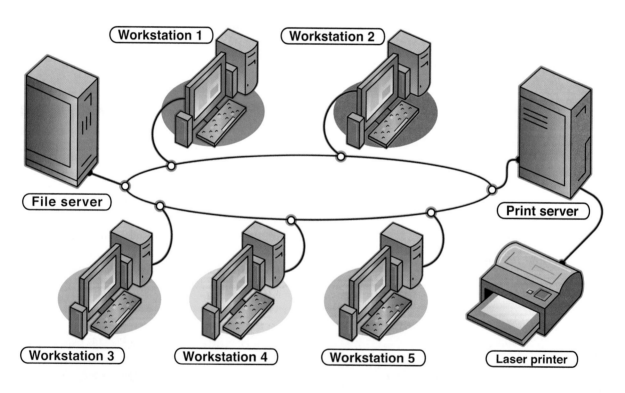

Figure 13.2.1 In a client/server network, users can share files stored on the file server and access a common printer, too.

Demonstrate Your Knowledge

Critical Thinking

1. Why are the networked computers at a school an example of a LAN?

_____

_____

2. If a family decides to network their home, why might they be likely to choose a P2PN?

_____

_____

3. Which system—a P2PN or a client/server network—is more likely to need a network administrator to be in charge of the network? Why?

_____

_____

Activities

1. Complete the following chart to compare the features of a P2PN and a client/server network.

Network Characteristics

Characteristic	P2PN	Client/Server
Typical size of network		
Control of file sharing		
Connection method		
Level of security		

2. Find a home, a shop, or another small business that has a LAN. Describe this network. Find out how many computers are connected, how they are connected, what other equipment is connected, and whether users are satisfied with the system.

Wide Area Networks

Objectives

- Identify the purpose and components of a wide area network.
- Explain the use of intranets.
- Compare and contrast the Internet and other wide area networks.

As You Read

Organize Information Complete an outline to help you note key facts about wide area networks as you read the lesson.

I. _____
   A. _____
   B. _____
II. _____
   A. _____
      1. _____

What's Online

In Lesson 13-3 of the iText, you will find more features and information for this lesson, including:

- Interactive tutorials
- As You Read worksheet
- Learn More interactivities
- Check Your Understanding interactive assessments
- Interactive lesson review

Key Terms

- wide area network (WAN) (p. 196)
- intranet (p. 197)
- backbone (p. 197)
- point of presence (POP) (p. 197)
- public data network (PDN) (p. 198)
- virtual private network (VPN) (p. 198)

What Is a WAN?

A **wide area network (WAN)** connects computers and other resources that are miles or even continents apart. A business with offices in many places can use a WAN to link its LANs in different cities. Then, users from any of the locations can, with the proper permissions, access the network. Each user can access files, printers, and other resources as if they were local. As far as users are concerned, a WAN "feels like" one giant LAN.

Once a WAN is created, users may not even realize the files they are sharing are remote. And that's the way it should be. Users should not worry about the physical location of the shared files, just that the files are available.

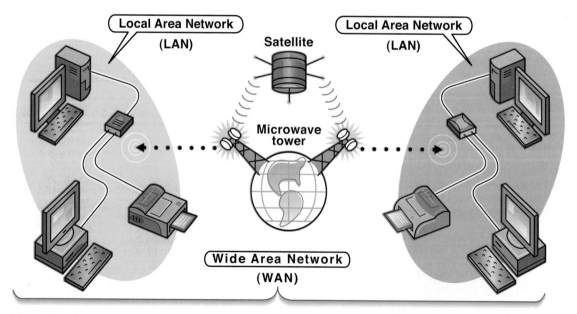

Figure 13.3.1 A WAN can link distant LANs through telephone lines or microwave signals.

© Pearson Education, Inc.

How Is a WAN Controlled? Like a client/server LAN, a WAN is controlled by a network operating system. A NOS is especially helpful on a WAN because there are so many users and resources to manage. The NOS also helps network administrators secure the resources throughout the network.

Is the Internet a WAN? Technically, the Internet is a WAN, but it usually isn't called that. Many people are more familiar with the Internet than with other networks. Thus, many organizations, including schools, set up their networks as **intranets**—private networks that look like the Internet. Intranets are used by businesses for company announcements and training. Anyone can access the Internet; an intranet is only for employees or members of an organization. Firewall software keeps others out of the intranet.

How WANs Work

A WAN needs to connect the resources together physically, and it needs to provide a way to access the connection.

Backbones **Backbones** are the high-speed lines, wired or wireless, that carry data through a network. Long-distance telecommunications companies carry some of the data traffic. Government and privately owned lines connect other WANs.

POPs Throughout the world, WAN providers offer local connections for users. That connection is called a **point of presence (POP)**. The most common example of a POP is an Internet connection. Think of your Internet provider. Does it offer services just in your city? Or does it offer services throughout the world? The popular service provider AOL®, for example, has thousands of local telephone numbers so that its customers can connect no matter where they are.

Career Corner

Medical Technician In addition to taking a patient's temperature and blood pressure, medical technicians are now trained to use high-tech devices, such as a new handheld device that can map a patient's DNA and provide an instant diagnosis. In addition to the high-tech training, technicians learn to use medical computer networks.

Figure 13.3.2 High-speed data lines, called backbones, enable networked computers to exchange information.

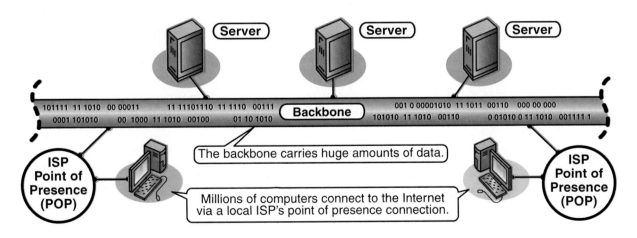

Types of WANs

Businesses and other organizations use the Internet for many purposes. They offer information about their company, for example, or a catalog of their products. For their own networks, however, they need something that is more secure and more dependable than the Internet. They use other kinds of WANs when money is involved or when timing is important. They have several choices:

- public data network
- private data network
- virtual private network

Public Data Network A **public data network (PDN)** allows many different companies to set up their own networks. Telecommunications companies own the PDNs and charge fees for the use of the network.

Private Data Network Some companies set up a private data network that cannot be accessed by outsiders. Having a private data network costs more than using a public data network.

Virtual Private Network A **virtual private network (VPN)** is a private network set up through a public network. VPN users connect to an Internet service provider (ISP) to access the network.

Real-World Tech

Networking the Navajo Nation   The Navajo Nation spreads across 26,000 square miles in Arizona, New Mexico, and Utah. The Nation's Diné College has seven campuses that are hundreds of miles apart. Only about half of the Nation's households have phone lines. How could the educational system take advantage of the Internet? The solution was to create a WAN using a variety of technologies. Small satellite dishes receive information while phone and dedicated data lines send messages out. The Navajo Nation's wide area network has expanded to overcome the wide open spaces in which its people live.

What group or institution do you think would benefit from a WAN? Why? Write your ideas below.

_____

_____

_____

Demonstrate Your Knowledge

Critical Thinking

1. Why are WANs so useful in the modern world?

_____

_____

2. Why might a company organize its network as an intranet?

_____

_____

3. What would a company need to be able to offer a PDN service to other companies who want to network their business?

_____

_____

Activities

1. Complete the following spider map to compare the Internet to other WANs.

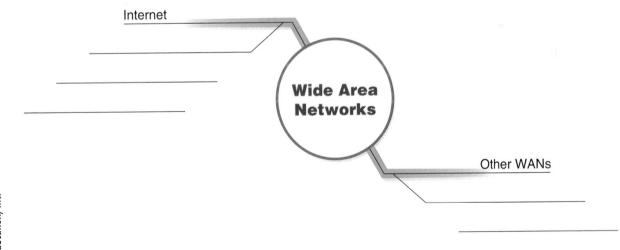

2. Working with a partner, choose an Internet service provider such as AOL®, AT&T, or your local cable company. Visit the company's Web site and find a list of its POPs. List five POPs in various parts of the United States and five in other countries.

Use the Vocabulary

Directions: *Match each vocabulary term in the left column with the correct definition in the right column. Write the appropriate letter next to the word or term.*

_____ **1.** network
_____ **2.** workstation
_____ **3.** protocol
_____ **4.** local area network
_____ **5.** collaborative software
_____ **6.** peer-to-peer network
_____ **7.** file server
_____ **8.** backbone
_____ **9.** point of presence
_____ **10.** virtual private network

a. network in which all computers are equal
b. computer connected to a network
c. local connection to a WAN
d. standard format and rules
e. set up on a public network
f. two or more computers linked together
g. program that lets people work together closely
h. high-speed line that carries network traffic
i. network set up in a limited area
j. the central computer in one kind of network

Check Your Comprehension

Directions: *Circle the correct choice for each of the following.*

1. Which of the following is NOT an example of a physical medium used to connect a network?
   a. telephone wires
   b. electric cords
   c. fiber-optic cables
   d. radio signals

2. If a company buys one large computer instead of many workstations, which of the following will it supply for its employees to work on?
   a. a file server
   b. nodes
   c. a point of presence
   d. terminals

3. Which of the following is another name for collaborative software?
   a. groupware
   b. network operating system
   c. local area network
   d. backbone

4. Which of the following do users of a client/server network have to provide?
   a. a client
   b. a file
   c. a protocol
   d. an access control

5. Which of the following is used to control a WAN?
   a. NIC
   b. VPN
   c. NOS
   d. POP

6. Which of the following is used to provide a local connection to a WAN?
   a. NIC
   b. VPN
   c. NOS
   d. POP

Think Critically

Directions: *Answer the following questions on the lines provided.*

1. How are a LAN and a WAN similar? How are they different?

_____

_____

2. Why might a P2PN be a good choice for a small network? Why might a
client/server model be a good choice for a large network?

_____

_____

3. Why is the Internet an example of a WAN?

_____

_____

4. What kinds of wires and wireless lines can be used as the backbone of a WAN?

_____

_____

5. Why are protocols important to LANs and WANs?

_____

_____

_____

Extend Your Knowledge

Directions: *Choose one of the following projects. Complete the exercises on a
separate sheet of paper.*

A. If your school library has computers, find out if the ones available for
students to use are workstations or terminals and why they are organized
this way. Also, find out how the computers in your public library are organized. If possible, try each system. Write
a brief report comparing and contrasting the operation and purposes of a
network using workstations and a system using terminals.

B. Conduct research in the library or on
the Internet to find more details about
each of the physical media used to create
networks, such as twisted pair, coaxial
cable, fiber-optic cable, microwaves,
radio waves, and infrared rays. Present
your findings in an illustrated chart.
Compare the details you discovered with
those your classmates found. What conclusions can you draw about the use of
these media in networks?

chapter 14

Personal Communications Basics

© Pearson Education, Inc.

Staying in Touch   How do you stay in touch with friends after school, on weekends, or during school vacations? How do you stay in contact with friends who have moved? You could make phone calls and hope someone answers, or send letters and then wait for a response. Today, however, many people use their computer to stay in touch with friends, family, and co-workers.

Computer technology allows you to stay connected with people who are both close by and far away. You can communicate through text messages. You can chat online with several friends at once. With the right technology, you can even chat face-to-face through a computer network. There's no need to feel out of touch!

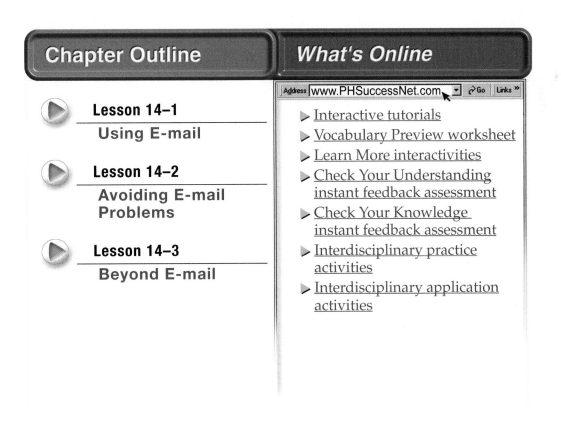

Chapter Outline

▶ **Lesson 14–1**
  Using E-mail

▶ **Lesson 14–2**
  Avoiding E-mail Problems

▶ **Lesson 14–3**
  Beyond E-mail

What's Online

Address www.PHSuccessNet.com   Go   Links »

▷ Interactive tutorials
▷ Vocabulary Preview worksheet
▷ Learn More interactivities
▷ Check Your Understanding instant feedback assessment
▷ Check Your Knowledge instant feedback assessment
▷ Interdisciplinary practice activities
▷ Interdisciplinary application activities

Using E-mail

Objectives

- Describe e-mail systems.
- Identify the key components of an e-mail message.
- Describe the process of creating, sending, and replying to messages.

As You Read

Sequence Information Use a sequence chart as you read to help you outline the process of receiving a message and responding to it.

In Lesson 14–1 of the iText, you will find more features and information for this lesson, including:

- Interactive tutorials
- As You Read worksheet
- Learn More interactivities
- Check Your Understanding interactive assessments
- Interactive lesson review

Key Terms

- attachment (p. 204)
- mailbox name (p. 204)
- server address (p. 204)
- e-mail server (p. 204)
- e-mail client (p. 205)
- alias (p. 205)

Figure 14.1.1 Every e-mail address has two basic parts—a mailbox name and a server address.

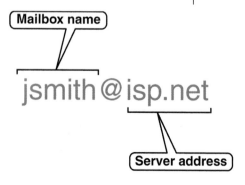

Evaluating E-mail

E-mail allows people to send an unlimited number of messages quickly and easily to anyone with an e-mail address. It is also less expensive than standard mail and voice, fax, and telephone messages. To use e-mail, all you need is a computer, an Internet connection, e-mail software, and an e-mail account.

E-mail also lets you attach files to a message. Anything sent with an e-mail message is called an **attachment.** Common attachments include word-processing documents, spreadsheets, photos, artwork, and movies.

Understanding E-mail

All e-mail addresses have two parts. The **mailbox name** is the part of the address before the "at" symbol (@) that identifies the user. The **server address** follows the symbol. It names the domain name of the computer that houses the mailbox. An **e-mail server** is a computer, operated by your Internet service provider (ISP), that handles three key jobs:

- accepts incoming messages
- sends outgoing messages
- delivers incoming messages

When you send a message, it goes from your computer to your ISP's e-mail server, which examines the address of the recipient—the person to whom you are sending the message. If the recipient uses the same ISP as you do, the message is delivered directly to the recipient's mailbox. If the recipient uses a different ISP, the message is sent to that server through the Internet. The receiving server accepts the message and delivers it to the recipient's mailbox.

Sending and Receiving E-mail

To send or receive e-mail, you use an **e-mail client,** which is a program that lets you create, send, receive, and manage e-mail messages. You may get the program from your ISP, as part of a productivity suite, or with a Web browser.

Composing E-mail To compose a new message, you click a button within the e-mail client. The client displays a form for you to complete.

First, you must specify the message's recipient. Depending on your e-mail client's features, you may select someone's name from an address book. You may also type the e-mail address, which can be a name or a combination of letters and numbers. For example, the e-mail address for Chris Rodriguez might be chris_rodriguez@isp.net or cjr615@isp.net. Instead of typing a complete address, you may be able to type an alias, or select it from a list. An **alias** is an easy-to-remember nickname for the recipient, such as Chris_R. The recipient's name or address appears in the To: line of the message form. Similarly, if you want to send a copy of the message to other recipients, you can add their names or addresses to the To: line or place them in the Cc: line. (The characters *Cc* stand for "carbon copy.")

Next, fill in the Subject line. The Subject line gives the recipient an idea of the message's content and may help the recipient decide whether to open it or delete it. Then, write the text message. You can add attachments by clicking a button and then clicking the name of the file you want to attach to the e-mail. Finally, click Send.

Netiquette are the rules for polite online behavior.

Think *About* **It!**
Circle each of the following online rules that help make e-mail more useful.

> Type a lengthy description in the Subject line.

> Vary fonts and type sizes in the message.

> Edit the original message so only the part you are answering appears in your reply.

> Don't write in anger.

> Be brief, but be polite.

Figure 14.1.2 Creating an e-mail message in Microsoft Outlook Express, a popular e-mail client

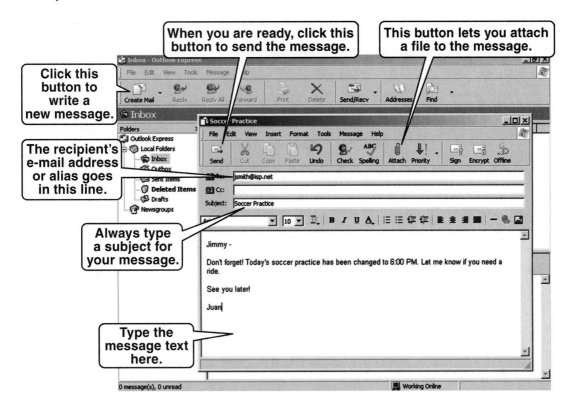

When you are ready, click this button to send the message.

This button lets you attach a file to the message.

Click this button to write a new message.

The recipient's e-mail address or alias goes in this line.

Always type a subject for your message.

Type the message text here.

Figure 14.1.3 Replying to an e-mail message

Replying to E-mail Suppose you received an e-mail message inviting you to a party. You can respond to the invitation by clicking Reply, which responds only to the person who sent you the message. You can also click Reply All, which responds to all the people who received the original message. Several things occur when a response is prepared:

- The client displays a reply form with the original sender's address shown in the To: field.
- The subject field may show *Re:* in front of the subject of the original message. (*Re* means "regarding.")
- The original message is copied into the body of the reply. Most e-mail programs give you the option of including the original text in your reply.
- You can type your reply above or below the original text.

Forwarding E-mail When you receive a message, you can pass it along to someone else. This is called forwarding a message. For example, you could forward the party invitation to your parents to ask them if you can attend. They will receive the message from you, but the Subject line may include the characters *FW:* before the subject text to show that the message has been forwarded. You can add your comments before the original message's text.

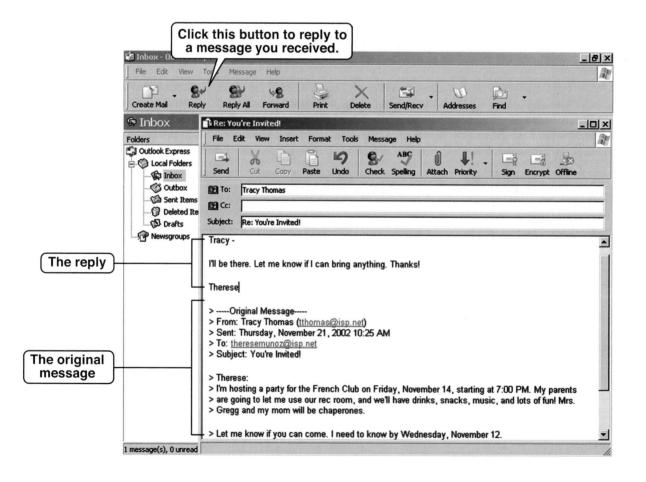

© Pearson Education, Inc.

Demonstrate Your Knowledge

Critical Thinking

1. How important is e-mail communication to you? Why?

_____

_____

2. Is it a good idea to fill in the Subject line of an e-mail message? Why or why not?

_____

_____

3. How can senders and recipients benefit from seeing the original message in a reply?

_____

_____

Activities

1. Complete the following chart to explain the key parts of an e-mail message.

E-mail Messages	
Key part	**Function**
To	_____
Cc	_____
Subject	_____
Text	_____
Attachments	_____

2. Make a list of classmates' e-mail addresses. Review the list and tally how many different server addresses are used. Which is most popular? Why?

Avoiding E-mail Problems

Objectives

- Examine problems related to e-mail.
- Define bounce messages, spam, e-mail viruses, and hoaxes.

As You Read

Compare and Contrast Use a Venn diagram as you read to help you compare and contrast various e-mail problems.

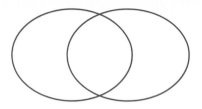

What's Online

In Lesson 14–2 of the iText, you will find more features and information for this lesson, including:

- Interactive tutorials
- As You Read worksheet
- Learn More interactivities
- Check Your Understanding interactive assessments
- Interactive lesson review

Key Terms

- bounce message (p. 208)
- spam (p. 209)
- e-mail virus (p. 210)

Failed E-mail

It is easy to send e-mail messages, but it is also easy to make mistakes. What happens when you make a mistake?

Using the Wrong Address One of the most common e-mail mistakes is entering an incorrect address in the To: field. When you do this, one of two things will happen:

- Your message will go to the wrong person if the incorrect address is someone else's valid address. Unless that person replies, you may never know what happened to your message.
- The e-mail server will return the e-mail to you with a bounce message.

A **bounce message** is a notice from the e-mail server telling you that your message could not be delivered. Bounce messages are often a result of an incorrect e-mail address. Also, a message may not be delivered if the recipient's mailbox is full. This happens because many ISPs limit the amount of server space available for each user's messages.

Avoiding Bounce Messages If you or your family changes ISPs, your e-mail address will change. In that case, be sure to tell everyone in your address book about your new e-mail address. Otherwise, people sending messages to your former address will receive a bounce message when they write to you.

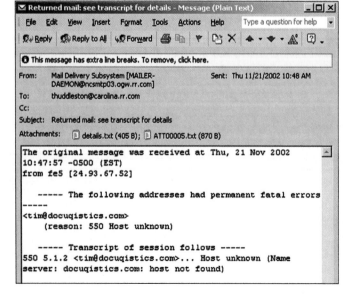

Figure 14.2.1 An example of a bounce message, due to an incorrect e-mail address

Junk E-mail, or Spam

Many e-mail users complain about the flood of **spam,** a term used to describe unwanted, or junk, e-mail messages and advertisements. Like physical junk mail, spam usually tries to sell something to the recipient. Spam can cause several problems:

- The recipient wastes time reviewing and deleting spam.
- Spam clogs e-mail servers, slowing Internet traffic.
- Spam often contains incorrect or misleading information.

You can sign up for e-mail newsletters at many different Web sites. Or you may subscribe to a mailing list that lets you use e-mail to exchange messages about some topic.

At first, you may welcome these newsletters and messages. However, the people who operate online newsletters and mailing lists may give your name and e-mail address to others, who may begin sending you unwanted messages. You may soon tire of all the unwanted spam that results from online subscriptions. Most newsletters and mailing lists give directions to unsubscribe to the e-mail. Of course, you can also delete unwanted messages.

Blocking Unwanted E-mail Stopping spam from reaching e-mail servers and clients is an ongoing battle. Some servers use technology to block "spammers." Some e-mail clients provide special tools, called filters or rules, which users can configure to automatically delete junk e-mail.

Technology @ Work

Bounce messages are a part of e-mail use. But what should you do when you get one?

Think *About* **It!**
Suppose you e-mail the school photographer to find out whether your class pictures are ready. However, you get a bounce message. Circle each action that might then be helpful.

▶ Retrieve the message from your Sent Items folder and check your typing.

▶ Confirm the e-mail address of the photographer.

▶ Resend the message to the same address.

▶ Send a reply to the bounce message asking for help.

Real-World Tech

Getting Advice by E-mail Advice columns that appear in newspapers and magazines exist on the Internet, too. Some are geared to specific groups, such as children or teens. As with all online resources, be cautious about where you send e-mail and any information you share.

There are many kinds of question-and-answer forums available online. What type interests you most?

_____

_____

_____

Dangerous E-mail

Some e-mail messages can damage programs and data.

E-mail Viruses   **E-mail viruses** are programs that can destroy data and cause network problems. Most e-mail viruses are sent as attachments to messages. When the recipient opens the attachment, a script or program can launch. This program can modify or destroy data and programs, or change the computer's settings.

Not all e-mail viruses are distributed as attachments. Most e-mail programs can create and open messages in HTML format. A virus programmer can insert virus code directly in an HTML-format message. If you receive an infected message in HTML format, all you have to do is view the message in your e-mail program. The virus then infects your computer.

Nearly all e-mail viruses copy themselves and then send themselves to everyone in your address book. When recipients see a message from you, they think it's safe to read. They open the message, and the destructive process repeats itself.

Be Wary of Attachments   Beware of any e-mail attachment that has an .EXE, .BAT, .COM, or .VBS extension at the end of its file name. These files are usually programs that can be used to launch a virus. If you're uncertain of an attachment, delete it and report it—don't open it! Running up-to-date virus protection software to scan e-mail for harmful attachments is an important safeguard.

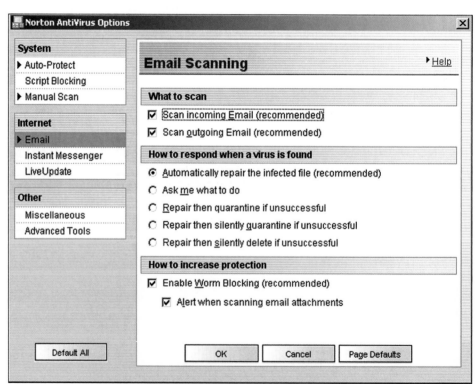

Figure 14.2.2 Configuring an antivirus program to scan e-mail messages

Demonstrate Your Knowledge

Critical Thinking

1. For what reasons might you not receive a reply to an e-mail message you sent?

_____

_____

2. Why should you think twice before subscribing to any online newsletter or mailing list?

_____

_____

3. How can receiving an e-mail virus affect the friends you send e-mail?

_____

_____

Activities

1. Complete the following concept web to identify the problems with spam.

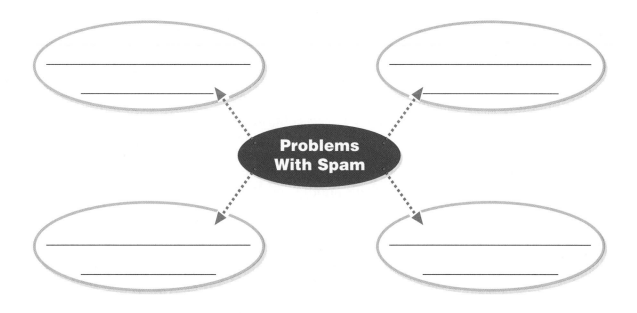

2. As a class, make a list of reasons you might receive a bounce message. Rank the reasons in order of frequency, from the most frequent to the least frequent reason. Identify things you can do to reduce the frequency of bounce messages.

Beyond E-mail

Objectives

- Compare and contrast technology-enabled conferences.
- Explain distance learning.

As You Read

Organize Information Use an outline as you read to help you organize information about advanced communications methods.

What's Online

In Lesson 14–3 of the iText, you will find more features and information for this lesson, including:

- Interactive tutorials
- As You Read worksheet
- Learn More interactivities
- Check Your Understanding interactive assessments
- Interactive lesson review

Key Terms

- teleconference (p. 212)
- videoconference (p. 213)

Meeting Through Technology

E-mail communication has advantages. It allows you to quickly send a message and, later, receive a reply. But what if you need to communicate with others right away? What if you need the benefits of a conversation? What if you need to talk to many people at once?

Teleconferencing Imagine a company with 50 salespeople located around the world. Getting all these people together to discuss a new product would be helpful. Flying them all to one city for a meeting would be very expensive, however. An e-mail message sent to all of them would not let them share ideas quickly with one another—neither would 50 individual phone calls from the boss.

In cases such as this, teleconferencing may be the solution. A **teleconference** uses computers that are connected by a network or the Internet. These connections allow people to communicate with one another in real time through their computers. Depending on the software they use, the participants may be able to speak to one another as if they were using telephones, and every participant can hear all the others. Teleconferencing software may allow users to "chat" by typing messages that appear on everyone's screen. Participants may also be able to share documents on-screen, as well, using a special feature called a whiteboard to view and edit the documents in real time. Teleconferences help companies in several ways:

- They save time and money.
- They are similar to in-person meetings.
- They are convenient.
- They allow all participants to communicate in real time.

Videoconferencing In addition to teleconferences, companies may use videoconferences. **Videoconferences** offer the advantage of not only hearing one another in a meeting but also seeing one another at the same time.

Special equipment is needed for a videoconference. Suppose a group of people in Boston, Massachusetts, want to meet with a group in Dallas, Texas. A room in each location must have a video camera and microphone connected to a computer, which in turn must be connected to the Internet or a network. The video camera focuses on the group or on an individual and projects the image onto the computer screen. As participants in each city speak, they can be seen and heard by participants in the other city. Information from a previously recorded meeting can also be shared by videoconference.

Videoconferences can also work like television. Imagine that the president of a company wants to speak to all the employees. To minimize costs and travel, the company does not want to schedule a meeting of thousands of employees and bring them all to one location. Instead, a camera can focus on the president, and the speech can be shown on monitors in each of the company locations. This is called a one-to-many meeting.

In a many-to-many videoconference, participants in several different locations can all see and hear one another. In this type of videoconference, each participant can be seated at his or her own computer, each with its own video camera, microphone, and network or Internet connection.

Career Corner

Wireless Developer How can devices like cell phones display content that you normally view on a PC? By using the wireless access protocol (WAP) and the Wireless Markup Language (WML), handheld devices can function as tiny browsers, displaying all sorts of content for their users. These protocols and languages allow devices to download content quickly and display it on a tiny screen efficiently. There is a growing demand for designers who understand WAP, WML, and other wireless solutions.

Spotlight on...

TELEMENTORING

66 *Students get a chance to work with people who are proof of the value of education. Academic performance improves as a result of a renewed motivation to learn. Started in 1995, ITP has served more than 11,000 students in nine countries in grades 4 through college.* 99

David Neils
Founder,
International Telementor Program

The International Telementor Program, or ITP, matches students with workplace mentors who help them complete projects. Students and their mentors communicate online. Students at Eisenhower Middle School in Topeka, Kansas, developed their school's first Web site with help from ITP mentors. And students in Pleasant View School in Baldwin Park, California, worked with mentors to create multimedia presentations on their state's history.

Technology @ School

Many students and teachers use distance learning.

Think *About* **It!**
Think about some of the ways schools might use distance learning. Circle each statement that identifies a sensible use.

▷ Small schools could offer a wider range of courses.

▷ Schools could let individuals or small groups pursue their interests.

▷ Schools could pair a sports team with a coach.

▷ A teacher in one school could share lessons with teachers on other campuses.

Learning From a Distance

Distance learning allows you to learn anytime, anywhere—as long as you are on a computer connected to the Internet. Many schools offer classes via distance learning, and they use a variety of technologies to deliver instruction to their students. In many cases, the instructor provides lectures and displays slides through a one-to-many videoconference, which students can watch on their home computers. Reading assignments can be done online, tests and quizzes can be done via the Internet, and students can work together via teleconference and e-mail. It is possible to study many different subjects through distance learning. You can even earn a complete college degree online.

Applications for Distance Learning To get people interested in using the technology of distance learning, it must be powerful and captivating. Instruction must offer more than slideshows and text. One possibility is to encourage interaction through real-time discussions, interactive quizzes, projects, and even games. Here are some uses for distance learning:

- Schools help students pursue a wide range of interests.
- Universities offer degree programs through the World Wide Web.
- Businesses conduct employee training in remote locations.
- Companies use the Internet to provide instruction and online help to consumers.

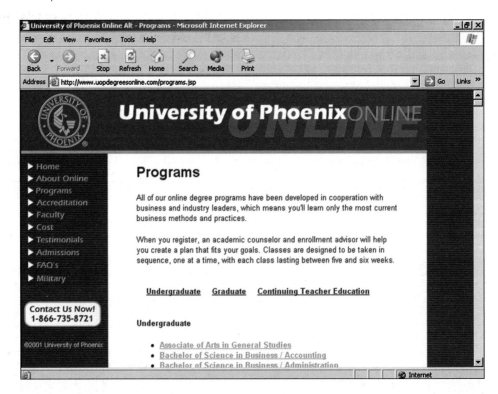

Figure 14.3.1 Many schools, such as the University of Phoenix, have an "online campus" that offers distance learning options for students.

Demonstrate Your Knowledge

Critical Thinking

1. Do you think teleconferencing can benefit families as well as businesses? Why?

_____

_____

2. How can schools use videoconferencing?

_____

_____

3. How could a group of coaches use the whiteboard feature in teleconference software?

_____

_____

Activities

1. Complete the following T-chart to compare and contrast a teleconference and a videoconference.

Teleconference	Videoconference

2. Research a Web site that offers distance learning courses. A company may offer a single class on one topic, or a college may offer a degree through distance learning. Print out the home page of the Web site.

Use the Vocabulary

Directions: *Match each vocabulary term in the left column with the correct definition in the right column. Write the appropriate letter next to the word or term.*

_____ 1. attachment
_____ 2. mailbox name
_____ 3. e-mail client
_____ 4. alias
_____ 5. e-mail server
_____ 6. bounce message
_____ 7. spam
_____ 8. e-mail virus
_____ 9. teleconference
_____ 10. videoconference

a. part of an e-mail address

b. a meeting that provides audio and visual contact for people in different locations

c. a notice that e-mail could not be delivered

d. junk e-mail

e. anything sent with an e-mail

f. a meeting via computers and a network or the Internet, which lets participants talk or exchange text messages

g. program sent in or attached to an e-mail message, which is intended to cause problems for the recipient

h. an ISP computer that accepts, sends, and delivers e-mail messages

i. software that lets you create, send, receive, and manage e-mail messages

j. nickname by which an e-mail user is known

Check Your Comprehension

Directions: *Complete each sentence with information from the chapter.*

1. In an e-mail address, the symbol @ represents the word _____.

2. The _____ is an Internet service provider's computer that routes e-mail.

3. In an e-mail message form, the _____ field identifies people other than the main recipient who should receive the message when it is sent.

4. When you _____ an e-mail message you have received, you send it to another person.

5. You will not get a bounce message if you enter an incorrect but _____ address.

6. Some e-mail clients have _____ and rules that you can configure to delete unwanted e-mail.

7. Beware of e-mail attachments that have _____ such as .EXE, .BAT, .COM, or .VBS in their file names.

8. Teleconferences and videoconferences save money because people don't have to _____ to attend a meeting.

9. Videoconferences can be used to communicate both live and _____ speeches.

10. Many schools now offer classes through the Internet, a practice known as _____.

Think Critically

Directions: *Answer the following questions on the lines provided.*

1. How do an e-mail client and an e-mail server work together to handle e-mail?

_____

_____

2. How can attachments both help and hurt e-mail communications?

_____

_____

3. What advantages do e-mail, teleconferences, and videoconferences offer to work-groups in different locations?

_____

_____

4. What is one way to avoid receiving a bounce message?

_____

_____

5. Could distance learning make use of a videoconference? How?

_____

_____

Extend Your Knowledge

Directions: *Choose one of the following projects. Complete the exercises on a separate sheet of paper.*

A. Picture phones allow you to see the person at the other end of a telephone call. A video camera that clips on your computer allows you to see the person with whom you communicate on the Internet. Research these technologies on the Internet. Compare and contrast their cost, features, and uses. Assess which, if either, you think will become more popular.

B. In small groups, brainstorm for the advantages and disadvantages of face-to-face communications, traditional letters, e-mail, telephone calls, teleconferencing, and videoconferencing. Then, create a list of situations for which each of these media might be the most appropriate communications choice.

Internet Basics

www.internet.

The Internet Connects the World No matter where you are on the planet, chances are good that the Internet is there, too. An international communication and information system, the Internet connects millions of computers and people.

People use the Internet at school, at work, and at home. At school, students and teachers use the Internet to do research and share information. At work, people use it to send e-mail, share files, and communicate with co-workers near and far. At home, people use the Internet to get help with homework, play games, and shop, among other activities.

The Internet has changed the way people around the world live and work. It is considered one of the most important and exciting inventions in history.

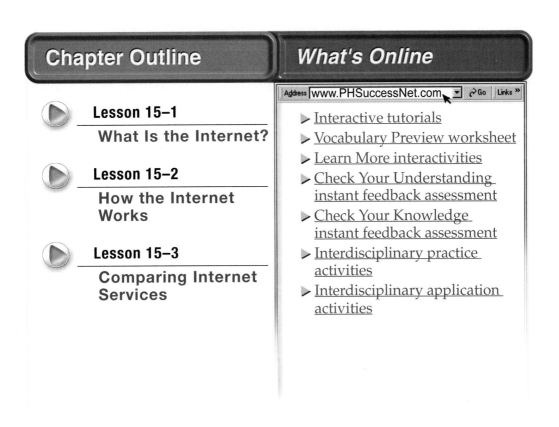

Chapter Outline

▶ **Lesson 15–1**
   What Is the Internet?

▶ **Lesson 15–2**
   How the Internet Works

▶ **Lesson 15–3**
   Comparing Internet Services

What's Online

Address www.PHSuccessNet.com ▾ ⟳Go Links »

➤ Interactive tutorials
➤ Vocabulary Preview worksheet
➤ Learn More interactivities
➤ Check Your Understanding instant feedback assessment
➤ Check Your Knowledge instant feedback assessment
➤ Interdisciplinary practice activities
➤ Interdisciplinary application activities

What Is the Internet?

Objectives

- Compare and contrast LANs, WANs, and the Internet.
- Describe how the three main parts of the Internet work together.
- Explain the advantages and disadvantages of the organization of the Internet.

As You Read

Organize Information Use a spider map to organize information about the Internet as you read.

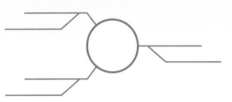

Key Terms

- Internet (p. 220)
- Internet client (p. 221)

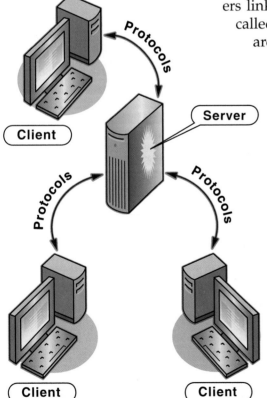

Client

Protocols

Server

Protocols

Protocols

Client

Client

Organization of the Internet

The **Internet** is a vast network that links together millions of computers around the world. It runs 365 days a year, 24 hours a day.

Structure of the Internet Two or more computers connected to one another are known as a network of computers. Computers linked together in the same building, such as a school, are called a local area network (LAN). Computers or LANs that are linked together over a large area, such as different parts of the country, are called a wide area network (WAN).

The Internet is a global WAN, a network of networks. It connects everything from single computers to large networks. The Internet can even connect computers that run different operating systems. This ability to share information with almost any computer makes the Internet a powerful tool for communication.

Servers The Internet is made up of three important parts: servers, clients, and protocols. Internet servers are the computers that provide services to other computers by way of the Internet. These services include processing e-mail, storing Web pages, or helping send files from one computer to another.

Figure 15.1.1 Like many networks, the Internet is made up of connected client and server computers, which use protocols to communicate.

Clients and Protocols **Internet clients** are the computers that request services from a server. When you connect to the Internet, the computer you use is considered a client. Protocols are the special sets of rules that allow clients and servers to connect to one another. Protocols tell computers how to format data and transmit it over a network.

Inventing the Internet

In the 1960s, people were working on ideas that later became the Internet. In 1969, the first four major computer centers in the United States were linked. By 1973, the network was international. In 1983, the Internet protocols went online for the first time. Two major groups worked on the development of the Internet: the United States military and university researchers.

United States Military In the 1960s, the United States government wanted to find a way to communicate in the event of a disaster or military attack. The military began to work on a system that would operate even if some communication connections were destroyed. The Defense Advanced Research Projects Agency (DARPA) of the U.S. Department of Defense focused on computer networking and communications. In 1968, this research led to a network of connected computer centers called the Advanced Research Projects Agency Network (ARPANET).

University Researchers With the military's leadership and funding, DARPA formed computing research centers at universities across the United States. From 1969 through 1987, the number of computers on the network increased from four to more than 10,000. These connections created the networks that became the Internet.

Technology @ Home

Staying current with changing technology is not always easy. But despite the challenges, one of the fastest growing populations of Internet users is women over 50 years of age. Many of them first learned to type on manual typewriters!

Think *About* **It!**
Listed below are other technologies invented since research for the Internet began in the mid-1960s. Circle each item you have in your home.

> food processor
> VCR
> cellular phone
> video game
> DVD

Figure 15.1.2 Today, the Internet includes millions of servers and connections all over the globe.

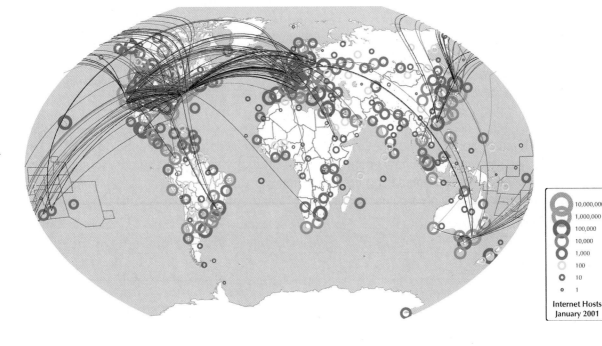

10,000,000
1,000,000
100,000
10,000
1,000
100
10
1

Internet Hosts January 2001

Internet Management

Who owns the Internet? The truth is, no specific organization or government does. The Internet is made up of many networks. Each network is managed by an organization, school, company, or government. So, although each part of it is managed, no one is in charge of the entire Internet. This provides both opportunities for growth and problems.

Freedom of the Internet One advantage to the open quality of the Internet is the ability to share information. Because much of the Internet is available for public use, there is a lot of freedom to get information from the Internet as well as to add to it. Anyone can make an idea or opinion accessible to anyone else.

Pitfalls of the Internet However, there are pitfalls to this open organization. People can post whatever point of view or information they want, even if it can sometimes be misleading or false. It is up to the users of the Internet to think critically about the information they find. If you have a question about anything you find on the Internet, ask an adult you trust about it.

Because the Internet is not managed and protected by a specific government or agency, each individual has to figure out how to best use it. The network developed from the ideas of the U.S. military and university researchers has now become a global, open system of communication and information.

Real-World Tech

Voting on the Internet? According to the Federal Election Commission, the Internet is not ready for U.S. citizens to vote on it. Safeguarding the privacy, security, and reliability of the voting process is important to ensuring a free democratic election.

While there have been some experiments with Internet voting, experts agree that it will be a long time before it is used in general elections. The Internet, however, can improve some parts of the election process. For example, the technology is in place for secure overseas military voting. Also, registration databases and vote totals can be sent over the Internet, saving time and money.

In what other ways might you use the Internet to find out more about politics? Write your ideas below.

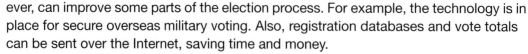

Demonstrate Your Knowledge

Critical Thinking

1. What is the difference between LANs and WANs and the Internet?

_____

_____

2. How do the three parts of the Internet work together?

_____

_____

3. How do you think the advantages of the organization of the Internet contribute to its disadvantages?

_____

_____

Activities

1. Complete the timeline to show the history of the Internet.

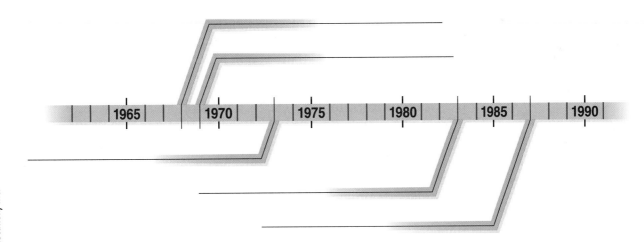

2. Conduct research to find out about the computers in your school. How many computers are there? Are they networked? How? Make a chart or diagram to show your findings.

How the Internet Works

Objectives

- Identify ways to connect to the Internet.
- Compare and contrast Internet Service Providers and online services.
- Summarize the need for protocols.
- Distinguish between Internet Protocol addresses and domain names.

As You Read

Outline Information Use an outline to organize information about how the Internet works as you read.

Key Terms

- Internet service provider (ISP) (p. 224)
- username (p. 225)
- online service (p. 225)
- navigate (p. 225)
- Transmission Control Protocol/Internet Protocol (TCP/IP) (p. 226)
- Internet Protocol (IP) address (p. 226)
- domain name system (p. 226)

Accessing the Internet

There are different ways to connect to the Internet. The reasons for various options are availability, location, speed, and price.

Dialup, ISDN, and DSL Access The least expensive way to get online is to use a dialup connection between a standard phone line and a modem. These connections are called "dialup" because your computer must connect to the Internet by using a telephone number to contact a server. When the session is over, the connection is broken.

Some Digital Subscriber Lines (DSL) require a special telephone line. Integrated Services Digital Network (ISDN) lines require a special ISDN adapter and modem. As a result, both services cost more than regular phone service. Furthermore, DSL and ISDN are not available in all areas.

Cable and Satellite Cable television companies offer Internet access through cable modems. This access is at speeds much faster than dialup modems. You need a network card in your computer, a cable modem, and cable access. Satellite access is also very fast for downloading files to your computer, but it requires a phone line and a modem for sending files to outside users.

Getting Online

After you have access to the Internet, you must select a way to get online. Choices include Internet service providers and online services.

Internet Service Providers An **Internet service provider (ISP)** is a company that provides a link from your computer to the Internet. For a fee, an ISP provides its subscribers with

© Pearson Education, Inc.

software, a password, an access phone number, and a username. A **username** identifies who you are when you access the Internet. An ISP does not guide you through the Internet—it only provides an easy-to-use connection to it. You can use either a local ISP or a national ISP.

Online Services   An online service connects your computer to the Internet. **Online services** are businesses that provide tools to help you **navigate,** or move to different parts of, the Internet. Online services are not the Internet. They provide special software that you load onto your computer. The software makes the connection to the service, which then guides you through content and activities. Three popular online services are America Online (AOL), Microsoft Network® (MSN), and CompuServe®.

Protocols

The Internet provides a way to link a single computer or smaller networks to a larger network. To transfer data from network to network, a set of standards, or protocols, is used to define how things should work. Protocols determine how networked computers communicate, formulate data, and transmit data.

Connections

Science Researchers interested in ending world hunger can now meet in a virtual 3-D laboratory to work together on projects.

Using the Internet, researchers can model different environments, such as a potato farm in the Andes Mountains. They then work together to improve the economy of a developing country through agricultural research.

Figure 15.2.1 Microsoft Network® is a popular online service provider with millions of subscribers.

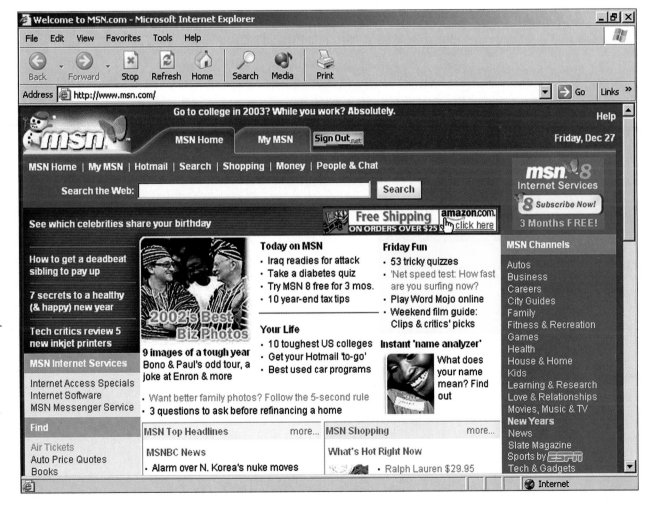

Technology @ Work

Businesses outside (and occasionally inside) the United States add a suffix to top-level domain names to identify themselves. These domain-name suffixes are commonly called sub-domains.

Think *About* **It!**

Identify the name of the country represented by each two-letter suffix.

- ▷ .jp
- ▷ .au
- ▷ .th
- ▷ .uk
- ▷ .us

Internet Protocols Internet protocols are referred to as **Transmission Control Protocol/Internet Protocol** or **TCP/IP.** *TCP* defines how one Internet-connected computer contacts another and exchanges information. *IP* defines the Internet addresses.

IP Addresses Each computer that connects to the Internet has to be uniquely identified. To do this, every computer is assigned a four-part number separated by periods called the **Internet Protocol (IP) address.** For example, the IP address for your computer might be 123.257.91.7. The administrator of the network to which your computer connects assigns your IP address.

Domain Names IP addresses can be difficult to remember, so a simpler naming system called the **domain name system** using letters as well as numbers was created. A domain name identifies one or more IP addresses. If you want to obtain a domain name, you or your ISP can contact a registering organization. It then contacts an organization called InterNIC, which keeps the master database of domain names.

How do domain names work? Let's say you want your computer to access information stored on another computer. Your local ISP's domain name server will contact the domain name server you are calling. The information to identify both computers will be exchanged, and the contact will be made.

Every domain name has an ending, or suffix, that indicates which type of organization registered the name. The following table lists these suffixes—called top-level domains—and the types of organizations they represent.

Top-level domain	Organizations represented
.com	Commercial businesses, such as companies
.edu	Private and public schools and universities
.org	Organizations, usually of a nonprofit nature
.gov	Government organizations only
.mil	Military organizations only
.net	Network organizations, such as Internet service providers

Demonstrate Your Knowledge

Critical Thinking

1. How do ISPs and online services differ?

_____

_____

2. What do TCP/IP protocols do?

_____

_____

3. How do IP addresses and domain names differ?

_____

_____

Activities

1. Complete the Venn diagram to compare and contrast options for accessing the Internet.

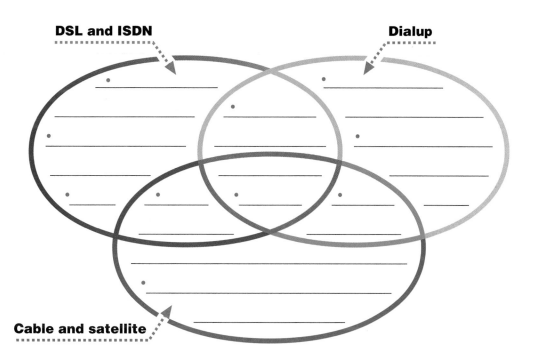

2. As a class, create a list of top-level domain names, such as .com, .edu, or .org. Then, in small groups, scan newspapers or magazines to see which domain names are most common.

Comparing Internet Services

Objectives

- Identify and describe kinds of Internet services.
- Summarize how to access information on the Web.
- Analyze the usefulness of e-mail in daily living.

As You Read

Identify Main Idea/Details Use a main idea/detail chart to identify the main idea and details of popular Internet services as you read.

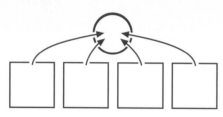

🔊 Key Terms

- Web browser (p. 228)
- portal (p. 228)
- search engine (p. 228)
- hypertext (p. 229)
- hyperlink (p. 229)
- uniform resource locator (URL) (p. 229)
- download (p. 230)
- upload (p. 230)

Internet Services

When you send an e-mail message to a friend, you use one kind of Internet service. Browsing the World Wide Web is done through another type of service. Different Internet services are used for accessing the World Wide Web, sending and receiving electronic mail, and conducting file transfers.

Intranets The Internet uses protocols that define how the client software and server software communicate. In the same way, some organizations have their own networks of services, called intranets, which are private. Employees can use e-mail, the Web, and other Internet technologies with their company's intranet. Intranets, however, are used within a company and are not open to the public.

Internet Software

The protocols for delivering an e-mail message are not the same as the protocols for displaying a Web page. Typically, there is different software for each Internet service. You use a **Web browser** to view Web pages. The two most popular Web browsers are Netscape® Navigator and Microsoft® Internet Explorer. You use a mail program to send and receive e-mail messages. This distinction, however, is beginning to vanish. Hotmail's Outlook® Web Access, for example, uses a Web site to access and send e-mail.

Portals Internet **portals** provide organized subject guides to Internet content. They usually offer search engines as well. A **search engine** is software that finds and lists information that meets a specified search. First, the search engine asks you to type a keyword into a blank field. Then, the search engine will give you the results of that search. Popular search engines include Yahoo!, Excite, and InfoSeek.

Accessing Information on the World Wide Web

The World Wide Web is a huge collection of hypertext documents called Web pages. In a **hypertext** document, certain words or pictures can serve as hyperlinks. A **hyperlink** is a link to another document on the World Wide Web.

Hyperlinks Usually hyperlinks appear underlined, in a different color, or highlighted. Sometimes there are buttons or images that can be clicked. When you move your mouse over a hyperlink, the pointer changes to an icon of a hand. You can click this hyperlink item to be transferred to another document.

URLs When you click a hyperlink, the Web browser retrieves and displays the document connected to that hyperlink. How does this work? Every document has a unique address, called a **uniform resource locator (URL),** which tells exactly where the document is located on the Internet. A hyperlink instructs the browser to go to the URL for that document.

Electronic Mail

For many Internet users, electronic mail, or e-mail, has replaced traditional mail and telephone services. E-mail is fast and easy. If you organize your e-mail addresses into groups, you can broadcast, or send, a message to a group in just one step.

Technology @ School

The Internet is available in thousands of schools across the country. Although students may be blocked from accessing inappropriate sites, they can contact scientists, take virtual field trips, and even watch frog dissections!

Think *About* **It!**
Before logging on to the Internet, think about the purpose of your visit. Underline each item below that you think is an appropriate use of the Internet at school.

- research a book report
- solve math problems
- e-mail a friend
- play video games
- create a database of your favorite books

Spotlight on...

TIM BERNERS-LEE

❝ The whole idea that you can have some idea and make it happen means dreamers all over the world should take heart and not stop. ❞

Tim Berners-Lee
Creator of the World Wide Web

In the 1980s, Tim Berners-Lee turned what was a system for keeping track of his random notes into a system for linking the work of scientists any-

where in the world. Berners-Lee designed the URL, or a scheme for locating Internet addresses; developed HTML, or a language for encoding hypertext; created HTTP, or a system to link hypertext documents; and built the first browser. Few people in history have had a greater impact on the way we communicate than Berners-Lee.

Figure 15.3.1 An e-mail message may travel a long way from the sender to the receiver.

E-mail Pros and Cons   E-mail is not free, and it's not instantaneous. However, you do not pay to send each e-mail, as you would a letter. The cost of your e-mail service is included in the fee you pay your Internet service provider or online service provider. In most cases, it takes minutes or more for an e-mail message to reach its destination. But it costs the same and takes approximately the same amount of time to send a message to someone in your own city as it does to send a message halfway around the world.

Transferring Files

File Transfer Protocol (FTP) lets you transfer files on the Internet. With an FTP client, you can transfer files from an FTP server to your computer in an operation called **downloading.** In **uploading,** you transfer files from the client to the server.

FTP can transfer both text files and binary files. Binary files are program files, graphics, pictures, music or video clips, and documents. Once you've stored a file on an FTP server, you can distribute the URL so that your friends can also download the file from the server.

One difference between using an FTP server and e-mail to transfer files is that with FTP, the file stays on the server until you take it off. With e-mail, a file that has been transferred will be lost once the e-mail message has been deleted. E-mail is considered a more secure method, however, because only the recipient of the e-mail message has access to the attached files.

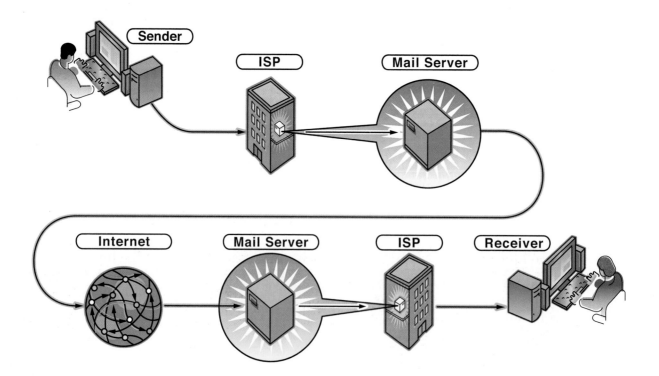

Demonstrate Your Knowledge

Critical Thinking

1. How are intranets different from the Internet?

_____

_____

2. How do hyperlinks work?

_____

_____

3. How do you think e-mail has impacted the daily life of its users?

_____

_____

Activities

1. Complete the following chart to compare and contrast e-mail and FTP.

E-mail	FTP
• Transfers files on the Internet	• Transfers files on the Internet
• _____	• Files stay on server until removed
• Only recipient has access to attached files	• _____
• _____	• Can send and receive both text and binary files
• Files are sent from sender's computer to receiver's computer	• _____

2. Twenty years from now, how do you think jobs in communications will change? How do you predict people will use the Internet? Write a short essay summarizing your predictions.

© Pearson Education, Inc.

Use the Vocabulary

Directions: *Match each vocabulary term in the left column with the correct definition in the right column. Write the appropriate letter next to the word or term.*

_____ **1.** Internet
_____ **2.** Internet client
_____ **3.** Internet service provider
_____ **4.** username
_____ **5.** domain name system
_____ **6.** portal
_____ **7.** hyperlink
_____ **8.** uniform resource locator
_____ **9.** download

a. highlighted text or graphic in a Web site that directs browser to another URL

b. made up of letters and numbers that correspond to one or more IP addresses

c. computer that requests services from a server

d. identification while on the Internet

e. address of documents on the Web

f. vast network of connected computers

g. a company that provides access to the Internet

h. to transfer a file from a server to a client

i. Internet service that provides a guide to Internet content

Check Your Comprehension

Directions: *Complete each sentence with information from the chapter.*

1. A network that covers a large area is called a _____.

2. The three main parts of the Internet are _____, servers, and protocols.

3. The two main groups responsible for inventing the Internet are the U.S. military and _____ .

4. A _____ is the least expensive way to access the Internet.

5. _____ are businesses that provide special software to guide users through Internet content and activities.

6. A _____ enables someone to search for a Web site with a keyword.

7. TCP/IP is _____ for the Internet.

8. The top-level _____ for most commercial businesses is .com.

9. A _____ is used to view Web pages.

10. You can send a _____ to someone by attaching it to an e-mail message.

◉ Think Critically

Directions: *Answer the following questions on the lines provided.*

1. Why did the U.S. Department of Defense begin to research computer networking and communications?

_____

_____

2. Why do you think it is important to think critically about the accuracy and validity of information you find on the Internet?

_____

_____

3. Why might someone use an online service rather than an Internet service provider?

_____

_____

4. How do you get a domain name?

_____

_____

5. Why do you think e-mail is so popular for daily communication at home, school, and work?

_____

_____

◉ Extend Your Knowledge

Directions: *Choose one of the following projects. Complete the exercises on a separate sheet of paper.*

A. Because the Internet is so easily accessible, it is important to learn how to protect yourself when you are online. Conduct research using the Internet to compile a list of Web safety tips. Include information about any acceptable use policy your school may have. Publish your findings, with permission from your teacher, on your school's Web site.

B. In small groups, conduct online research using keyword strategies to learn what kinds of Internet access are available in your area. Find out how much the services cost and the benefits of each. If possible, get information from companies competing for the same services so you can compare prices. Compile your research in a chart. Then, summarize your findings as a class.

chapter
16

World Wide Web Basics

A Global Source of Information Think about a comprehensive source of information—one that grows by thousands of new documents every day. Such a resource would contain a wealth of information.

Actually, you don't have to suppose such a resource into existence. It already exists—it's the World Wide Web. You can turn to the World Wide Web to check out products, get help with schoolwork, find out about current events, and do many more tasks.

However, along with offering a lot of wonderful information, the Web is also home to some inaccurate and potentially harmful information. It is up to you to evaluate the information you find on the Web.

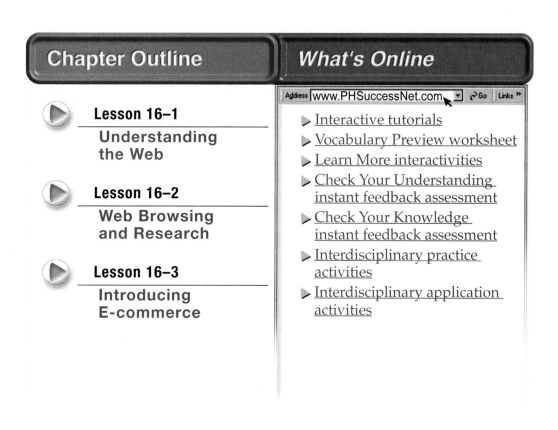

Chapter Outline

Lesson 16–1
Understanding the Web

Lesson 16–2
Web Browsing and Research

Lesson 16–3
Introducing E-commerce

What's Online

Address www.PHSuccessNet.com

- Interactive tutorials
- Vocabulary Preview worksheet
- Learn More interactivities
- Check Your Understanding instant feedback assessment
- Check Your Knowledge instant feedback assessment
- Interdisciplinary practice activities
- Interdisciplinary application activities

Understanding the Web

Objectives

- Explain the creation of the World Wide Web.
- Contrast the Internet and the World Wide Web.
- Describe a Web site.

As You Read

Organize Information Use a summary chart to help organize details as you read.

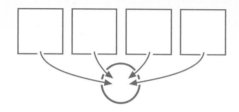

What's Online

In Lesson 16–1 of the iText, you will find more features and information for this lesson, including:

- Interactive tutorials
- As You Read worksheet
- Learn More interactivities
- Check Your Understanding interactive assessments
- Interactive lesson review

🔑 Key Terms

- browser (p. 236)
- graphical browser (p. 236)
- Hypertext Markup Language (HTML) (p. 237)
- Web page (p. 238)
- Web site (p. 238)
- Web server (p. 238)

Creating the Web

As early as 1980, a few people were trying to connect documents stored on different computers by means of a private network or the Internet. These connected documents, it was thought, could someday create a "web" of information that would be instantly available to anyone.

In 1989, Tim Berners-Lee developed a way to retrieve one computer's Internet address while working on another computer. The resulting programs and protocols led to the creation of the World Wide Web, which is now a widely used part of the Internet. Berners-Lee made this new technology freely available to everyone and pleaded with other researchers to help develop ways to expand the World Wide Web, or the Web, as it is commonly called.

In 1992, Marc Andreesen and other students at the National Center for Supercomputing Applications (NCSA) developed a browser called Mosaic®. A **browser** is a program that enables users to navigate the Web and locate and display Web documents. Mosaic® was the first useful **graphical browser,** one that could display graphics as well as text.

In 1994, Andreesen introduced Netscape® Navigator. A year later, Microsoft® released Internet Explorer®, and that same year the Web was opened up to public and commercial use. Navigator® and Explorer® soon became the most popular Web browsers.

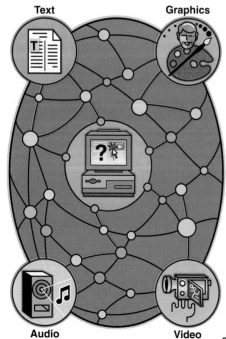

Text   Graphics

Audio   Video

Figure 16.1.1 The Web gets its name from the web of connections it creates between computers all over the planet.

The Internet and the Web

Many people use the terms *Internet* and *World Wide Web* as synonyms. In fact, the World Wide Web is just one part of the Internet. Every computer on the Internet has a unique IP, or Internet Protocol, address. Every document on the Web has a unique address, too, called its uniform resource locator, or URL.

Like e-mail, newsgroups, and file transfer, the Web is a service supported by the Internet. Although these services share the Internet and many of its resources, each is different, with its own set of protocols and applications.

Networks and Documents   The Internet is a network of networks. It provides the supporting structure for certain services. The Internet connects millions of computers. Any computer in the world can connect to any other computer as long as both are connected to the Internet.

The World Wide Web is a huge collection of documents linked by hypertext. Hypertext allows readers to click links to get to other documents. Writers format documents and add the hyperlinks by using **Hypertext Markup Language,** or **HTML.** People all over the world create and format Web documents by using standardized HTML codes called tags. These documents are saved, or "published" to a server on the Internet. Then, when the documents are accessed by a Web browser, each portion—text, images, sound, or animation—appears with its intended formats.

© Pearson Education, Inc.

Spotlight on...

MARC ANDREESEN

❝ *I think the browsers are obviously important. I think also the servers are important. And the single most important thing that has happened is the thousands of people that have created applications using this stuff that none of us thought of or ever would have thought of.* ❞

Marc Andreesen
Web browser developer

That's Marc Andreesen's perspective, in 1995, on the popularity of the Web. Browsers existed before Andreesen's work on linking documents. The graphical browsers he helped develop, however, were a real breakthrough. With graphical browsers, Web documents could include illustrations, photos, animation, sounds, and videos. Through his work on Mosaic® and Netscape® Navigator, Andreesen greatly contributed to the growth of the World Wide Web.

Understanding Web Sites

A **Web page** is a document on the Web. A **Web site** is a collection of related pages. Moving from one Web page to another is called browsing. When you type a URL or click a link in your Web browser, it sends a request to the computer on the Internet that contains the page identified by the URL. That computer is called a **Web server.** It stores Web pages and responds to requests from Web browsers. When the server receives your request, it sends the document to your computer, and your browser displays the page on your screen.

Most Web sites have a primary page called the home page or index page which appears when you first enter the site's URL. A URL can also contain other information to identify a specific page on a Web site.

Protocol The first part of a URL specifies the protocol required to access the document. A protocol is the set of rules used by Internet computers. For the Web, the Hypertext Transfer Protocol (http) is used.

Domain Name The next part of a URL, such as www.fbi.gov, is the domain name of the server that stores the Web site. This part of the URL usually takes you to the site's home page.

Path The remainder of a URL, if any, defines the path to the document's location on the Web server. Like any computer, a Web server stores files in folders, so the path lists the folder and subfolders, if any, containing the desired document. Thus, a URL such as http://www.fbi.gov/employment/ identifies a folder named "employment" on the site's Web server.

Resource File Name At the end of a URL, you may see the name of a file—the specific Web resource for which you are looking. The resource may be an HTML document or a Web page, a video clip, a text file, or another type of resource. The file name extension identifies the type of resource.

Figure 16.1.2 The parts of a URL

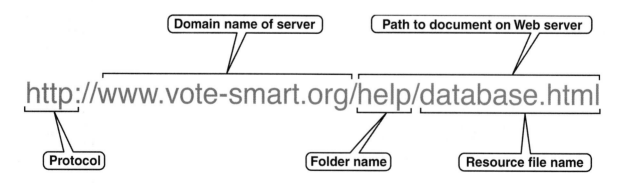

Demonstrate Your Knowledge

Critical Thinking

1. What do you think are the three key events in the history of the Web?

_____

_____

2. What is the key difference between the Internet and the World Wide Web?

_____

_____

3. What is the difference between a Web server and a Web browser?

_____

_____

Activities

1. Complete the following timeline to chart events in the history of the Web.

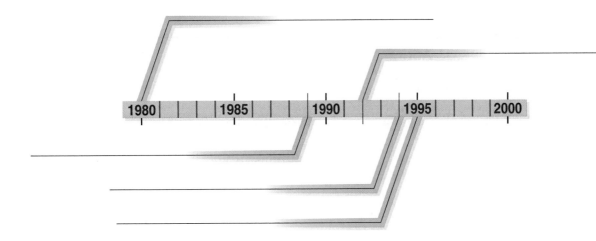

2. Open any Web page other than a default home page. Copy the URL from the address box, and label each part of the URL. Review your labels with a partner.

Web Browsing and Research

Objectives

- Explore Web navigation tools.
- Explain how to improve search results by applying keyword and Boolean searches.
- Suggest ways to evaluate Web pages.

As You Read

Organize Information Use an outline to organize ways of accessing and evaluating Web pages as you read.

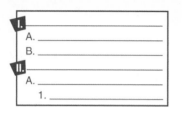

What's Online

In Lesson 16–2 of the iText, you will find more features and information for this lesson, including:

- Interactive tutorials
- As You Read worksheet
- Learn More interactivities
- Check Your Understanding interactive assessments
- Interactive lesson review

Key Terms

- navigation button (p. 240)
- Back button (p. 240)
- Forward button (p. 240)
- Boolean search (p. 241)

Figure 16.2.1 All popular browsers feature navigation buttons, an Address box, and tools for creating a list of frequently visited Web sites.

Browsing the Web

Although their look is different, Netscape® Navigator and Microsoft® Internet Explorer share some common features.

Navigation Buttons Located on the browser's toolbar, **navigation buttons** let you perform certain operations quickly. When you click Refresh or Reload, the browser again downloads the page you are viewing. When you click the **Back button,** the browser reloads the previous page. The **Forward button** moves ahead to pages previously viewed before Back was activated.

Address Box If you type a URL in the Address box and press Enter, the browser will take you to the Web page located at that URL.

Favorites or Bookmarks The Favorites feature in Internet Explorer® and the Bookmarks feature in Netscape® Navigator let you create a list of frequently visited Web pages. Then, rather than retyping the URL, you can return to any bookmarked or favorite page by clicking its name in the list.

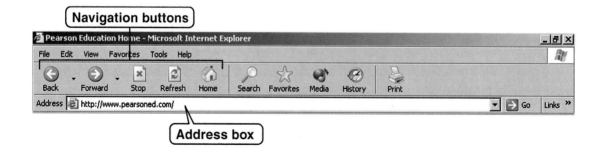

Finding Information on the Web

Because the Web is so vast, it can be hard to locate information on a specific topic. Subject guides and search engines can help focus that task.

Subject Guides   Many Web sites offer subject guides to the Web, pages grouped together under headings like Careers, News, or Travel. These guides include only pages that provide useful information about the subject.

Search Engines   If you cannot locate what you are looking for in a subject guide, use a search engine such as Google®, Lycos®, or HotBot®. Type one or two keywords that describe the subject you're looking for, and then click Search. The search engine will display a list of Web pages that contain the keywords you specified. For example, if you type the word *dog* as your keyword, the search engine will list Web pages that contain that word.

You can improve your chances of getting worthwhile results by conducting a **Boolean search.** To conduct a Boolean search, type an operator such as AND, OR, or NOT to link the keywords in the search box. For example, if you use the word *telescope* as your keyword, the search engine will list pages containing information about every type of telescope. But if you are primarily interested in reflecting telescopes, you can use the Boolean search *telescope AND reflecting* to see pages that include both terms and ignore pages that include only one of them.

Connections

Social Studies The Web is a terrific resource for finding historical and other social studies information, such as information about your state. Some states, like Texas, make it easy for you. The Texas Historical Association and the General Libraries at the University of Texas in Austin sponsor "The Handbook of Texas Online," a multidisciplinary encyclopedia of the history, geography, and culture of Texas.

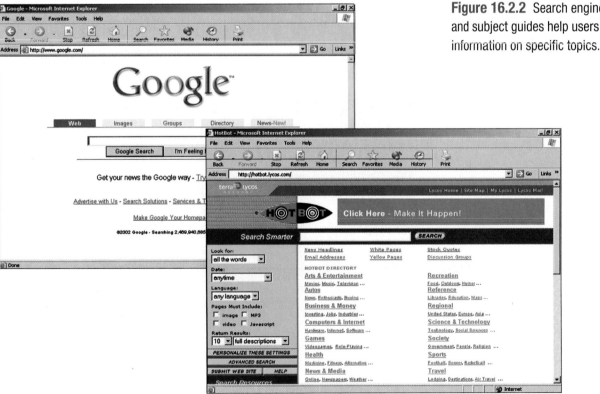

Figure 16.2.2 Search engines and subject guides help users find information on specific topics.

© Pearson Education, Inc.

Think *About* **It!**

Think about the types of activities in which a middle-school computer club might engage. Circle each item below that you think would be a good club project.

▷ create a club Web site
▷ encourage members to shop online
▷ learn to generate video and audio on the Web
▷ post gossip about classmates
▷ search for homework help

Evaluating Information on the Web

You can find excellent and reliable information on the Web. As with print references, you can also find some Web pages that are biased, objectionable, misleading, inaccurate, or dangerous.

Guidelines for Finding Reliable Information   Verify any information you find by checking another source. The freedom of the Web leads to a greater potential for error, since pages may not be checked for accuracy of the information they contain. Ask yourself these questions about any information you find on the Web:

- Who is the author of the page? Is that author qualified to write about this topic?
- Does the author indicate the source of the information presented?
- Does the information appear to be accurate? Are there misspelled words and bad grammar that might indicate poor quality of content?
- Is the information presented logically and thoughtfully?
- Does the language seem balanced and objective, or is it biased and argumentative?
- What is the purpose of the page? Is the author trying to sell you something or convince you to believe something? Who benefits if the information is accepted?
- Who provides the server for publishing this Web site? Who pays for the page?
- Does the page show when it was created or revised? Is the page up to date?

Figure 16.2.3 The Web can be fun and useful, but it is up to users to decide whether Web-based information is reliable.

Demonstrate Your Knowledge

Critical Thinking

1. How might you return to a Web page you accessed earlier in a session?

_____

2. To find information about dolphins, what Boolean search strategies could you apply to avoid pages relating to the Miami Dolphins football team?

_____

3. Why is it important to evaluate the language and purpose of a Web page before you accept the information stated on it?

_____

_____

Activities

1. Complete the following cause-and-effect chart to show the effect of using various browser commands.

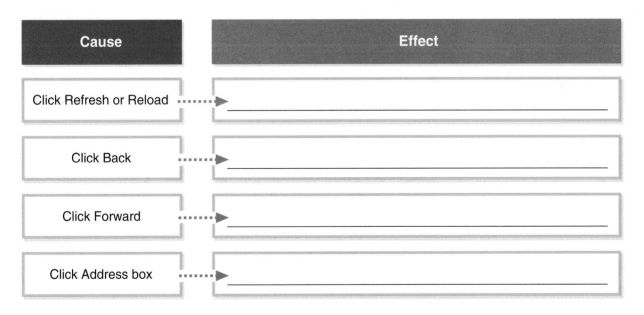

Cause	Effect
Click Refresh or Reload	_____
Click Back	_____
Click Forward	_____
Click Address box	_____

2. As a class, choose a keyword to search on the Web. Work in small groups to find this keyword and have each group use a different search engine. Identify the source and evaluate five of the Web pages that result from the search. Compare your findings with those of other groups. Discuss how you might refine a keyword search to make it more effective.

Introducing E-commerce

Objectives

- Compare and contrast methods of e-commerce.
- Identify reasons for the success of online shopping.
- Explain how Secure Electronic Transactions and vendor liability coverage protect consumers.

As You Read

Organize Information Use a spider web to help you organize ways to use e-commerce as you read.

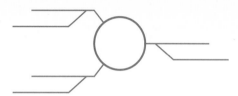

What's Online

In Lesson 16–3 of the iText, you will find more features and information for this lesson, including:

- Interactive tutorials
- As You Read worksheet
- Learn More interactivities
- Check Your Understanding interactive assessments
- Interactive lesson review

Key Terms

- e-commerce (p. 244)
- Secure Electronic Transactions (SET) (p. 246)
- certificate authority (CA) (p. 246)

Electronic Commerce

Electronic commerce, or **e-commerce,** is the use of telecommunications networks or the Internet to conduct business. E-commerce is not new; companies have used wide area networks, or WANs, to do business for years.

Thanks to the Internet and affordable computers, e-commerce has become accessible to anyone who has an Internet connection and a Web browser. More and more Internet users are researching products, shopping, opening bank accounts, and trading stocks online. Many businesses realize that they may lose customers if they do not have an online presence.

Online Banking

In online banking, customers use a Web browser to access their accounts, balance checkbooks, transfer funds, and pay bills online.

Personal Finance Programs Programs such as Microsoft® Money or Intuit's Quicken® have features that can help you budget your money, analyze your spending habits, balance your checkbook, and make account transactions. One drawback to these programs is that you can access your online account only from the computer on which you keep your Money® or Quicken® data. Another potential problem is that anyone with access to that computer and your password can view this data.

Web-Based Banking Web-based online banking allows users to access their accounts in financial institutions. All the data is stored on the bank's computer, not your own, so you can access your account from any computer that has an Internet connection. You can learn about different types of services and interest rates, transer funds, or even pay bills online.

Online Shopping

When many people think of e-commerce, they think of shopping online. Online shopping has grown in popularity due to security features built into popular Web browsers.

The Buyer's Point of View The World Wide Web is an excellent resource for researching products, services, and prices. At many sites, buyers can read product reviews posted by other buyers. At other sites, they can find vendors and product ratings.

The Seller's Point of View One of the main advantages of online business is low startup cost. For a small investment, a vendor can open a Web storefront and sell products online to a wider variety of customers than one physical location offers.

Amazon.com, for example, was launched in 1995. This company set out to change how consumers buy books. Rather than visit a bookstore that stocks from 10,000 to 40,000 titles, consumers around the globe can log on to Amazon.com and search a database of more than three million titles.

Another example of a company that uses e-commerce extensively is eBay.com, which provides a place for buying and selling all kinds of products online.

Almost anyone with financial resources can set up a checking or savings account at an online bank.

Think *About* **It!**
Think about the advantages an online bank account offers. Below, circle each statement that identifies an advantage.

➤ lets you check your account any time
➤ lets you make deposits anytime
➤ helps you avoid math mistakes
➤ helps you plan your spending
➤ prevents overspending

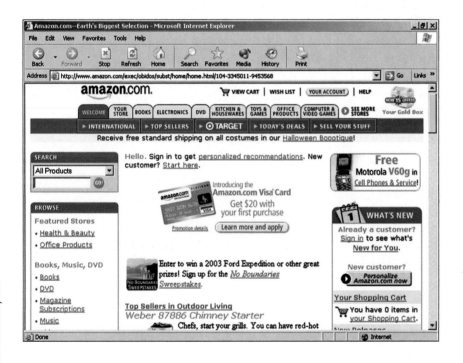

Figure 16.3.1 Amazon.com is a popular e-commerce Web site.

Secure Electronic Transactions

To protect both merchants and customers, Visa, Mastercard, and American Express worked together to develop a program called **Secure Electronic Transactions,** or **SET.** Both buyers and sellers use digital signatures to identify themselves. To ensure that the signature certificates are valid, both have to be endorsed by a third-party **certificate authority,** or **CA,** a company that verifies people's identities from support documents provided for this purpose.

To participate in SET, customers have to use somewhat difficult programs. Thus, few online merchants are currently interested in SET.

Since many credit card companies offer liability coverage, SET may be unnecessary, at least for now. Under the Fair Credit Billing Act, a credit card company cannot hold the account holder responsible for more than $50 of fraudulent charges.

Basic Online Security

Even if you and your favorite merchants don't participate in SET, you can still conduct business securely over the Web. If a Web page is secure, your browser will tell you. Look for a pad-lock icon, which appears in the browser's status bar. If the pad-lock is closed (locked), the page is secure. If the padlock is open (unlocked), the page is not secure.

Another security indicator appears in the browser's Address bar. If the page is secure, it should use the secure http protocol, indicated by *https* in the Address bar. This means that the Web site encodes all the information you send to it, so even if someone else gets the information, it will be unusable.

Figure 16.3.2 Your browser can tell you whether you are using a secure Web site.

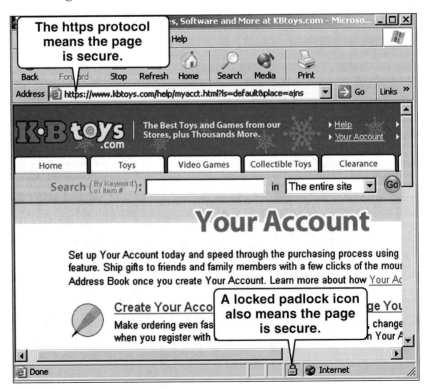

© Pearson Education, Inc.

Demonstrate Your Knowledge

Critical Thinking

1. Name a way the Internet has expanded e-commerce for businesses or consumers.

_____

2. What advantages might customers find at an online store like Amazon.com compared to a traditional store? What disadvantages might they find?

_____

_____

3. Which online security measure helps protect personal information on credit cards?

_____

Activities

1. Complete the following Venn diagram to compare and contrast two forms of online banking.

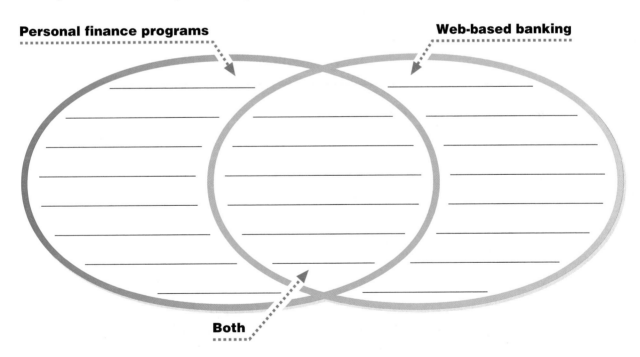

Personal finance programs

Web-based banking

Both

2. Go to Amazon.com and find reviews of your favorite book, as well as the prices of hardcover and paperback editions. Then, use a search engine to access another online bookstore and use keywords in a Boolean search to find the same information. Decide which site you might buy the book from. Explain your reasons to the class.

Use the Vocabulary

Directions: *Match each vocabulary term in the left column with the correct definition in the right column. Write the appropriate letter next to the word or term.*

_____ **1.** graphical browser

_____ **2.** HTML

_____ **3.** Web server

_____ **4.** Web page

_____ **5.** Web site

_____ **6.** navigation button

_____ **7.** Boolean search

_____ **8.** e-commerce

_____ **9.** Secure Electronic Transactions

_____ **10.** certificate authority

a. tool that lets users perform routine operations with a browser

b. a way to improve searches by linking keywords

c. computer that houses Web sites and sends documents to users

d. a collection of related documents on the Web

e. organization that validates digital signatures

f. conducting business through a network on the Internet

g. Web navigation program that shows pictures and text

h. the use of digital signatures to protect online buyers and sellers

i. single document on the Web

j. markup language used to format Web documents

Check Your Comprehension

Directions: *Circle the correct choice for each of the following.*

1. Which government agency supported the Internet in the early years?
  a. Federal Bureau of Investigation
  b. National Science Foundation
  c. Federal Communications Commission
  d. Internal Revenue Service

2. Which of the following is NOT part of a complete URL address?
  a. protocol
  b. server
  c. path
  d. author

3. Which of the following browser tools will most easily help you revisit a Web site you enjoyed?
  a. Favorites or Bookmarks
  b. Forward
  c. Refresh or Reload
  d. Address box

4. By which of the following does a search engine search?
  a. URL addresses
  b. Favorites
  c. Bookmarks
  d. keywords

5. Which of the following has contributed the most to the growth of e-commerce?
  a. traditional stores
  b. advanced Web browsers
  c. affordable computers
  d. personal finance programs

6. Which of the following provides a guarantee for digital signatures?
  a. online banks
  b. online stores
  c. certificate authority
  d. liability coverage

Think Critically

Directions: *Answer the following questions on the lines provided.*

1. Why is the URL of a page describing a particular book available on Amazon.com more detailed than the URL of the company's home page?

_____

_____

2. Do you think you should be more careful in accepting information from a Web page than from a printed article in a reputable newspaper? If so, why?

_____

_____

3. Which Web browser features or tools do you find most useful? Why?

_____

_____

4. How might you identify an online bank with which you would like to do business?

_____

_____

_____

Extend Your Knowledge

Directions: *Choose one of the following projects. Complete the exercises on a separate sheet of paper.*

A. Browsers provide other features and functions in addition to those listed in this lesson. For example, as you begin to type an address, Microsoft® Internet Explorer reveals a list of sites you've already visited that begin with the same letters. Work with a partner and explore the functions of a browser. Position the mouse over other buttons to see what appears. Click the buttons to see what happens. Visit the online Help feature to find out more about it. Create a chart in a word-processing program and enter your findings.

B. The Web has been praised for the wealth of knowledge it provides for users around the world. It is also criticized for the dangers it makes possible and for the temptation it offers some people. Conduct online or library research to learn the praises and objections people have for the World Wide Web, and take notes. Participate in a debate on the advantages and disadvantages of the resource.

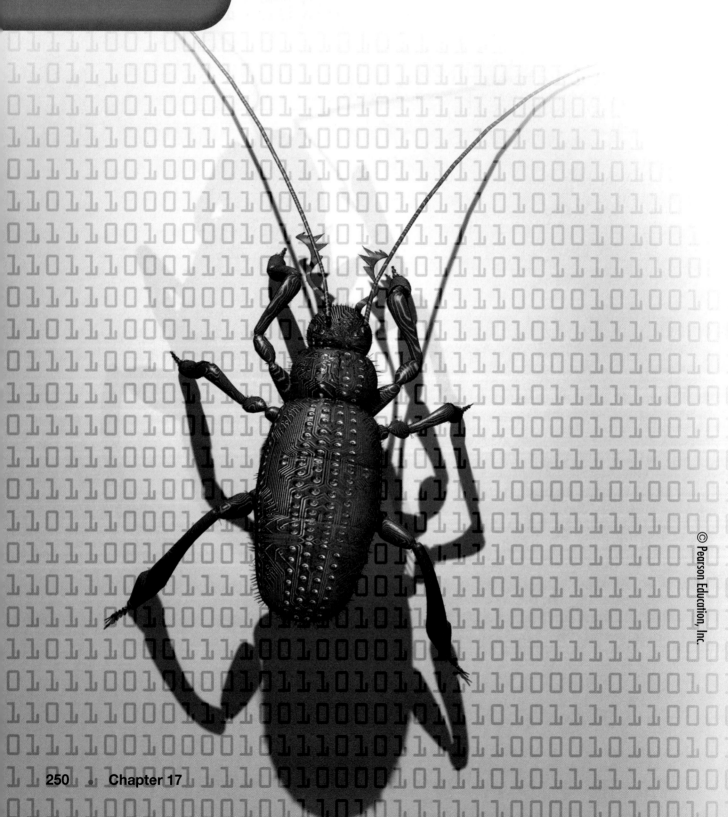

chapter 17
Issues for Computer Users

© Pearson Education, Inc.

Computers and Safety Computers are tools and, like other tools, they are controlled by the person using them. People can use computers to learn, to communicate, and to have fun. However, people can also use computers to snoop into another person's private life or to commit crimes. Careless computer users can pass computer viruses from their machines to those of other users. What can make computers dangerous is the same thing that makes them helpful: They can store vast amounts of data.

When people learn to use tools, they learn to use them with care and to protect themselves and others from harm. Computer users need to learn ways to protect themselves, too.

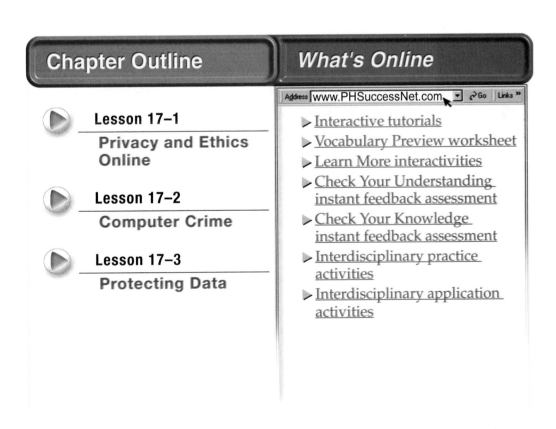

Chapter Outline

▶ **Lesson 17–1**

   Privacy and Ethics Online

▶ **Lesson 17–2**

   Computer Crime

▶ **Lesson 17–3**

   Protecting Data

What's Online

Address www.PHSuccessNet.com ▾ ⟲Go Links »

▷ Interactive tutorials
▷ Vocabulary Preview worksheet
▷ Learn More interactivities
▷ Check Your Understanding instant feedback assessment
▷ Check Your Knowledge instant feedback assessment
▷ Interdisciplinary practice activities
▷ Interdisciplinary application activities

Lesson 17–1

Privacy and Ethics Online

Objectives

- Summarize the danger of sharing personal information on the Internet.
- Explain copyright laws.
- Give examples of rules in acceptable use policies (AUPs).

As You Read

Organize Information   As you read the lesson, use an outline to help you organize basic information about privacy and ethical issues.

What's Online

In Lesson 17–1 of the iText, you will find more features and information for this lesson, including:

- Interactive tutorials
- As You Read worksheet
- Learn More interactivities
- Check Your Understanding interactive assessments
- Interactive lesson review

🔑 Key Terms

- copyright (p. 253)
- fair use (p. 253)
- plagiarism (p. 253)
- ethics (p. 254)
- acceptable use policy (AUP) (p. 254)

Privacy in Cyberspace

Many consumers share personal information about themselves, their habits, and their finances. Sometimes, however, such information is gathered without a person's knowledge or approval.

How Businesses Obtain Personal Information   Some businesses gather information from public records kept by the government. They may also access information that people volunteer about themselves in several ways:

- Web site registration—Many Web sites require visitors to fill out registration forms.
- Online purchases—Some Web sites gather information about people who buy their goods or services.
- Warranty registration—Products of all kinds come with a warranty that enables the user to get help if the product breaks or fails. To take advantage of a product warranty, you usually must register with the manufacturer. Some warranty registrations ask for a great deal of personal information.
- Sweepstakes entries—Many people fill out sweepstakes entry forms hoping to win a prize. In doing so, they provide important personal information.

What consumers may not know is that companies that gather personal information often sell it to other organizations, such as marketing companies, whose job is to sell products and services to consumers. As a result, marketing companies have access to enormous quantities of data about people. This information is stored in large computerized databases.

Protecting Privacy Some people say that individuals should have the right to refuse to provide information about themselves, as well as the right to have information about themselves removed from a database. Although such a guarantee does not yet exist in the United States, you can protect your privacy. The main thing you can do is be careful to whom you give out personal information about yourself.

Copyright Laws

Laws that involve **copyright** protect individuals and companies from the theft or misuse of their creative, literary, or artistic work. It is a crime to copy this kind of work without the permission of the person who owns the copyright to it.

Fair Use The idea of **fair use** means you can use a portion of a copyrighted work without permission in certain cases. Fair use applies when a limited portion of the work is used for research or as part of schoolwork. Reviewers also have the right to quote part of an original work in their reviews.

Using Digital Information Computers and the Internet make it easy to copy someone else's work. Using material from a Web site or a book without crediting the source is **plagiarism.** This is copying someone else's work and passing it off as your own. You should always follow the rules of fair use and acknowledge the source of information you use.

© Pearson Education, Inc.

Career Corner

Writer Professional writers learn how to properly cite and use sources to avoid plagiarizing them. Writers must be able to apply strong language skills to develop their own ideas and express things in their own words—not in the words of sources. Writers work in many different media, including books, magazines, newspapers, television and radio, and the Internet.

Spotlight on...

SHAWN FANNING

  I gave up sports so I could spend more of my spare time at the computer learning about programming. . . . Looking for a challenge beyond entry level courses, I started to start writing a Windows-based program of my own.

Shawn Fanning
Founder, Napster™

The first computer program Shawn Fanning developed was Napster™, a software applica-

tion that allowed people around the world to share music files. Music publishers protested that Napster™ violated their legal right to the music they sold, but Fanning replied that the Napster™ software did no such thing. It did not copy the music files—only the people using the Napster™ software could do so. Eventually, however, Fanning gave in to strong pressure from the music companies. Napster™ closed in 2002 after attempting to evolve into a subscription service for sharing music.

Technology @ School

Gestures, facial expressions, and tones of voice—which people use in conversation to add meaning—are missing from e-mail.

Think *About* It!

Beside each item below, write *T* if you think your intent would be clearly communicated on computer. Write *F* if you think it could be miscommunicated.

➤ fact

➤ sarcasm

➤ anger

➤ question

➤ joy

Figure 17.1.1 Your school district's AUP provides guidelines for using your school's computers, network, and Internet access.

Acceptable Use Policies

People who practice **ethics** behave morally. One way you can act ethically is to follow your school district's **acceptable use policy, or AUP,** while using computers at school. These policies identify for computer users the responsibilities of Internet use. They spell out certain rules of behavior and explain the consequences of breaking those rules. Many businesses use AUPs, too, to govern the way workers use company-owned computers.

Policy Guidelines A school district's AUP may include the following ethical guidelines:

- Users agree not to visit objectionable Web sites that contain content that does not meet community standards.
- Users agree not to use inappropriate language, such as language that is profane, abusive, or impolite.
- Users agree not to copy copyrighted material or to damage computer equipment belonging to the school.
- Users agree to respect the privacy of other people.

Possible Penalties Users of school computers who do not follow these rules may face consequences. They might lose privileges or be suspended from school activities. Very serious violations, such as using a school computer to threaten someone, may require police involvement.

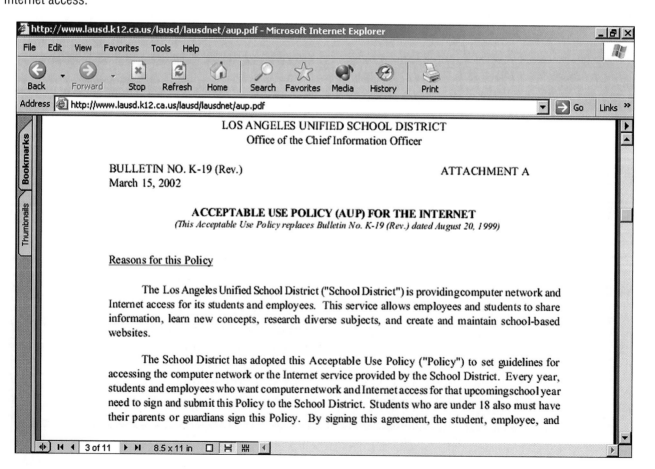

© Pearson Education, Inc.

Demonstrate Your Knowledge

Critical Thinking

1. What can happen to personal information you volunteer on Web sites?

_____

_____

2. What kinds of work do copyright laws protect? How does the concept of fair use apply to these laws?

_____

_____

3. What are two widely accepted examples of school districts' acceptable use policies?

_____

_____

Activities

1. Complete the Venn diagram below to compare and contrast fair use and plagiarism.

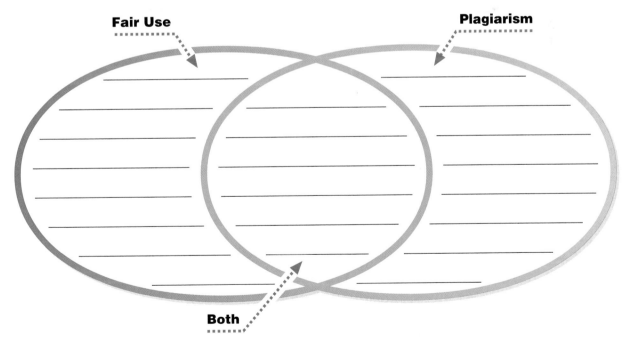

2. Use the Internet to research the life of someone in whom you are interested. Write a brief summary of the person's life. Cite your sources of information.

Computer Crime

Objectives

- Summarize how computer crime costs businesses money.
- Identify different types of cybercrime.

As You Read

Organize Information As you read the lesson, use a word web to help you identify various risks associated with computer crime.

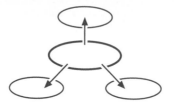

Key Terms

- computer crime (p. 256)
- cybercrime (p. 256)
- downtime (p. 256)
- virus (p. 257)
- worm (p. 257)
- Trojan horse (p. 258)
- software piracy (p. 258)

The High Cost of Computer Crime

The Internet has opened the door to new kinds of crime and new ways of carrying out traditional crimes. **Computer crime** is any act that violates state or federal laws and involves using a computer. The term **cybercrime** often refers specifically to crimes carried out by means of the Internet. Due to computer crime, businesses lose money in the following ways.

Staff Time Even if intruders steal nothing from a business, they still cost companies money. Staff must make the network secure again and consider how to stop security breaches.

Downtime Security breaches also cost a company in terms of **downtime,** or a temporary stop to work. System administrators sometimes shut a network down to prevent the loss of data. While the system is down, workers cannot do their jobs. A company can lose business if customers are affected by downtime.

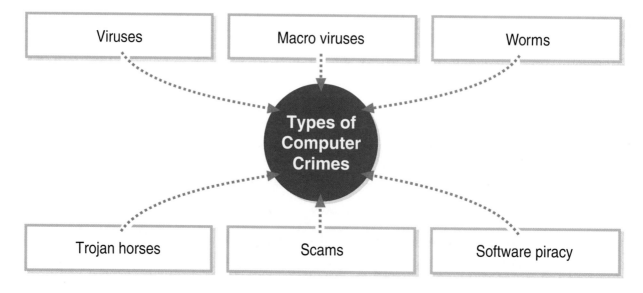

Bad Publicity Many companies refuse to announce that a computer crime has been committed against them. For example, if customers learn that someone has stolen their personal information from a company's network, they may decide that the company is not able to keep such informtion safe. This can cause customers to stop doing business with the company.

Types of Computer Crime

There are many different kinds of computer crime. Some of them require criminals to have a deep knowledge of programming.

Viruses A **virus** is a program that performs one or more tasks that the user doesn't expect. Some viruses are designed to do real harm, such as delete files, slow down network traffic, disable programs, or allow an unauthorized person to access the victim's computer. Most viruses are designed to hide themselves, avoiding detection by the victim for as long as possible.

If a virus is copied to your computer, the machine is said to be "infected." A virus can infect your computer in a number of ways. You might receive an infected disk from a friend. You might download an infected file from a Web site or receive it attached to an e-mail message.

Most viruses can affect only the operating system in which they were written. However, they can spread from one computer to another.

Macro Viruses A macro virus takes advantage of the macro languages in application programs, such as word processors or spreadsheets. Macro viruses launch themselves when an infected file is opened. These viruses are different from normal viruses because they can work on different operating systems.

Worms The most common computer viruses work by hiding inside another program. When you run the program, the virus activates and does its work. A **worm** is a type of virus that doesn't need to be hidden inside another program. Nevertheless, worms are commonly hidden inside document files in the form of macros.

In most cases, a worm's job is to replicate itself as much as possible, consuming the victim's disks and memory. Worms often spread by traveling through network connections. Many e-mail viruses, such as the I Love You virus, are actually worms. They distribute themselves by creating e-mail messages and mailing themselves to other computers.

Did You Know ?

Spyware is software that sends information about you and your Web-surfing habits back to companies from whom you downloaded freeware or shareware, or for whom you completed online registrations.

Spyware programs install themselves on your system without your knowledge. Most spyware claims that it tracks habits anonymously; that is, without naming specific individuals. Its goal is to gather data and then draw conclusions about a group's Web habits.

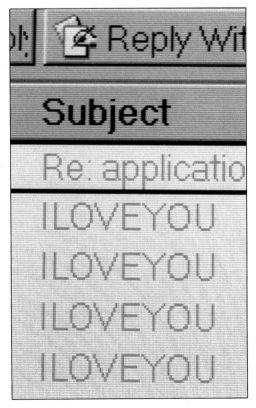

Figure 17.2.1 E-mail viruses are easily launched and spread.

Language Arts Where did all the unusual names for destructive software come from?

- A computer virus is named for the kind of virus that causes infectious diseases like the cold and the flu.

- A worm is named for a tape-worm, a kind of organism that lives in the intestines of another creature and lives off the food that creature eats.

- A Trojan horse takes its name from an ancient Greek story about soldiers who entered a fortress by hiding inside the body of a giant replica of a horse, which the defenders allowed in. The soldiers hidden inside the horse attacked and defeated the defenders.

Trojan Horses A **Trojan horse** is a program that does something useful but at the same time, hidden from view, does something destructive. It can damage the system it enters, including erasing all the data on a hard drive. A Trojan horse might come in the form of a simple game. When the victim plays the game, however, the program does something else in the background, such as opening a port on the computer. Someone can then use this port to access the computer through the Internet.

Scams Some computer crimes have nothing to do with programming. Criminals use a computer to commit theft. Internet advertisements and e-mail messages might claim that you can make huge sums of money with very little effort. According to these ads, all you have to do is send some money to receive full instructions. This is a scam—a trick to get your money.

Software Piracy One kind of computer crime is very widespread. It is called **software piracy,** the illegal copying of computer programs. One business group estimates that about one third of all software in use is pirated.

Most programs that people buy are licensed only to the purchaser. In other words, it is illegal for you to copy such a program and give it to a friend. It is also illegal to accept a copy of software from someone else. Software piracy is the easiest computer crime to prevent. Make sure that you pay for all the software you use that requires payment.

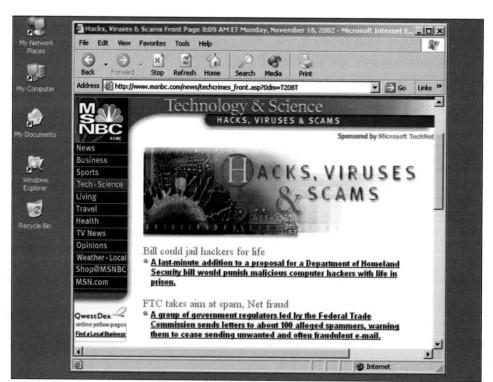

Figure 17.2.2 The federal government has passed laws aimed at computer crimes.

Demonstrate Your Knowledge

Critical Thinking

1. In what ways does computer crime cost businesses money?

_____

_____

2. How do computer crime and cybercrime differ?

_____

_____

3. What kind of damage can computer viruses cause?

_____

_____

Activities

1. Complete the chart below by describing what these computer crimes do.

Types of Computer Crimes

Type	Description
Virus	
Macro virus	
Worm	
Trojan horse	
Scam	
Software piracy	

2. Read the license agreement for a software program. How is the manufacturer impacted by pirated copies of the software it develops for sale? How can you prevent software piracy?

Lesson 17–3

Protecting Data

Objectives

- Describe ways criminals obtain passwords.
- Discuss ways to protect your computer from being accessed by others.
- Explain how to prevent data loss.

As You Read

Summarize As you read the lesson, use a chart to help you summarize ways to protect information on your computer.

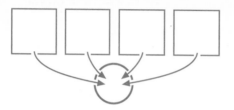

What's Online

In Lesson 17–3 of the iText, you will find more features and information for this lesson, including:

- Interactive tutorials
- As You Read worksheet
- Learn More interactivities
- Check Your Understanding interactive assessments
- Interactive lesson review

Key Terms

- packet sniffer (p. 260)
- power surge (p. 262)
- Uninterruptible Power Supply (UPS) (p. 262)

Password Theft

Many computer crimes start when an unauthorized user hacks, or gains unauthorized entry, into a computer network. This often happens when the intruder learns the password to access the victim's computer and the network. Following are ways such criminals learn passwords.

Guessing Too often, computer users choose passwords that are easy for them to remember, such as birthdates, names of pets, names of celebrities, and names of family members. Unfortunately, these passwords are also easy for intruders to guess.

Finding Sometimes people keep passwords written on pieces of paper near their computer. Other times, criminals simply look over someone's shoulder as he or she types the password and use it later. An intruder can also search the trash in the hopes of finding user IDs and passwords.

"Sniffing" Some criminals may use packet sniffers. A **packet sniffer** is a program that examines data streams on networks to try to find information, such as passwords and credit card numbers.

Pretending Some intruders pretend to be network administrators. They call network users and ask for their passwords, claiming that the passwords are needed to solve a problem in the system.

© Pearson Education, Inc.

Figure 17.3.1 Use passwords that are simple for you to remember but will not be easily guessed by others.

<label>footer</label>
260 • **Chapter 17**

Modifying Network software makes the people who administer a system into superusers. Intruders who have superuser access can modify virtually any file on the network. They also may change user passwords to ones they know.

Protecting Your Personal Data

It is in your best interest to protect your computer and its data. Here are some ways to help protect personal information.

Change Passwords Frequently Experts recommend that passwords have at least six characters, use uppercase and lowercase letters, and include some numbers. Remember, too, to change your password every few weeks.

Browse Anonymously When you go online, surf from sites that protect your identity. Anonymizer and IDZap are two sites offering this service.

Use a Different E-mail Address Although you may not be able to do this at school, on a home computer you can sign up for a free e-mail account from a Web site such as Hotmail® or Yahoo! Mail. Use that address when you register at Web sites or participate in other public Internet spaces. This will protect you from receiving unwanted mail, or spam, at your primary e-mail address.

Avoid Site Registration Be careful of Web sites that require you to register. Do not fill out a registration form unless the site clearly says that the data will not be shared with other people without your approval.

One way companies generate mailing lists for spam messages is by checking the addresses of people in chat rooms and in Web discussion groups. If you use these services, you can minimize spam at your primary e-mail address by using a secondary e-mail address for these chats. You can then trash the spam when you want.

Think *About* **It!**
Circle each contact to whom you would give your secondary e-mail address.

- friend
- movie promotional site
- Web site from which you ordered a DVD
- chat room
- Web site where you receive support for your computer

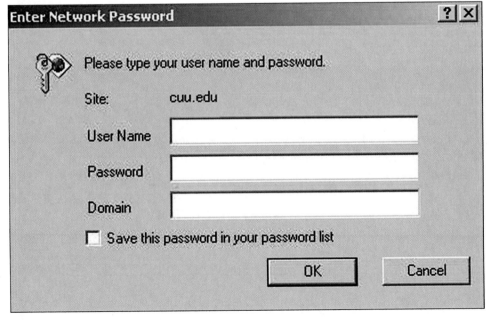

Figure 17.3.2 You may be required to provide a user name and password before accessing a computer network.

Technology @ Work

Backing up your files is the best way of making sure that data survives a hard-drive crash.

Think *About* **It!**
Think about the files you cannot afford to lose. Underline ONLY those files that you think are vital to back up regularly.

➤ data files

➤ programs that can be reinstalled from a CD-ROM

➤ games that are played from a CD

➤ files you downloaded and used once

➤ macros you created

Protecting Your Computer Data

A computer contains parts that break, just like any other piece of equipment. It's important to protect the data on your computer in the event of a power or hard-drive failure.

Power-Related Problems Just like any other device that runs on electricity, a computer can be affected by power fluctuations or outages. These problems can lead to the loss of data. A **power surge,** or a sharp increase in the power coming into the system, can destroy a computer's electrical components.

You can help protect your computer from power problems by attaching an **Uninterruptible Power Supply,** or **UPS,** between your computer and the power source. This battery-powered device goes to work when it detects an outage or critical voltage drop. It powers the computer for a period of time. A UPS can also protect against power surges by filtering sudden electrical spikes.

Backing Up Data You can limit the amount of data lost due to a power problem by saving your work regularly. The only way to completely protect your computer against data loss is to back up your work. This protects your data in case the computer's hard drive fails. To back up files, copy them onto a floppy disk, CD, or some other removable media. Store backup files away from the computer in case of a disaster.

Real-World Tech

Backup Technology One problem with computer backups was that the typical media—floppy disks—could not hold much data. Even high-capacity removable storage media such as Zip® and Jaz® drives could be quickly filled with space-hogging files.

Rewritable CDs (CD-RWs) or a second hard drive make backing up easy and cost-effective even when large amounts of data need to be stored. For some even larger files, removable tape cartridges can hold 20 gigabytes or more of information.

How do you back up your computer files? Write your answer on the lines below.

_____

_____

_____

Demonstrate Your Knowledge

Critical Thinking

1. What can computer criminals do after they gain access to a computer?

_____

_____

2. What are three ways someone might obtain your password?

_____

_____

3. What are three guidelines for safeguarding a password? Do you follow these suggestions? Why or why not?

_____

_____

Activities

1. Complete the concept web below to identify ways to protect personal and computer data.

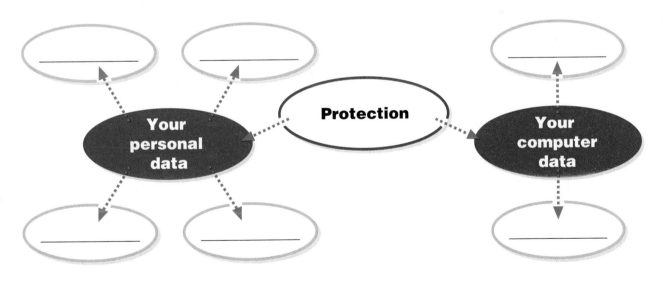

2. Interview someone who has lost files on a computer. Find out if he or she had backup files to help retrieve the work. Ask if he or she backs up files differently now and, if so, how. Share your findings with the class.

Use the Vocabulary

Directions: *Match each vocabulary term in the left column with the correct definition in the right column. Write the appropriate letter next to the word or term.*

_____ **1.** copyright
_____ **2.** fair use
_____ **3.** plagiarism
_____ **4.** computer crime
_____ **5.** cybercrime
_____ **6.** downtime
_____ **7.** software piracy
_____ **8.** packet sniffer
_____ **9.** power surge
_____ **10.** uninterruptible power supply

a. device that aims to prevent interruption of power to a computer
b. using a computer to break the law
c. using the Internet to break the law
d. when workers cannot work because a network is temporarily not available
e. illegal copying of software programs
f. right to control use of creative work
g. illegal copying of creative material owned by another person
h. sudden spike in electrical current to a computer
i. copying of creative material that is allowed in schoolwork or in a review
j. method of finding another's password

Check Your Comprehension

Directions: *Circle the correct choice for each of the following.*

1. Which of the following should you do cautiously because it could result in sharing personal information without your approval?
 a. buying software
 b. copying software
 c. registering at a Web site
 d. getting warranty protection

2. Which of the following is illegal according to copyright laws?
 a. buying a music CD
 b. listening to a music CD
 c. playing a music CD
 d. copying a music CD

3. Which of the following would be an example of disobeying an acceptable use policy?
 a. giving out another student's password
 b. informing the teacher of e-mails that contain bad language
 c. staying away from restricted sites
 d. using equipment properly

4. Which kind of destructive computer program can move from one operating system to another?
 a. macro virus
 b. Trojan horse
 c. virus
 d. worm

5. What is an example of a password that is easy to guess?
 a. a combination of numbers and letters that makes no sense
 b. a four-letter nickname
 c. ten letters that do not spell a word
 d. eight randomly chosen numbers

6. Which of the following practices may help reduce the loss of data?
 a. installing software
 b. using a password
 c. backing up files
 d. power surges

⬤ Think Critically

Directions: *Answer the following questions on the lines provided.*

1. Why is it a good idea to keep personal information confidential?

_____

_____

2. Why might a school want students and staff to sign its acceptable use policy?

_____

_____

3. Give examples of computer crime and cybercrime that illustrate the difference between the two terms.

_____

_____

4. What are the consequences of software piracy? How can you help prevent piracy?

_____

_____

5. Which methods of protecting your privacy and your data do you follow?

_____

_____

⬤ Extend Your Knowledge

Directions: *Choose one of the following projects. Complete the exercises on a separate sheet of paper.*

A. Review rules your school district may have for computer use as part of its acceptable use policy. Categorize policies based on appropriate use, vandalism or destruction, and consequences of violations.

B. Use the Internet to investigate a cybercrime. Write a brief report outlining what happened, what damage resulted, and whether the criminal was caught. If he or she was caught, describe how. State what consequences the criminal must face.

Numerals

@ in an e-mail address, a symbol used to separate the user name from the name of the computer on which the user's mailbox is stored (for example, frodo@bagend.org); pronounced "at"

10 baseT an Ethernet local area network capable of transmitting 10 megabits of data per second through twisted-pair cabling

3-D graphics adapter a video adapter that can display images that provide the illusion of depth as well as height and width

3-D rendering transforming graphic images by adding shading and light sources so that they appear to be three-dimensional

40-bit encryption a minimal level of encryption supplied with most Web browsers

A

acceptable use policy (AUP) a school district's policy identifying the rules of behavior of student and staff Internet users; p. 254

active cell the highlighted cell in use in a spreadsheet application; p. 93

alias an informal name by which an e-mail user is known; p. 205

analog a type of system that sends electrical signals that match the human voice and other sounds; p. 173

animation the process of showing many images in rapid sequence to make them appear as if they are in motion; p. 145

application software a program that allows you to create documents, listen to music, or play games on the computer; pp. 13, 59

archival storage a storage device for information that is not frequently used; p. 36

ascending order the sorting of data by increasing value; p. 117

attachment a file sent with an e-mail message; p. 204

AutoContent wizard in Microsoft PowerPoint, a series of dialog boxes that helps the user create a new presentation; p. 140

autocorrect a feature that fixes common spelling mistakes as they are typed; p. 78

AutoFill a spreadsheet command that automatically enters related, sequential data (such as the days of the week) into a connected set of cells; p. 197

autosave a feature that automatically saves a document at set increments of time; p. 78

AutoShapes a list of ready-to-use shapes in the Draw tool; p. 144

B

backbone high-speed lines that carry data through a network; p. 197

Back button a tool that lets users reload the previously viewed page in a browser; p. 240

backup utility a program that automatically copies data from the hard drive to a backup storage device; p. 54

bandwidth the amount of data that can travel through a network connection; p. 186

Basic Input/Output System (BIOS) a set of programs, built into a PC's ROM chips, that controls the function of the computer's keyboard, disk drives, monitor, and several other components; the programs also help the computer start itself when the power is turned on; p. 33

bit a number that is a building block for computer languages; short for *binary digit*; p. 4

bitmapped graphic an image formed by a pattern of dots; p. 124

bits per second (bps) the amount of data that can be sent in one second; p. 177

Boolean search a type of search that uses an operator to link keywords; p. 241

bounce message a notice that e-mail could not be delivered; p. 208

broadband the general term for all high-speed digital connections of at least 1.5 megabits per second; p. 187

browse to find information in a database by looking at records one at a time; p. 116

browser a program that enables users to navigate the World Wide Web and locate and display Web documents; p. 236

byte a group of bits combined into groups of eight or more; p. 4

C

cathode ray tube (CRT) a common type of monitor that produces images by making phosphors glow; p. 25

Cave Automatic Virtual Environment (CAVE) a virtual reality environment where images of the virtual world are projected on the walls of a real room; p. 165

CD-ROM drive the most common read-only optical storage device; p. 41

cell the box on a worksheet where each column and row meet; p. 92

cell address a unique name by which each cell on a worksheet is identified; p. 92

cell reference the shorthand command that tells a spreadsheet program to use the information inside a certain cell; p. 108

central processing unit (CPU) a piece of the computer's hardware that processes and compares data and completes arithmetic and logical operations; p. 8

certificate authority (CA) a third-party organization that validates digital signatures; p. 246

chart a graphical image, such as a pie or a set of columns, used to visually display numerical data, making it easy to understand and analyze; p. 98

Glossary

client a workstation computer attached to a network, which is controlled by a server; p. 194

client/server network a network system that uses a central server computer; p. 194

clip art a graphic that has already been created for use by others; p. 134

Clip Art Gallery a collection of images and sound that is ready to use; p. 145

Clipboard a tool that temporarily stores cut or copied text; p. 81

collaborative software software used to share calendars, documents, or hold meetings through a network; p. 192

color palette a display of options in a paint or draw program that allows the user to choose the color a tool will place in an image; p. 128

command an instruction that tells a software program what action to perform; p. 20

commercial software copyrighted software that must be purchased before it can be used; p. 64

compatibility the ability to share files between two different application programs or operating systems; p. 13

computer a machine that changes information from one form into another by performing input, processing, output, and storage; p. 4

computer crime any act that violates state or federal laws involving use of a computer; p. 256

copyright the right to control use of creative, literary, or artistic work; p. 253

crash to suddenly stop working; p. 48

cybercrime the use of the Internet or private networks to violate state or federal laws; p. 256

D

database an organized collection of information that may or may not be stored in a computer; p. 107

database management system (DBMS) a software program used to manage the storage, organization, processing, and retrieval of data in a database; p. 112

data type settings applied to a database field, which allow the field to store only information of a specific type and/or format; p. 108

default a preset option in a program; p. 84

demodulation the process that changes the analog signal received by a modem to the digital signal used by a computer; p. 176

descending order the sorting of data by decreasing value; p. 117

desktop the workspace on a computer screen; p. 50

digital a connection that uses computer codes to send voice, data, and video on a single line; p. 173

digital camera a camera that records and stores photos in a digital form that the computer can work with; p. 22

Domain Name System (DNS) a naming system using letters as well as numbers to identify one or more computers on the Internet; p. 226

download to transfer copies of files *from* a remote computer to a local computer by means of a modem or network; p. 230

downtime a temporary stop to all work on a network; p. 256

draw program a program used to create and edit vector images; p. 126

driver utility software that contains information needed by application programs to properly operate input and output devices; p. 54

E

e-commerce the use of telecommunications networks or the Internet to conduct business; p. 244

e-mail client a program, on a user's computer, that enables the user to create, send, receive, and manage e-mail messages; p. 205

e-mail server a program, on an Internet service provider's server computer, that sends, receives, and delivers e-mail messages to client computers; p. 204

e-mail virus a program sent in an e-mail message to deliberately cause computer problems for the recipient; p. 210

encoder a software program that converts a file from one format to another; p. 161

ethics moral principles; p. 254

export to format data so it can be used in another application; p. 132

Eyedropper a tool that picks up and works with a specific color from an image; p. 129

F

fair use the act of getting permission to copy or use copyrighted material for research, schoolwork, or professional publication; p. 253

fax machine a device that makes a digital copy (a "facsimile") of a document, then transmits the data to another device, such as a computer modem or another fax machine; p. 178

fax modem a computer modem that can send and receive faxes; p. 178

fiber-optic cable strands of pure glass that transmit digital data by pulses of light; p. 174

field the part of a database that holds an individual piece of data; p. 108

file a unit or grouping of information that has been given a unique name; p. 39

file compression utility a software program that reduces the size of a file for storage or transmission purposes; p. 54

file server the main computer in a client/server system; p. 194

file sharing making files available to more than one user on a network; p. 192

flat-file database a database that can work with only one file at a time; p. 112

floppy disk drive a storage device that reads floppy disks; p. 40

formula a mathematical expression used to link and perform calculations on numbers in worksheet cells; p. 94

Forward button a tool that lets users move ahead to previously viewed pages in a browser; p. 240

frame rate the number of still images displayed every second on video tape; p. 158

freeware copyrighted software given away for free; p. 65

function a commonly used formula that is built into a program; p. 94

G

garbage in, garbage out (GIGO) a phrase that stresses the importance of inputting accurate data in a database; p. 110

graphic anything that can be seen on a computer's screen; p. 123

graphical browser a Web navigation program that shows pictures and text; p. 236

graphical user interface (GUI) a visual display that allows the user to interact with the computer by using graphical objects on the screen; p. 50

graphics tablet a piece of hardware used for drawing; p. 130

group to combine separate vector images into one image; p. 133

H

hard drive the most commonly used type of secondary storage device, which stores bits of data as aligned particles on the surface of a magnetic disk; p. 40

hardware the physical parts of a computer; p. 8

head-mounted display (HMD) a helmet that wraps around the head; used for virtual reality experiences; p. 164

Help menu a set of directions for program functions; p. 69

hyperlink a link to another document on the World Wide Web; p. 229

hypertext a type of document that is published on the World Wide Web; p. 229

Hypertext Markup Language (HTML) a page description used to format Web documents; p. 237

I

icon an on-screen picture that represents an object, resource, or command; p. 50

image editor an advanced paint program that edits bitmapped images; p. 126

impact printer a printer that uses keys or pins to strike an ink ribbon to create an image on paper; p. 26

import to bring information into a program from another program; p. 132

information overload the result of a computer user being overwhelmed by the amount of information generated by his or her computer; p. 116

infrared light waves that cannot be seen by the human eye; p. 174

input raw information, or data, that is entered into a computer; p. 4

insertion point a mark that indicates where entered text will appear in a document; p. 77

insert mode the method of entering text in which the type is placed into a document without removing any previously entered text; p. 80

install to prepare to run application software by copying all or part of the program onto the computer's hard drive; p. 65

integrated software a program that combines the basic features of several applications into one package; p. 61

interactive multimedia a program that uses different types of media (such as text, sound, animation, and others) to convey its message, and which allows the user to choose the content that will be displayed next or direct the flow of the content; p. 156

interface a means for users to control or operate the computer; p. 48

Internet a vast network that links millions of computers around the world; p. 220

Internet client the computer and related software that requests a service; p. 221

Internet service provider (ISP) a company that provides the actual link between a computer and the Internet; p. 224

Internet protocol (IP) address a four-part number separated by periods that identifies each computer connected to the Internet; p. 226

intranet a private network used for a specific organization, which looks and works like the Internet; p. 197

K

key field an element that links tables in a relational database; p. 112

L

label text or a combination of numbers and text typically used for titles or explanation in a worksheet; p. 96

launch to start an application program; p. 68

layer to stack parts of a bitmapped image on top of another level; p. 133

liquid crystal display (LCD) a monitor that produces images by sending electrical signals to crystals; p. 25

local area network (LAN) a network in which all workstations and equipment are near each other; p. 192

local loop the network that connects to the phone company's central office; p. 173

M

mailbox name a part of an e-mail address before the "at" sign; p. 204

maximize to make an application window as large as possible; p. 69

memory specialized chips, connected to the computer's motherboard, which store data and programs as they are being used by the processor; p. 33

menu bar the bar generally located below an application's title bar where a set of commands is listed; p. 69

microwave a high-frequency radio wave; p. 174

minimize to make an application window as small as possible; p. 69

modem a device that allows a computer to transmit data to other computers through telephone lines; p. 176

modulation the process that changes the digital signal from a computer to the analog signal of a telephone; p. 176

multimedia describes a program that uses different types of media (such as text, graphics, video, animation, or sound) at the same time; p. 156

N

navigate to move to different parts of a network or program to find resources or files; p. 225

navigation button a tool that lets users perform routine operations with a browser; p. 240

network two or more computers connected to each other to share resources; p. 188

network interface card (NIC) a hardware device that physically connects a computer to a network; p. 188

network operating system (NOS) a set of programs that manages and secures a network; p. 194

node anything connected to a network, such as a computer, printer, or fax machine; p. 189

nonimpact printer a printer that uses spray or powder to create an image on paper; p. 26

Normal view in PowerPoint, a split screen that shows a Slide view and an Outline view; p. 142

Notes Page view a presentation view in which a slide is displayed on part of the screen and a text box is shown on the other part; p. 142

O

object-oriented database a database that stores objects, such as sound, video, text, and graphics; p. 113

office suite a program that combines several programs and all of their features; p. 62

online service a business that provides access to the Internet as well as to custom content, discussion groups, news, shopping services, and other information that is available only to its paying subscribers; p. 225

on-screen presentation a display of slides on a computer screen; p. 150

operating system a system that allows hardware devices to communicate with one another, run efficiently, and support software programs; p. 13

optical storage device a storage device that uses laser beams to read the information stored on the reflective surface of a disc; p. 38

order of evaluation the rule that tells a spreadsheet program which operation to do first in a multiple-operation formula; p. 101

Outline view the display in presentation software that shows the text from each slide in outline form; p. 142

output the result of a computer's processing, displayed on-screen, printed on paper, or heard through a speaker; p. 6

output device any piece of hardware that shows the result of computer processing; p. 24

overtype mode the method of entering text in which existing text is deleted as new type is entered; p. 80

P

packet sniffer a program that examines data streams on networks to find information such as passwords and credit-card numbers; p. 260

page format the arrangement of text on a page; p. 86

pagination the automatic division of a document into pages; p. 78

paint program the basic program for working with a bitmapped image; p. 126

peer-to-peer network (P2PN) a small network that usually includes from two to ten computers but no server; p. 192

peripheral separate input, output, and storage hardware; p. 10

personal information manager (PIM) program a program responsible for storing phone numbers and addresses and creating schedules; p. 60

physical media the wires, cables, or wireless transmitters and receivers used to connect the computers in a network; p. 188

pixel a single point in a bitmapped graphic; p. 124

placeholder an area within a slide layout designed to hold data, such as text or pictures; p. 144

plagiarism illegal copying of creative material owned by another person; p. 253

Plug and Play (PnP) capability of Windows-based PC operating systems to detect new, compatible devices; p. 54

pointer a cursor that shows your location on a computer screen; p. 21

point of presence (POP) a local connection to a wide area network; p. 197

portal an Internet service that provides an organized subject guide to Internet content, news, weather, sports, e-mail, etc.; p. 231

power surge a sharp increase in power coming into the computer system; p. 262

presentation software a specialized software that is used to create and display visual information; p. 140

primary storage memory chips that are built into a computer, such as random access memory (RAM); p. 36

print area a portion of a worksheet intended to be printed; p. 98

processing a task a computer carries out with data; p. 5

protocol standard format and rules for handling data; p. 190

public data network (PDN) a network that allows different companies to set up their own networks; p. 198

public domain software a program distributed for free without a copyright; p. 65

R

random access memory (RAM) special chips that store data and instructions while the computer is working; p. 8

random access storage device a storage device that lets the computer go directly to the needed information; p. 38

read-only device a storage device that allows users to access information but not save or change it; p. 37

read/write device a storage device that allows users to access information and save it to the device; p. 37

record a part of a database that holds data about a particular individual or item; p. 108

relational database a database in which shared key fields link data among tables; p. 112

repetitive strain injury (RSI) nerve damage in the hand caused by continued use of a keyboard or mouse; p. 22

Reply to respond to the sender of an e-mail message; p. 206

Reply All to respond to all people who received an e-mail message; p. 206

report an ordered list of selected database records and fields in an easy-to-read format; p. 118

report template a pattern that controls how data will be displayed in a database report; p. 118

resolution for a bitmapped image, the number of pixels in a certain section of the image; p. 125

S

scanner a device that lets you copy printed images into a computer by changing the image into a digital form; p. 22

scroll to move from one part of a document to another on the screen; p. 70

search engine software that finds a list of Web sites that meet a specified search; p. 228

secondary storage computer disk drives such as the hard drive and CD-ROM drive used to store large amounts of data; p. 36

section a part of a document that contains specific format settings; p. 86

Secure Electronic Transactions (SET) a standard that uses digital signatures to protect buyers and sellers who use credit cards online; p. 246

select text a software feature that allows the user to highlight, or select, any amount of text in a document for editing; p. 81

selection tool a program tool that can select a portion of an image to be moved, enlarged, or edited; p. 130

sequential storage device a storage device that requires a computer to scan from the beginning to the end of stored information; p. 38

server address a part of an e-mail address after the "at" sign; p. 204

shareware a copyrighted software that can be sampled before it is purchased; p. 65

simulation a virtual reality program that mimics a specific place, job, or function; p. 166

slide a separate page in a presentation program on which information is organized; p. 140

Slide Show view a display of slides in a presentation shown one after the other in the order they appear in the document; p. 142

Slide Sorter view a display that shows all of the slides in a presentation on one screen; p. 142

software programs that tell a computer what to do and how to do it; p. 12

software license the document that contains permission for a buyer to install and use a program; p. 66

software piracy the illegal copying of computer programs; p. 258

sort to arrange data in a specific order; p. 112

sound card a circuit board chip that converts sounds in analog form into digital form and vice versa; p. 158

spam unrequested e-mail messages and advertisements; p. 209

speech recognition a type of software that lets you use a microphone to input information and commands by speaking aloud and that converts your words into data, commands, or responses; p. 22

spreadsheet a software program used for processing numbers that are stored in tables, such as budgets or financial statements; p. 92

standalone program application software that specializes in one task; p. 80

storage devices, such as hard drives and CD-ROM drives, that permanently hold data and program instructions for a computer to use; p. 6

storage device a computer component that retains data even after the power is turned off; p. 32

style a set of formats for similar elements in a document; p. 85

stylus a pointing device used for drawing on a graphics tablet; p. 130

synthesize to create sounds imitative of actual musical instruments using a computer; p. 161

system requirement the minimum equipment a computer needs to run an application; p. 64

system software programs that help the computer work properly; p. 12

T

table the underlying structure of a relational database characterized by rows and columns; p. 108

Transmission Control Protocol/Internet Protocol (TCP/IP) the set of rules for formatting and transmitting data over the Internet, used by every computer that is connected to the Internet; p. 225

telecommunications the process of sending information over a telephone network; p. 172

teleconference a live meeting using computers and telecommunications equipment that allows two or more people in different locations to participate; p. 212

template a preformatted version of a certain type of document; p. 140

terminal a keyboard and monitor attached to a shared, central computer; p. 189

title bar the top row of an application window where the program name and often the name of the document is shown; p. 69

trace to convert pixels into lines; p. 134

transparency a see-through sheet of acetate that is laser-printed; p. 150

Trojan horse a program disguised as useful but that is destructive to the data on a hard drive; p. 258

twisted pair a pair of copper wires that are twisted together and commonly used as a networking medium; p. 174

U

ungroup to separate combined vector images into individual images; p. 133

uniform resource locator (URL) the unique address given to a document on the Internet; p. 229

uninstall to remove a program from a computer; p. 66

Uninterruptible Power Supply (UPS) a device that aims to prevent interruption of power to a computer; p. 262

upload to transfer copies of files *to* a remote computer from a local computer by means of a modem or network; p. 230

username the online identity of a person who is accessing the Internet; p. 225

utility software programs that are used to maintain and repair the computer; p. 14

V

value a number, such as a whole number, a fraction, or decimal; p. 96

vector graphic an image that is created using paths or lines; p. 124

video capture board a special card that plugs into a computer to convert video signals into a format a computer can understand; p. 158

videoconference a meeting that provides audio and visual contact for participants in different locations; p. 213

video editor a program that combines and edits video and audio files; p. 158

virtual private network (VPN) a private network set up through a public network; p. 198

virtual reality (VR) a realistic, three-dimensional world a user can "enter" and explore; p. 164

virus a program or piece of code that can destroy files; p. 257

Virtual Reality Modeling Language (VRML) programming language used to create virtual worlds on the Internet; p. 165

W

Web browser a program used to view Web pages; p. 228

Web page a single document on the Web; p. 238

Web server a program that maintains Web sites and sends documents to users; p. 238

Web site a collection of related pages on the Web; p. 238

wide area network (WAN) a network that connects computers and other resources over great distances; p. 196

wizard a series of dialog boxes that provides a step-by-step guide to a certain task; p. 140

word-processing program a program that creates documents through writing, editing, formatting, and printing functions; p. 76

word wrap the automatic starting of a new line when the previous line is full; p. 78

worksheet a grid made of vertical columns and horizontal rows in a spreadsheet program; p. 92

workspace the blank white area where the graphic will be worked on in a paint or draw program; p. 128

workstation a computer connected to a computer network; p. 189

worm a computer virus that spreads over the network without user execution; p. 257